BUTCH
THE WINGS OF FOOTBALL

A TRUE STORY TO BE TOLD

by Gail Butcher

BUTCH: The Wings of Football

Written/compiled by Gail Butcher and family
Original material © Gail Butcher

Published by Gail Butcher

All proceeds from the sale of this book will go to the Richard Butcher Memorial Trust

Registered Charity Number: 1151743

Further information available at www.richardbutcherfamilymemorial.com

Editing, layout and typesetting by Coinlea Services
www.coinlea.co.uk

Front cover design by Gail Butcher

ISBN-13: 978-1502594747
ISBN-10: 1502594749

Contents:

Introduction

To paraphrase *Forest Gump*, a film our son Richard dearly loved: "Life is like a box of chocolates. You never know what you might get." Our son needed stability in his life, and we, as his family, always stood by him in whatever he wanted to do. Football was his life, and his passion was his football career. He always appreciated our help and financial and emotional support, especially in the early days, when you needed your parents' support to help you follow a dream, if you were so lucky to make the grade.

This book has been dedicated to, and celebrates the life and career of, our son Richard Butcher, a professional footballer who sadly passed away at the age of just 29 years old on 10th January 2011.

Our friends, including managers and players in the football world, have contributed to this book to help us, as Richard's parents, raise money for the Richard Butcher Memorial Trust. The proceeds will go towards a football pitch and clubhouse for the local community in Northampton, to help young footballers of the future to follow their dreams.

If you'd like to make a donation, you can do so via JustGiving here: **http://www.justgiving.com/rbmt**

Alternatively, please text RBMT21 £2 to 70070 or BUTC29 £5 to 70070.

Thank you for your support, and please don't hesitate to contact us if you'd like to help raise funds in the future. Queries can be addressed to Mrs G Butcher.

Website: http://www.richardbutcherfamilymemorial.com/

Email address: richard.butcher3@ntlworld.com

Registered Charity Number: 1151743

Richard you followed your dream and we followed it with you

1: Acknowledgements & Thanks

Richard's mother Gail:

I have to say that for us to claim authorship for this book seems unfair, as we have so many authors who have taken part in the book. We would like to thank each and every one of them.

All through our son's career I collected every single paper and programme that Richard featured in. I would like to say that without all the fantastic media attention our son received through his football career, parts of this book could never have been put together. As parents we would like to thank all the football clubs our son played for, especially those who are featured in this book, and thank the newspaper reports for giving us the memories we will be able to treasure forever.

A huge thanks to the following people for their contribution to this book, which has been invaluable: Gail Butcher, Richard Butcher, Glenn Butcher, Martin Fletcher, Darren Mackenzie, David Mackintosh (Leader Northamptonshire Council), (Michael Hortin, Journalist BBC Lincolnshire). The managers, mentors & coaches: Gary Simpson, Kevin Wilson, Carl Shutt, Big Keith Alexander (RIP), Ronnie Moore, Darren Ferguson, Peter Jackson, and Keith Oakes. From Northampton: Ali Gibb, Andy Morrow, Carl Heggs, David Savage, Garry Hughes, Gary Thompson, Matthew Finlay, Kevin Wilson, and Paul Curtis. From Rushden: Carl Heggs. From Kettering: Ian Bowling, Lee Howarth, Craig Norman, Carl Shutt, and Dale Watkins. From Lincoln City: Ian Bowling, Sam Clucas, Peter Gain, Ben Futcher, Paul Morgan, Keith Oakes, Gary Simpson, and Simon Yeo. From Oldham Athletic: Mark Hughes, Andy Liddell, Ronnie Moore, and Chris Porter. From Peterborough United: Darren Ferguson, Ben Futcher, Peter Gain, Keith Oakes, Gary Simpson, and Gavin Strachan. From Notts County: Jim Rodwell, Lawrie Dudfield, Ali Gibb, Jason Lee, and Gavin Strachan. From Macclesfield Town: Paul Morgan, Gary Simpson, and Simon Yeo. Then of course there was Richard Butcher himself.

8   Acknowledgements & Thanks

All images reproduced with kind permission of the respective football clubs and official photographers, all of whom have done their reputations and fans proud.

2: Past and Present

Throughout this book Richard will sometimes be referred to as 'Butch' as this was the nickname given to him by friends, since his name was Richard Butcher, which his father also shares.

We married at a young age, just 16 and 19. The day we took our wedding vows was on the 4th of October, 1980. The ceremony took place at the Northampton Guild Hall with a reception at Far Cotton Working Men's Club, and my father-in-law helped us to afford a weekend in London as a honeymoon present. To raise our spending money, at the wedding reception we held an auction, which was a lot of fun. With some of the money that was generously given to us by family and friends we bought a Silver Cross pram ready for our new arrival.

On our return from London, our married life started out with our living separately—my husband lived at his family's home and I lived at mine, as there was no room at either house for both of us. Nearer the time for our son's arrival, my sister Dawn moved out, and this allowed both my husband and me to move into my mum's house, so we could at least be together.

Richard's dad, a skilled tradesman, lost his job when Luxury Yachts closed. But my dad, Tony, came through and helped his son-in-law to get into Air Flow Stream Lines to help us have a steady income. This forged a good family life ready for us to bring up our children. At the time, this was all very difficult for my parents, having their young daughter getting married at just sixteen and having a baby, but they stood by me and helped as much as they could.

Richard was born at 6.42 am on the 22nd January 1981 in Northampton General Hospital, almost a month ahead of schedule; he was due on the 14th February. I spent three days in slow labour that seemed to go on forever. I thought our son would be a big baby as I got so large with my pregnancy. Going from a petite eight stone to thirteen stone, I had found myself having to take a rest as I waddled around town, and yet, at 6 lb. precisely, he was smaller than expected.

Our son was born with a worrying lump on the side of his head and jaundice. His father likened him to an alien, but they instantly bonded. He was a wide-eyed beautiful boy, lying there so alert from the minute he was born with his curly dark hair and lovely brown eyes. I wanted him kept close by me at all times, so worried was I that he was going to disappear. I could not believe he was all mine.

RICHARD'S MUM AND DAD WERE MARRIED AT NORTHAMPTON GUILD HALL

Richard's brother Glenn would also be a small baby and another early morning debutant, weighing in at 6 lb. 1, at 4.50 am in December, 1982. Glenn was born with lovely blue eyes and blond hair. He was such a well-behaved baby we fell in love with him instantly. I really enjoyed having the boys close together, with less than two years between them.

I can remember taking Richard to the doctor's one day, and he said to me, "Do you want to know how tall your son will be?" He measured his feet and said, "At least 6 feet tall." With me and his dad not being so tall, I could not believe it, but Richard obviously took after his Great-Nan as he inherited her height.

We lived in our first home just a year. This is where some of our memories will always be. When I got married at sixteen and had my baby boy it was the best thing that had ever happened to me in my life. It was hard but worth it. Richard's father and I made ends meet. But then, what mum and dad wouldn't put their family first and tailor their lives and careers around building a home for those you love?

Married life for us started out living apart until we then moved in with my parents. For the first six months of Richard's little life we stayed in a small bedroom no bigger than a shoe box. With his cot taking up the room and a large double bed pushed up against the wall, we spent many a time constantly going up to the council to see if a place was available. When we got the call about our first home, I just couldn't wait! I packed my suitcase and the pram, and off we went. It was great having our own home. Finally! I thought.

It was a lovely little two-bedroom house with no central heating to keep us warm and ice hanging from the windows inside and out. Our curtains didn't draw to a close as they were not wide enough, and we only had wire to hang them on, but we were happy. Lots of people helped out. My dad brought us a fire and my mother-in-law gave us a cooker, and I would use my Nan's old radiogram to play some records. All my washing was done by hand. I would take to boiling the nappies on the stove to bring them up nice and white. We had a close relationship with the neighbours. We even shared a washing machine at times, as we didn't all have one. We would put fifty pence in the electric meter; when it ran out we would light the cooker and make fish-finger sandwiches by candle light, all hugged up together. Our life sounded tough then but to be honest they were the best days of our life. Having to save for things gave us a sense of pride; we were taught if you can't afford it don't have it. We brought our children up with the same morals as our mothers and fathers and grandparents before us.

I can recall once going to bed and taking Richard to keep him warm. He was only one year old but had started walking at nine months. I took the kettle with me and a jug to warm his milk up in the night. When Richard woke in the night, I gave him his bottle and he went back to sleep—or at least I thought he had. He sneaked out of bed and kindly placed his dad's alarm clock in the jug of water, causing him to be late for work. As the water in the jug had turned to ice, the clock sat solid, and we were unable to move it.

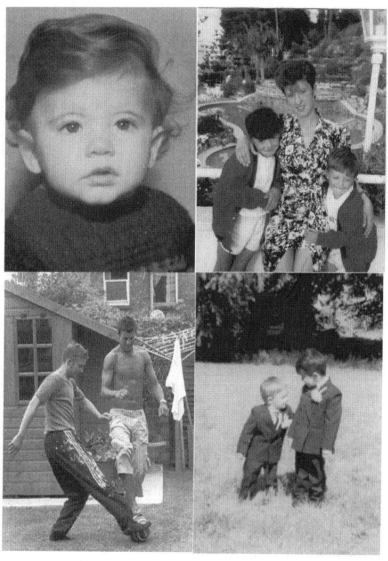

We contacted the council to ask about central heating, but they declined and said there was no money left in the pot, so we would have to use any form of heating we could to keep us warm. We spent just a year in this house before moving on to our little terrace house in Euston road, Northampton which needed a lot of work done to it. This is where we would stay for over thirty years. Again, this was a very cold house with heaters set out everywhere. We would then start work on our home with help from family and friends.

One evening when Richard was around six, he couldn't sleep, which was unusual for him. He asked to come down and sit with me for a while. At this time I was watching the great film 'Ghost'. I didn't think he was taking much notice of the film as we were talking about other things.

His dad was working nights at that point, but he would always call me on his break to check that we were all right. Richard took the phone from me and said, "Dad, will you be okay walking home? I am just worried something might happen to you." Then I realised it was the film that had gotten our son worried after what had happened to poor Patrick in the film. His dad reassured him that he would be okay and not to worry because he would be walking home with a friend. His place of work was only ten minutes away.

My first job, when leaving school, was working for Church's shoe factory with my mum; that's when I found out that I was expecting Richard. Then I worked as a cleaner at Mereway Upper School for a few years before joining the Northampton General Hospital working weekends and during the week as a ward orderly. I did night shifts on the labour ward, and worked on the old people's and maternity wards.

The experience of being a mum, even a young one, particularly helped me to help others who were having their first child. I used to say to them, "It's like tooth-ache; once it's over and the pain goes, the joy begins." I met so many lovely people at that hospital. Maternity and cancer wards, you might think, are so different, but both are so full of human kindness. People gave me so many gifts. I don't know why, because I was only trying to help them with their discomfort.

I then moved on to work for a bank, Barclaycard, on a handy, flexible nine am to one pm shift, and sometimes stayed until three for extra money, with the kids safe at school. Richard Sr. had moved up to become a setter and then a skilled tool maker at Air Flow, where he would work until they closed down in 2004.

I would take the kids to school, get to work by nine in the morning, finish at two, then come home and do the housework. I would then pick up the kids from school, do the dinner, and sit down for a while for some family time. Shortly after hubby had come home from work, I went out again between five and nine. I would set about getting the kids' clothes ready for school and lay them out for the morning.

Eventually, I had to leave my Barclaycard job to look after Richard and Glenn's great granddads. For eight years Great Granddad Tom lived with us at home and Great Granddad Bill lived in a self-contained flat, so he needed support from his family. Three of us would share to help support him. Daughter Sheila would go in the morning, I would go in the afternoon, and Glenda, my mum, would go after a full day's work. Granddad Tom who lived with me was suffering from dementia, and Bill had had a stroke, but both Richard and Glenn eagerly helped them more than they knew.

Caring for your loved ones is very difficult at times when they suffer with dementia. I would lie awake at night worrying if Tom, my granddad, was going to climb out of the window or open the door and run down the street when I was asleep. It is no fun and games. I would sleep in an armchair to keep an eye out for him. I can remember Richard helping me lift his Great Granddad Tom up the stairs as I could not lift him when Richard's dad was out at work. When he had finished his shift he, too, would eagerly pitch in and help get my granddad into the bath as it was a man's thing, and I would shave him and cut his hair. He would laugh when looking in the mirror and say he wanted his hair cut, too. I would go along with it and say, "But he has got to pay, Tom." We all dug in deep to support our loved ones; that is how life should be.

We often took Granddad Bill out in his wheelchair to do a bit of shopping. I can remember buying his favourite blueberry muffin in the shopping centre. We would then buy a cup of tea and he would get his cake out to eat it, and, to my horror, once we were asked to leave because we had not bought the blueberry cake in the cafeteria. It really upset me because my granddad Bill so looked forward to his shopping day out, and whenever we went after that, he didn't feel he wanted a cup of tea; he would wait until I got him home. We often took granddad Tom out for a game of skittles or cards before his dementia got the better of him. It's so hard watching your loved ones deteriorate before your very eyes. Granddads Tom and Bill both sadly passed away within three months of each other.

I have to say, and I speak for many others who support their loved ones at home, that it did cause its own health problems for me at times. Lack of sleep and all the lifting would lead me to be quite tired at times. It really is twenty-four-hour care. There were times when I was unable to leave the house even to go to the shop because of my granddad's dementia. For his own safety we always had someone around him; he was never left alone. I was also looking after my family and YTS lads from Northampton who moved in at that time.

Having had Richard at such a young age, it made us both grow up so quickly, but, despite working so many hours to just get by, we so enjoyed being parents, through both the good times and the bad. We never had the help the young people get today—no nursery fees paid or child tax credits, no chance of further education—you just took any job that would pay the bills and put food on the table and clothes on your back. I can remember going for a cleaning job once, and they asked, "Have you come for the secretarial job?" I replied no, because it didn't fit around my family life at the time. I think they found it quite strange that I would want the cleaning job, being so young.

Holidays were so precious for us all. We made time count. The material things in life are not that important. Finances were getting better, but to have a holiday was important so we used to save the Sun newspaper tokens to ensure a summer holiday. We saved hard for a first holiday abroad to Spain, but our savings didn't allow for the flight. We took off on a coach which took us twenty-four hours to get there. The kids didn't seem to mind, but the trip was harder than I thought.

As Richard's mother I have fond memories of our boys Richard and Glenn who spent a lot of good times together on holiday down on the beach. They would run up and down in the waves as Richard said it would make his legs stronger. In doing so they both became very fit. I think their dad gave up after a while as he couldn't keep up. That's when you know you're getting on a bit. His dad would often join in to play football with the boys and would race amongst the waves. What a sight to see.

On our return home the boys would sometimes annoy the neighbours. The times our son used to kick the ball at our local garages down the street upsetting them. They used to knock on the door and say, "We know Richard loves his football, but can he please do it somewhere else?" Our son would always be polite and full of apologies.

Glenn speaks of his time with his brother:

We would play football at every opportunity. We used to play in the garden, pretty much breaking most things that got in our way. One day we broke a statue of an angel. The head came clean off, but thanks to a little bit of luck we managed to balance it back on.

Mum remembers it being a windy day. She stood in the kitchen and a sheet of cardboard blew across the garden, and she thought it had chopped the statue's head off. She said, "Look at that!" and we boys, well, we just killed ourselves with laughter; that was another ornament we had broken.

The time we went fishing was not so funny. A friend threw back his rod, but when it came forward the hook grabbed my ear, and it really hurt. Richard was so worried and upset for me; he cut the fishing wire and weights and walked me to KFC. Because I was so upset they gave me a free-bee, although we did end up down the hospital to get the hook removed. … That's not the only time we managed to get into trouble. When playing football we also used to play in the living room, breaking the ornaments on the mantelpiece. That did not go down too well, either.

I look back now and can't believe what we got away with. We were always playing football in the street, setting off the odd car alarm and breaking the occasional window. I remember when Richard managed to put the ball straight into the top corner of our friend's window. His father, the ex-heavyweight boxer John Cullen, came to the front door. It was a scary old time when he asked "Who did that?" Thankfully, Richard put his hand up as I, Paul Martin, and Ash, to name a few, stood very silent, before John replied, "Don't worry, I'll get it fixed." We thanked our lucky stars that day, I can tell you. He was a lovely man. Otherwise, things could have been a whole lot worse that day. But we were all very close as friends, and all looked out for each other. Our parents never allowed us to go too far, and we always had to stay in groups. We had a great relationship with our friends, always in and out of each other's houses.

There were times when Richard and Paul Cullen would have this thing about marmite. They would eat it by the spoonful to see who could eat the most. The two marmite boys were worse than the milky bar kids.

My brother was a typical big brother, he used to love to wind me up, play-fight with me and play tricks on me. I always remember on car journeys we would both get some sweets. He would eat all his before trying to get some of mine off me. He used to say "Glenn, please don't make me fat." So I used to keep feeding him my sweets, trying to make him fat.

We also used to play cards on a regular basis. He could never play properly as he just had to win. Then he would often stand up afterwards with cards falling all over the floor.

Richard was so hyperactive, always on the go. He never went to bed before ten, but when he did, he would get in the bed and wake me up to have a good old chat. We got a double bed in the end. I got fed up with him leapfrogging from one to the other. Even when I was a baby, my mum told me my brother would climb into my cot, causing the bottom to fall out with the weight of the two of us.

I can remember Mum coming home from work one day. She went upstairs into Richard's bedroom, always clean and tidy, mind you, but there was this awful smell. She said, "Where is that smell coming from? I will have to clean this room to find out." She set about doing so, and, to her horror, she found a big white rat hiding behind the chair—in a cage, mind. She shouted, "Richard, where did you get this from?" It turns out one of his friends couldn't keep it anymore, so he decided to give it a home.

As we got older it was nice to have a brother who played football. He used to get me free Cobblers tickets every other week when he was doing his apprenticeship at Northampton as a YTS lad. These were tough times for Richard, as there was a lot of pressure on him to do well. He was very dedicated to football even when temptation was there. As a young footballer he found women were never far away, and his friends would want him to go to town and have a drink. He did go out from time to time, but football always came first with him.

Yet, at the end of the day, it doesn't matter what you do for a living, my brother was just a normal person wanting to do what normal teenagers do. Richard would always take the time to come home, even after becoming a pro footballer. He enjoyed spending quality time with his long-term friends who kept in touch throughout his career. He was always interested in what his friends had been up to, far more than wanting to talk about himself.

Even when the season was finished he would train hard, getting me to race him around the Sixfields Lake up near our hometown club, the Cobblers. I ran for the town at the time, so I could give him a bit of a run for his money. We would have some great races, and that still brings back some great memories.

Richard was and still is a great brother because he was always so great to have around. As kids, he would look out for me, and as we got older things never really changed. Sometimes, though, I think he thought he was my dad and not my brother. He was very protective and hated the thought of someone taking advantage of his family. One day he drove all the way from Lincoln to see my boss, as he thought I was being taken advantage of. I got a call out of the blue. He said, "Hi, Glenn, I am sitting with your boss, you need to come now." This is just one example of how protective he was towards me.

He was very caring, and every time I went to visit him, he insisted on giving me petrol money, so it didn't cost me anything. Watching Richard play football was hard sometimes. They don't get paid a lot of money at that level, but people still like to give you abuse. It's hard to sit there and say nothing if someone says something about your brother. I think people forget they're just normal people. We are from a normal terraced house in a normal street, and we are more down-to-earth than most typical back-street kids.

That's another thing: my brother never forgot his roots and always had time to talk to anyone. He thought a lot about people that came to watch him and could not believe how people could pay money to watch him play. He signed autographs happily, but always struggled to understand why people wanted his. We walked through Lincoln City one day, and a couple came right up to him and asked if they could have their photo taken with him. He was always polite and did as they asked. He never saw himself as a star, just a normal person, but he was a star to me, though, and I miss him loads every day. Although my brother wasn't lucky enough to be a David Beckham, he would often score wonder goals just like one of his heroes. But he was privileged to play alongside Wayne Rooney's brother and many other players he so admired while playing for Macclesfield Town.

Richard's Father says:

Our son started his football career when playing for Parkland Tigers Under-12s and Northampton Timken Colts Under-13s. Soon after that things began to get more serious. Matthew Finlay was one of our son's teammates, and he also got that all-important YTS with Richard. The big break came when our son attended the Northamptonshire Football Association Centre of Excellence Under 13s. He was then invited for trials for Northampton Town Youth team and, if I recall correctly, there were around eighty lads from all over the county as well as the Milton Keynes area. They had a number of sessions and games with Richard showing up very well, and he was selected for the Northampton Town Under 14s side. As our son progressed through the different age groups the trials consisted of a minimum 3 x 20 minutes a game, with teams consisting of six to seven players per side. The assessment was done by at least four qualified coaches. Things became a lot more serious, and that is when you start thinking to yourself, *is there a chance he could possibly make it as a professional footballer?* Although they were exciting times, I can remember driving to Derby County on one occasion, and we arrived well over an hour before we needed to be there. Richard was not very happy with me for getting there so early, but I am not great at driving and was worried about getting lost and missing the match.

Richard's Mum Gail:

A point that comes to mind on how important the lower league football clubs are: the large wages that follow the premiership and championship sides could easily help out our lower league clubs. Just one week's top-flight player's wage donated could help a small club like Northampton, Macclesfield Town, or Lincoln City survive. After watching Clarke Carlisle's football programme on TV about depression, suicide, and football secrets, I found it really hard to hear when some had gambled all their wages away, only to be left with nothing at the end of their careers. Most of the lower-league football lads, I would say, will never get the chance to earn the sort of wages some of the top-flight players are lucky enough to earn.

Richard's Father:

I tried to contact Clark Carlisle as our son was a pro footballer, and my depression and his mother's was so severe after losing Richard. And I had a number of other issues I wanted to talk to him about which I was hoping he could follow up for me.

Richard's Mum Gail:

Although the money's not bad at some clubs, I think we really need the PFA (Professional Footballers' Association) or top flight football organizations to come and help support our lower league flight. I have to admit some non-professional lads whom I have met since Richard's death do now take the time to follow the score line at our lower league clubs outside of their home town Northampton known as the 'Cobblers'. Macclesfield Town kindly donated a football kit to a local team who have renamed themselves as the 'Butcher Locos' in memory of Richard. They wear the kit with pride and seem to have a massive 'kick' in their steps, as most of these lads find it hard to even find regular work through no fault of their own.

We need to support our young kids of today and our future generation of footballers. This is what our charity is about. We have a great passion towards what we have been trying to achieve, as this has been set up in memory of Richard to help do something for our young generation of footballers. We all dream that our children will be playing for Man United or Arsenal one day, but we also have to encourage them to look at the wider picture right from a young age.

Richard's father and I followed our son's path along with him; he worked so hard to see his dreams come true. With any teenager, it is a very difficult time as they approach leaving school, what with the distractions of girlfriends, and all the other things that teenagers like to do. Any parent will tell you these are very challenging times.

Richard was no exception; he was always very popular with the girls. He was always very dedicated to his football, but he did need the full support of his mum and dad to keep him on the right track. From a mum's point of view I didn't like football much. In the early days I thought Richard had two left feet (he was two-footed as the trademark 'twenty-yarder' would show) but I soon got into the swing of things. It was a case of, "if you can't beat them, join them." I was always very proud of my son, he was my first little treasure, he so enjoyed his football. We enjoyed watching him as a young lad, mind the cost of football boots—three pairs at a time—and he always had the best. You need a lot of time and support to give, as there are lots of ups and downs, twists, and welcome breaks, to chasing the dream.

Richard's Father:

The little kicks and flicks were always exciting to watch. As a father I can remember going to the park or behind the police station on a number of occasions and having Richard kick the ball at me. It was like a rocket, and I always came home with bruises on my legs. My son always asked me if I would like to have a kick-about with him, and Glenn, and a few of his friends.

PARKLANDS TIGERS F.C
RICHARD BUTCHER

But going to a match was always worrying for me. Would he have a good game? If he did, Richard felt great, and so did I, and to have a win made it even better still. The stress and strains on finance that football can bring to you and your child and family will be a hard one, because it is a long path. Chasing the dream but also knowing it can end at any time, never knowing where they will move to or how well they will perform, or even get on in their chosen career. For most families, times are hard and some young lads never get to follow their dream because of the finances and time being so very hard to come by, especially if you're not lucky enough to be well off. Or the travelling will be too much for you due to work commitments, which can force your child to miss out on a career he or she most enjoys; although there are no guarantees in football.

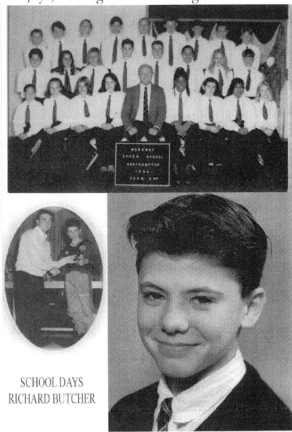

SCHOOL DAYS
RICHARD BUTCHER

The local schools Richard attended during this time were: Queen Eleanor Lower School (1985–1989), Delapre Middle School (1989–1993), and Mereway Upper School (1993–1997).

Richard's Mum Gail:

Whenever we walked into the playground after the weekends to collect Richard's nephews and cousins from school, the Headmaster, Mr. Bob Buntline, from Delapre Middle School, and Mr. Masters were always so interested in how Richard was doing. They would look out for him all the time and always knew when he had scored a goal. Richard also signed a photo of each club he played for and gave each school a copy of an album for a keepsake. It told his story. He was talked about in assembly to show young lads what they could achieve if they didn't make the Man United Team, which is what all our kids dream about.

Richard's best drama teacher, Mrs. George Atkinson, sadly passed a few weeks before our son. We had talked about this with him before his passing. Her funeral took place at the time Richard had died, and his funeral was being organised. It was so hard to believe. They both ended up being talked about together in our local Northampton Chronicle paper. She was also my teacher as a child, and Glenn's, too. Even the teachers you stay close to after leaving school are always still interested in what you are doing.

NAME   is my Life

Name : Richard Tony Butcher
Address : 114 Easton Rd., Northampton
Weight : _____   Shoe Size : 4
Colour of eyes : brown   Hair : black
Number of brothers : 1   Ages : 7
Number of sisters : 0   Ages : 0
Family Details : Me my mum and dad and brother are like the same because me and my mum have had black hair and brown eyes but my dad and brother has blu
Pets : one mouse
Hobbies : football
Future jobs Miner   Pocket money 3£
Main jobs at home : 0
Hero : Gary Linker   Ambition : football player

Favourites :   book : The dragon
food : chips and fish   TV prog : Bad boys
football team : Everton
singer/pop group : New kids on the block

Teacher Mr. David Fox:

Richard was in my class for a year at Delapre Middle, and then I knew him for a year after that for year-eight game lessons on the Far Cotton Rec. So, in a way, this feels rather like writing a school report all over again, but I only have positive things to say about him and that may be enough.

In fact, in Richard's year group at Delapre, we had a number of very good, very keen little footballers and Richard was the most talented of them. They were a happy bunch, and their skill and enthusiasm made them a pleasure to watch. Richard just loved to play football, and I remember not just his ability as a young lad, but also the support and encouragement he gave to his teammates. He played the game with a smile and could appreciate a pass or a tackle against him just as well as he loved to make that pass or score that goal himself. He was a selfless player, and to see that quality in someone so young was something I always admired in him.

In class, entirely by chance, I had Richard sitting in front of me just on the other side of the desk. I think it's just how the alphabetical order worked out, because he never gave me the least cause for concern, either with his work or his behaviour. He was polite, conscientious, and hard-working. No matter how boring he may secretly have found this lesson to be, he was far too polite and well brought up to show it! Yes, sometimes his eyes would go to the window, and I knew he would much rather be out there playing football, but I could hardly blame him for that. Richard was reliable, modest, and with a good sense of humour. If all our pupils were like he was, teaching would be very easy.

Richard's Father:

We knew it was always going to be football, though Richard was given the opportunity to work at Top Man for his work experience through the school. To be fair he looked really good in a suit, but I think he only lasted the day and that evening he phoned Paul Curtis, who was in charge of the Northampton Town Youth Team, to ask if he could do his work experience there. Paul was quite happy for our son to do that and did say, "I don't know why you did not ask to come here in the first place."

Richard even played some games for the youth team before he left school. It had got to be around that time that Northampton Town FC had decided who they were going to take as YTS trainees. These were very stressful times for us as parents, and Richard of course, as he had his heart set on this opportunity just as all the other lads and their parents had. I can remember the evening; it was during training when, one by one, the lads, along with one of their parents, were called in to see Paul Curtis. Gail waited outside; she must have had everything crossed for luck. It was great news for Richard, as he got offered that prized YTS place with Northampton Town FC. We were obviously over the moon, but it was also very difficult to see some of the other lads, along with their parents, who came out in tears. They had not been so lucky, and we felt for them as did Richard, even during his time of pride and joy. I don't know what made us prouder, to be honest.

We had a few of the YTS lads stay with us for a time. There was all the washing hanging round the house, the fighting for the bathroom, and constant grooming of hair. Richard's mum cooked all the dinners and made all the lunch-time pack-ups. These were famous with the 'first-teamers' who used to nick them when they had a chance. Gail always liked to feed them well, and made sure their food and diet was nutritious and healthy—that's vital for a player at every stage of his or her development. She was working and looking after her granddads as well, with Glenn and Richard helping, but Gail always loved a full house and never minded looking after them. We had the loft converted, so they all had their own space, and we had ours.

In Richard's younger days, from a travelling point of view and because I hated driving, we always left early so Richard would never be late for any games. Some of the youth matches you went to were a long way. You would do a full day at work, rush home, have dinner and then off you would go to a game. Sometimes I would have to try and get a day off as I knew it would be too much for me.

I liked to be involved with Richard's football as much as I could and Gail came along too when she wasn't working. She worked nights sometimes but she also had Glenn to care for. He was our son too; we wanted him to have a good start and to feel he was an important part of our family. He would want to do other things and we needed to be there for him too. Sharing our time out to the both of them was so important. But when you are both working and you so want to be involved with your kids and enjoy the time with them you will do anything to be there for them.

It made things easier when Richard passed his driving test. It helped so much as he would go off to the game early and then we could go along a bit later. We got his first car for him and set him all up as he didn't have much money at that time being YTS. But it gave him his freedom and made him more confident and he was able to help the other lads out and take them to football if they were stuck for a lift.

It would also give Richard some freedom with the girls, even though football would always be his number one priority. He did however have one very lucky escape with childhood sweet-heart Gamma, his long-term girlfriend during his school days at Mereway Upper. One evening, the two were enjoying a bit of TV—doubtless an informative documentary—when a car came crashing through the window and into the lounge. The two were miraculously spared injury, although Richard required a precautionary neck brace that, allegedly, slowed him down on all fronts, for a few weeks at least.

Richard's Mum Gail:

Richard's dad wanted to call his son Everton when he was born, but I wouldn't have it, and even when he got older he still complained and moaned because I wouldn't let his dad have his way. He was Richard the 5th in a long line in the Butcher family.

Richard Sr.'s first job was a yacht fitter. As a qualified carpenter and cabinet maker he would kit out the yachts, achieving a sense of pride and accomplishment. But his apprenticeship and stay lasted just the four years as in 1981 the company shut down, which led to many skilled-job losses.

Thanks to his father-in-law he was able to continue to fend for us, his family, with a job at Air Flow Stream Lines. Starting on the shop floor as an operator, he progressed to setter before becoming a skilled tool maker. After twenty-three years Air Flow closed down, robbing Northamptonshire of another skill base, along with the British shoe trade, where members of our family had also worked over the years. A quick stint at Pinnacle Mobile Homes and Widney Cabs as a machine operator in 2005 was equally short-lived as both closed down. Richard's dad moved to Carlsberg UK in 2005 and is still working there putting in the twelve-hour shifts on various machines, as well as carrying out inspections and checks.

As a dad, he has always looked after his children, working hard, and always willing to help, be it his time, his advice, his craftsmanship skills, or even a few quid here and there. I can remember him making a wooden shoe at work with laces threaded through it to help his son learn to tie his shoe laces up, and it worked! It really was a clever piece of kit.

We both would give the last penny we had to help our children if they needed it. We went short on a number of occasions in order for both Glenn and Richard to move into their first houses. This seems to be the norm now, for many parents to help their children get on the housing ladder if they are able to offer the financial support.

Richard's father's interests are largely sporting, but in particular football, with Everton and Northampton on the list. He likes 50s and 60s music—indeed he has friends in The Jets who also suffered a sad loss in the family, Young Kyle Cotton, just the tender age of ten years old; such a beautiful young man we all came to love. Our family enjoyed going to gigs, and Richard and Glenn would have DA hairdos similar to their dad's. Richard and Glenn grew up with rock and roll and enjoyed spending time with the Cotton family and their sons.

Whilst my husband has never been a lover of dancing, except when he has had a few, both Richard and Glenn loved dancing and could both jive, thanks to the patience of me teaching them. Perhaps it was starting out as such a young couple that ensured that we never quite lost the inner child, as we enjoyed camping out in the back garden with the boys.

We never pushed Richard into wanting to be a footballer; we were so proud of both of the boys in whatever job they chose to do. Just so long as they tried their best, even should they fail, we would always be there to support them emotionally and financially to the best of our abilities. Richard's brother Glenn was unlucky to inherit his dad's knees, which have caused him problems over the years. He also enjoyed running for the county and had a great love for football. And he was a very good player, I might add.

I can remember going to bingo one day we were struggling for money. At the time I never used to win but just this once I did. I came home from bingo, my husband said "did you win?" I said no and threw the money round the house; just seven hundred pounds but this helped us afford the kids' uniforms and a weekend for the kids at Billing Aquadrome theme park. Although it rained all weekend, we had great fun with the boys rowing up and down the river in their little boat with an umbrella.

However, when it came time to cook breakfast we did have a little visitor: a mouse, yes a mouse, who decided to eat all the chocolate biscuits as well as breakfast; he must have been quite fat when he left.

Close friend Martin Fletcher recalls a funny moment:

Me and Butch were going on holiday to Kavas. We were all very excited, and the day before the flight I got a call from a few friends whom Butch knew saying they would like to have a catch up. Well, after we had all reminisced on growing up together, I said to Butch, "I will have to get off now. Pick you up in the morning." He said, "Okay, mate."

Butch always took his time to get ready. It took him hours to do his hair style like Beckham, who, no doubt, was one of his idols. I turned up in the morning to pick the lads up, and what a shock I had! Ten bald men standing in front of me! They had found some clippers and had shaved each other's hair off! I really could not believe my eyes. He got in the car and all the way he kept saying, "Does it look good?" I had to reassure him from that moment on.

It was funny to see, as I thought I would never see the day Butch had no hair. But to make it even better, it had just been announced on TV that Beckham had shaved all his hair off. Butch said, "See? Beckham has copied me." That made him a happy boy again.

I kept in touch with Butch on and off on the phone, and went to visit him with my daughter at his home in Lincoln. Your lives take different paths, but whenever we spoke, it was like he had never been away—my best friend, Butch. I miss you, Buddy, every day.

Richard Mum Gail:

As a mum, I remember the day after that, when Richard was nicknamed 'microphone head', as his hair was so dark and thick. I really didn't like it when he was bald, and neither did he. I was so pleased when it grew back.

The softer side to Richard was that he was so very kind and caring. One Mothers' Day, Richard and his brother Glenn decided to make me a Mothers' Day breakfast. He must have been around ten at the time. He must have put just about everything you could think of on the plate: sausages, egg, bacon, beans, tomatoes, toast and not to mention a cup of tea. They were so very proud when they handed me the tray and got quite upset when I couldn't eat it all.

He was so thoughtful; he would buy presents like a plaque that would say DAD'S SHED and a little plaque with a rose on which said I Love My MUM. Richard's gifts were always unusual and came from the heart. Every card he wrote, he would thank us from the bottom of his heart for our support for helping him follow his dream; but it was Richard who made it happen with all the hard work he put in and the sacrifices he had to make.

He asked me once what I would like for my birthday. I said, "I don't need anything. I have my little family, that's all I need." He said "What do you want?" I couldn't think of anything. I saw a large fish in the corner shop which would look nice by our pond so I said "I love that fish in the shop window." He said "You're joking, Mum." I said "No, it's lovely," so off he went and came back with this great big fish ornament, which sits happily by my pond. Richard always thought it was ugly but I love it.

School friend Darren Mackenzie remembers:

Richard always attracted the girls, attractive lad; he played football at school, so he had the girls in his hand. But Richard's sole focus was football. Yes, he had girlfriends, but football was his heart.

When I was about twelve or thirteen my family moved away from the area to the other side of town, so we never got to finish our schooling together. But this never really kept us apart, as I used to bike over to Cotton most weekends, to do, guess what? That's right, play football. With me now being at another school from Richard, it led to interesting school football derby matches: Weston Cavell Upper vs. Mereway Upper; Richard, the star of Mereway School team—with me the Weston Favell goalkeeper. We would always joke and laugh during a game, and Richard always tried so hard to score past me, which, luckily, he never did. I would always say this to him every time I saw him, and you could tell it annoyed him, which meant the next game he would come out harder and better. You could see from a young age he was going to be a good footballer.

After we had finished school, we all went our separate paths, Richard into football, and me into the army, so contact between us slowed down. But I would still make a habit of watching his games and having the odd chats, even though we kind of lost touch with each other. I was on tour a bit, and Richard's career had really picked up. I did always follow his progress, and also would try and get to some of the games when on leave.

I remember one game when Northampton Town played Lincoln. I went up to the game just because Richard was playing, and I took my brother-in-law and nephew Spencer along with me. Richard was playing, and I recounted our times together to my nephew. Then, after the game, I shouted over to Richard. He was looking very oddly towards me, but walked over and when he got close he realised who I was. I remember him saying, "Sorry, mate, I thought you were a Cobblers fan who wanted to get me." We spoke for about thirty minutes pitch-side, and Spencer was star-struck as I asked Richard to sign his programme; Spencer was in his element.

After that, we kept in contact a little more. Richard was a cracking bloke, and from the impression I get from his mum, Gail, a cracking son also. He was just a nice guy, knew his roots in life, and always stayed grounded. He had respect, you know, so he always gave his family and friends time.

The morning I found out about what had happened, I was gutted, and felt ill, I couldn't believe it. I was in shock, but I stayed away from the family for a while, to give them space, before I contacted Gail and sent her my condolences. It was then that I started helping Gail with her charity work. Richard is forever part of Far Cotton and he would love to help local youngsters to follow their dreams and maybe even realise them as he had done. RIP, Butch, Never forgotten—and always in our hearts.

Richard's Mum Gail:

Our son's life has always revolved around his family, but he solely focused on his football career. I am sure fans saw the honesty and passion Richard put into his career and life in general. His dream and our dream came true, but the loss we feel as a family only a mother and father can feel. We will never feel the same or be the same. We miss the daily phone calls and the daily contact, especially his dad. As a father to a son, football was their passion. Having a child missing from your life is like no other. There are no words to explain how we have felt.

The tragedy is: no parent should outlive their children; it is so wrong somehow. You feel as though you lose your way in life. Since our son's passing the days seem so long, and the nights too. To Glenn it feels like he has lost a mum and to Richard Sr. it feels like he has lost a wife, but I get so wrapped up in my own feelings that nothing seems to matter, even if I do try not to show it. But everyday life is a struggle to the point when nothing matters; the days and nights can pass without a trace and leave me unable to deal with just the small things in life. Just to go shopping or even to look at clothes I find so difficult, as I would say in passing, "That's a Richard top. It would look nice on him," or certain foods he would like, or a dinner I cook that I know was his favourite. When shopping, I am constantly looking for 'my son'. I see someone who looks just like him, and, for a moment, I want to shout, "Richard, over here, it's Mum!" but then I realise it's not him; I sleep with his jumper, and spray his after-shave just so I can smell him 'just one more time'. I talk to him, and kiss his photo good night. I look for any shadow in the dark, or even a twinkle of light, or a soft cold air across my face, just to feel him around me one more time. I light a candle at his grave, and then I come home and light one right next to his photo. It becomes a ritual you want to do just to make you feel that little bit closer. I look at his photos and can see his strength, his muscles, his arms and legs, and I want to reach out and touch him, he seems so real. How could this be? Where has he gone?

Football made Richard's life such a joy. He always said scoring a goal was like nothing else. The feeling was overwhelming for him and for us. He found it hard when the fans asked for his autograph. He struggled to understand why anyone would want it. Richard had a passion for football, and we shared that life with him. He made us so proud to be his parents.

We both tend Richard's grave, going there to try to make sense of a true tragedy. When we recently got a mail-order butterfly set for our five-year-old granddaughter she, Elise, insisted on letting them off at his graveside with myself and Richard's grandparents.

Our son died the day before her birthday, so she likes to think they share it together. She always places a candle in her cake, and we light it for him. Elise is a special little lady at the age of just six years old. She kisses Richard good night, and sends her letters of love to an uncle she misses very much. She places flowers on his grave, and sings her songs to him like he's around her all the time. We try to show Elise the family values we always showed to Richard and Glenn when growing up, and to show her we can still love our son her uncle although he's not here.

RICHARD'S NIECE ELISE, RELEASING BUTTERFLIES
AT RICHARD'S GRAVE

He has a lot of young nephews who still don't understand where he's gone, and the younger ones, Kyle, Brogan, and Robbie, keep photos hanging in their rooms and watch CDs of his 'fantastic' goals regularly and are so very proud of their uncle Richard, but they find nothing to celebrate in losing him, and missing out on the time they could have spent with him. We try to tell them Richard's okay, and that he's having lots of fun where he is today.

We as parents miss our first-born. As any parent will tell you, it leaves a massive hole in your life. Richard's dad suffered a heart attack while this book was being written. It has no link to our son's death, but he underwent a triple bypass, so losing Richard and then nearly losing his dad was a massive shock to myself and son Glenn.

Glenn recalls:

I was on holiday at the time when I got the call. I could not believe it. I managed to get a flight back straight away, so I could be with my dad. It was a very difficult time and a scary moment as my dad had been told that if he didn't have the operation he could die at any time. He was classed as critical and he was rushed off to Harefield in an instant. He's always been so fit, just like Richard; never been ill in his life. He always looked after himself so well. We were told the main cause of what happened at the age of just fifty-three was stress. The turmoil of losing Richard, and the entire heartache that went with it, obviously took its toll.

Richard's Mum Gail:

We have worked so hard for the Richard Butcher Memorial Trust since Richard's death. As a mother I had to throw myself into something that involved my son. After having great support from the local community who signed a petition to support a football pitch and club house for the community, what could I say?

2,000 people signed it in just two months. Not all football is a wealthy gain, but it helps a lot of young lads who want to follow their dream. I thought I could help by raising money to give these young lads something to shout about. But you do have to be a committed parent when it comes to a football life with your child. I had already started my charity but I can remember watching 'Surprise Surprise' and a lovely lady was on who had lost her daughter and had set up a charity in her memory to raise money to build a community centre for her local community. The whole community stood by her and her dream came true. I was so emotional after watching that. I felt the lady was an inspiration to me and to others for what she had achieved after her daughter's death, and this gave me the incentive to carry on.

I have shared my story and Richard's with you with the hope it will give the young people of today an insight of what a footballer's life can be like and what it has felt like for us and many other families to lose someone so young. The book will take you through Richard's career and his personal life with us, his family and friends.

3: Northampton Town 1997 – 1999

Richard had been part of the Northampton Town Youth Development Centre of Excellence since 1994. We hoped all the shooting practice behind the police station would be worthwhile, and would pay off in the future. Richard always kept his feet on the ground, knowing it could be a long shot.

Some of the Centre of Excellence home games were played at Raunds Town where Richard met Keith Burt, the manager. Richard ended up playing for them when he was released from Northampton. Richard was naturally looking forward to reporting to Sixfields on Monday 30th June 1997 at 10 am. The letter cheered him up knowing he was going to get an extra £5 a week in his pay packet, and he was looking forward to going on a preseason youth tour to Barcelona to play against young European footballers in the International Friendship Cup of Spain. I had to look for a sponsor around our local area to help fund the trip. I asked Mereway Upper School and they were quite happy to make a donation towards the trip, and Richard's family pulled together and made up the rest up.

The money Richard earned was quite small. Richard would receive just £42.50 a week for his first year at Northampton Town and for the second year just £47.50. It was substantially less than the players brought over from Ireland, who made five times that amount, but Richard didn't care. He would have played for anything to get his chance of becoming a pro footballer, even for nothing at that time.

It was an exciting time for Richard at the Cobblers when Northampton had won the Third Division Play-off final against Swansea 1–0. 32,000 Cobblers fans, including us, Richard's family, followed the Cobblers with pride, and the team went on to have another good season but lost 1–0 to Grimsby in the Second Division Play-off final 24th May 1998. 40,000 fans followed the Cobblers to Wembley, which was an incredible sight to see.

Richard enjoyed the fact that he was a silhouette on the flags all the way down Wembley Way to the iconic National Stadium. He was also on the front of all three of the match programmes that covered the play-off finals taking place at Wembley that weekend. He was very shy about it, but very proud, and so were we. It was very exciting at the time; all the family went along. I made a number of phone calls to try and get one of the flags to keep with my collection, but to no avail.

Meanwhile, here are some highlights of our son's youth years at Northampton Town.

He enjoyed his time in Holland in 1996. The Cobblers' Under-18s picked up the top sporting award at the Clamber Cup for their conduct on and off the pitch. The lads reached the quarter finals of the competition. They finished with four wins and three draws in their eight games.

1998 Northampton Town–Fulham, one game that is close to our hearts as my Nan supported Fulham. Long-term injuries to Ian Clarkson, Tony Dobson, and Damian Matthew, allowed striker Andy Morrow, and Garry Hughes, and our son, central midfielder Richard Butcher, to be drafted in for the FA Cup squad. He was an ever-present youth lad who had already been given three reserve starts.

There is one special game that comes to mind that Richard so enjoyed playing in with his time at the Cobblers—the family fun kick-off at Sixfields with around 5,000 fans who turned out in freezing conditions 11th January 1999, Cobblers reserves–2 Arsenal reserves–0, but nine experienced Arsenal players would feature and take to the pitch: England legend Tony Adams, Nigel Winterburn, Stuart Taylor, Remi Garde, and Nelson Vivas, David Livermore, Michael Black, Paolo Vernazza (Sub William Huck 76) Omer Riza,(Sub Julian Gray 67) Sub unused, Ashley Cole. Ref. Andy Woolmer (Kettering Town). The Cobblers team were Andy Woodman, Michael Warner, and Scott Woods, Garry Hughes, Colin Hill, Richard Hope, Richard Butcher, James Hunt, Chris Lee, Kevin Wilson, and David Seal, (Subs Andy Morrow 68, Brad Piercewright 82, Adam Hancock, 82).

In 1999, the Cobblers youth team Richard was involved in at Northampton town took a bow at Sixfields. They were the proud winners of the Football Youth Alliance Division One title. Kevan Broadhurst's side finished unbeaten in their section, and were unlucky not to qualify for the merit division. Our son also scored far fewer goals with his time at Northampton Town.

Paul Curtis, the Director of Youth Development at Northampton, knew the pain of rejection and was therefore keen to be as hands-on as he could be.

Paul Curtis said:

As for myself, I was released by Charlton Athletic as a 16-year old in 1979 (the youth structure was light years away from what it is now, maybe for the better?), and played once for Dartford U18s. I was seen by a Charlton scout, and was then invited back and signed in November (leaving 'A' levels). After a few seasons in and out of the 1st team, maybe 90-100 games, I signed for Northampton in 1985. I left in 1986. There are one or two things that made me despondent with pro football, but, again, it does revolve around a previous manager, so I can't say much. Suffice it to say, I got a job with the ex-chairman, played for Corby Town, and actually earned more than being a pro footballer (certainly not unusual then or now). I was invited back as a coach by a former teammate who was the manager in 1991, and I stayed until 2003.

Richard was one of those players that I worked with at a younger age, with my youth team manager working on a daily basis with him as an apprentice aged 16. Richard always showed potential, and was a strong, athletic, and competitive midfield player who at an early age had been earmarked by myself as a potential first team player, especially given the way in which the first team played at that time.

Richard was to tidy Denis Casey's physio room, clean the boots of new striker Carl Heggs, and, in so doing, benefit from football's time-honoured pro–apprentice relationship. Carl, or Mr. Heggs, as he is now respectfully referred to as, signed for Northampton in 1998 for £25,000. This was just three months after the famous Third Division Play-off final that had seen the Cobblers beat his previous club Swansea 1–0 leaving tumbleweed blowing through the town of Northampton as the faithful flocked to Wembley. Although he was not a prolific goal scorer, Carl was a combative six-footer who made things difficult for the opposition by creating vital space and affording the opportunities through knock-downs for his strike partners to plunder. Carl took Richard to heart at Northampton and would remain a friend for life.

NORTHAMPTONSHIRE FOOTBALL ASSOCIATION
Centre Of Excellence
Under 13's - Final Season 1993-1994

RICHARD BUTCHER NORTHAMPTON TOWN F.C
PHOTOS TAKEN BY; PETE NORTON

NORTHAMPTON TOWN F.C ; RICHARD BUTCHER AND TEAM MATES
PHOTOS TAKEN BY : PETE NORTON

Garry Thompson ran the reserve side which topped the Capital
League for most of the 1997/98 season and gave Richard, even as a
first year scholar, four games in a competitive and experienced
environment during the first season, and a dozen or so in the second.
The first team requirements saw Butch leap-frog on the one hand,
but, in the long term, it cost his development and ultimate progress

to a pro deal. Football can be like that. Your chances come through luck, and windows of opportunity that change and slam with the wind.

Garry Thompson recalls:

In my job as reserve team manager of Northampton at the time, I came across a big gangly midfield player. Part of our brief was to keep an eye on the youth team players. At the time Paul Curtis was in charge, followed by Kevin Broadhurst. Assistant manager Kevin Wilson and I watched a fair few games and this big gangly midfield player turned out to be Butch. If you saw Northampton play at the time you would have said this kid was tailor-made for Ian Atkins' style of football, a big strong box-to-box midfielder, but he had some real ability, and more importantly a strong desire to play and win games.

I always found him a very chirpy lad, involved in any shenanigans that the youth players would be doing, and always badgering me for games in the reserve team as he was keen to progress. But the biggest compliment I can pay the kid was his focus and determination. I met his mother, Gail, on many occasions after games, and we would always have a chat, and Butch was a credit to her and the family. As life would have it, I reconnected with Butch a few weeks before he died, as I was working for Sill Sports soccer agency. I gave Richard a call, and we had arranged to meet, but changes in training times made us change dates a few times and, unfortunately, we never got the chance to meet up again. But busy, bubbly, loud, and funny, in a good way, would be my description of Richard.

Richard's Mum Gail:

Our son had nothing but good reports to say about Garry Thompson. Richard thought he was a great manager, and the one thing I can say is he did believe in Richard. Many a time I sat on the terraces watching the game, as some of them were played in the afternoon, and many a time Richard was having a great game, but Garry Thompson, at times, found it very hard to keep Richard on the pitch—not through any fault of his own, I might add; Garry was put under pressure to take him off the field. He was a great manager and a great friend, and it was a pleasure to know him. Richard thought very highly of him. I can remember making the YTS pack-ups for them to take to training. Along with Richard, the first-team lads seemed to take quite a shine to them, as I could not believe the lads were so hungry. When they arrived back home the lads ended up hiding them in the roof at Sixfields Stadium in the hope they would get their lunch.

Carl Heggs reflects on his career and friend Richard Butcher:

I was lucky to have Richard, who cleaned my boots as part of the time-honoured apprenticeship in football. He was a genuine, nice kid, always smiling and would make the days a pleasure. Most gave their lads £10 at Christmas, but I gave Richard £100 and he was so chuffed. But he deserved it, because he worked so hard on and off the field and always wanted to listen and learn, the friendly banter and laughs aside. I only got just over 50 goals in my career, and was more a thorn in the opposition's side all game, with others getting the glory, but this was Richard, too. You have to chase and chase to save those throws and corners, something Richard became very good at. These actions of the unsung heroes are vital to the team, and I think most fans respect that.

Ian Atkins was a set-piece manager with a strong, forceful, and direct style with lads like James Hunt and Sean Parrish at the heart of a midfield that was always going to be hard for young Butch to break into. I was then transferred to rivals Rushden for £100,000, with Northampton needing the money after an unlucky relegation (16 players out during the season is tough for anyone, but especially on the Cobblers' resources) with the board making the decision and not the manager.

A player has to have the right manager and the right style if they are going to make it, and I was fortunate to have that with Ian who signed me three times, including rescuing me from that horrible time at Rushden. That is massive at our level, where you are just a touch better than most of the mates you leave behind. The Messi's of this world will fit in, but then they will also have the outstanding quality around them to help them, too. With us, it is the effort you put in, and the hope that it inspires your team-mates to respond and really put a great shift in. That Northampton season was brilliant for me, as

I made three of the most important friendships of my life with James Hunt, for one, now godfather to my children.

One of Richard's great pals and a team-mate, Matthew Findlay:

Myself and Richard started playing football together from the age of 12 for Timken colts. Then, at the age of 13, we both went to the Cobblers Centre of Excellence. We signed for the Cobblers YTS like a shot in 1997 and that was a dream come true for two local lads because both myself and Richard jumped at the chance to sign for our home town club.

After a tough first year for all of us—it's a tough adjustment getting used to full time football—we went on to win the Midlands Section Division One League in our second year. We had a good side with a lot of local players in it, including Brad Pearceright, Adam Hancock, Ian Burt, Andy Morrow, Scott Woods, Gianni Santoro, James Gould, and Ryan Thompson. We were a close-knit team and got along well, which I feel really shone through when we won the league. We had some good players in the team, of which Butch was one. I think with a little bit more luck, and a little bit more determination, like Butch had, maybe a few more of those players could have gone on to play the pro game.

We all looked up to the pros, as this is where we all wanted to be some day. Richard was a dedicated footballer, always taking great pride in all that he did on and off the pitch. On the field he always worked hard—box to box—and he was a big strong powerful lad who was hard to knock off the ball. He used to weigh in with his fair share of goals from midfield, but he could never score past me in training for all his effort. He was one of the fittest players at the club even at the age of 16.

The daily routine was to get to Sixfields by 9.30 am and make sure all the training equipment and boots were ready for the first team. I looked after about seven first-team players' boots—those of Andy Woodman, John Fran, Roy Hunter, Richard Hope, Ali Gibb, and James Hunt. Richard used to take care of Dennis Casey's phyiso room and his boots, and a few players' boots, which included the legendary Carl Heggs. Both of them got on really well.

From Sixfields we would travel to training at Moulton College, which is where the majority of the training was done. Good times were had on that mini bus on the way to training, with Butch being at the centre of it! So many good times were had with all of us together; you really can't beat the banter of all the lads being together.

Sometimes we had to drive our own cars to training. I can still see Butch in his white Astra, not going above 30 mph ever. After a couple of hours training it was back to Sixfields to have lunch, that's if we had any left, as the first team used to rifle through our lunch boxes. Sometimes we would train again in the afternoon or have a gym session, or, depending on which day it was, we would all have a quick game of one-touch. Butch was always the biggest stitch-up merchant of them all. He would love to get everybody out, and then do a little song and dance to rub it in. Then it was the task of getting all our jobs done—which used to take hours—this was the worst part of the day as we had to do the boots, changing rooms, and cleaning the balls etc. Then, as long as all the jobs were done and the manager was happy, it was home time usually about 4 or 5.

The manager for our first year was Paul Curtis, who was the Youth Development Director, and in our second year it was Kevin Broadhurst. I would say a good majority of our time spent at Northampton was enjoyable, especially the second year when we won the league, and we all got plenty of football in the reserves. We all got released in May 1999, apart from Andy Morrow who had already signed pro. All the boys were completely gutted as this was all we wanted and dreamed of doing. After we got released, I and Butch both got a job together as well as playing for Raunds Town, but he didn't last long in the job and it was clear to see he was destined to be a footballer.

It was always a pleasure to play football with Butch, as he really was a top bloke both on and off the pitch, and I'm proud to call him one of my mates. I have never heard anybody say a bad word about him; he really was a genuine bloke.

Richard's Mum Gail:

Our son was a lovely young man who was very private and liked his own company. Richard's confidence was building with the support of us, his family. He also had an extensive diet and fitness regimen and had a disciplined approach right up to his death. He would only take supplements from Boots the Chemist for calcium and cartilage bone protection.

Richard's diet was fish, pasta, rice, chicken, sweet potatoes, baked beans, and fruit smoothies. I can remember buying him a book which told him about every vegetable there was to eat, and what they do to help support a healthy body. He followed the book to a T.

As parents we always encouraged exercise. 'Friday night with Friends' always gave us an excuse to have fun with the boys with our aerobics workout and for us, as mums, to try and lose a few pounds. We always had to follow Richard's exercise regimen. He was very good; he could have had his own video.

When he became a teenager he would also spend time with his dad going to the gym. Of course, I joined in too. He was always very serious about his physical and muscular development and body shape. One of his favourite workouts was the cross-trainer with his head phones on singing away to himself.

The phrase 'model professional' is a term used far too frequently in the footballing world these days, but one person who certainly fitted that bill was our son. There were many times he could have given up, with the glamour of football league nearly taken away, but he had that spark and determination to fight on and to never give up on the career he loved so much, which you will come to understand while reading this book.

David Savage, the former Republic of Ireland, Northampton, Oxford United, and Millwall midfield legend, was a close friend of Richard.

Dave Savage tells us about the young fighter:

When I arrived at Northampton in 1999 the game had changed so much since my trainee days at Brighton & Hove Albion in 1990. Gone were the gruelling tasks of cleaning the senior players' boots, collecting the sweaty kit, and scrubbing down the changing rooms daily after the players had left. In my opinion, we were breeding a generation of young players who didn't understand the sacrifices, or have the discipline needed to make a living from the game. The first-team changing room was always seen as a sanctuary that young players aspired to be a part of. To enter without permission when I was a trainee was to risk the wrath of the senior players.

The class of 99 was very different, however. They could be found laughing and joking with first team players, with no real idea of how hard it is to get there. But there was one young player who caught my eye. He had all the attributes needed to progress. Physically he was tall and strong. He could pass well, and had an eye for goal, but more importantly, his attitude was his strongest asset. His name was Richard Butcher, or 'Butch' as he was known to his friends. He reminded me of the 'old school' trainee. Richard was very respectful of all the senior players and he was always asking how he could improve his game. Richard would often be found in the gym after training, and working on his finishing, which would become a trademark of his later in his career. Although Butch never made his name at Northampton, I had no doubt he would have a good career in the game.

When I was asked to write a piece for this book, I wanted to get across how different Butch was to most footballers. Football is the type of game that breeds selfishness, looking after number one, and living up to a stereotype. So I hope this story gives you an idea of the type of lad Butch was. It was December, Lincoln City were playing Oxford Utd. Butch was playing for Lincoln, while James Hunt and I (former Northampton Town players) were playing for Oxford. We won the game 1–0 but Richard played extremely well and seemed almost embarrassed that he'd outplayed two players he'd looked up to as a trainee.

But it was what happened outside the changing rooms afterward that will give you an insight into what type of man Richard was. As myself and 'Hunty' were leaving Butch gave us both an early Christmas card. Now, you might think nothing unusual in that, but let me explain. I have never before or since received a card from another footballer. I have never given one to another footballer, let alone one I hadn't seen for two years. The reason for this is because I would be the victim of changing room jokes for the rest of my career and, I'm ashamed to say, myself and James looked on it as a strange thing for Butch to do.

As I said before, football breeds selfishness. Richard, as well as being incredibly meticulous and organised, didn't care what way footballers were supposed to act. He did what he thought was the right thing to do. If more players were like Butch, the game would be a whole lot better for it, and I just hope Richard and the young boys and girls of Northampton get a fitting memorial; one that represents the local boy who, no matter where he played, never really left home.

Your purchase of this book will not guarantee that someone makes it, for football is an imprecise science. Richard found that, despite rejection, amidst adulation and praise; indeed, he would only keep at it and, ultimately make it, through his parents' writing an incredible amount of letters asking for trials. But it will provide facilities and bring parents and children together as they, too, chase the dream. Thank you. Richard's spirit will live on at Far Cotton, paving the way for parents and children to foremost enjoy the people's game, but also to dare to share that dream.

Richard's Mum Gail:

Dave Savage has always shown what a caring young man he is. He has shown so much support towards the charity since Richard passed, but foremost, he has been a friend to us, Richard's family, who needed him at this sad time. He now works at B&Q and always has a smile to give and a caring word to say. His mother, Ann, has also given us her support through internet chatting. This has been a difficult time for him to deal with Richard's death, as well as to help his family through their own sad losses in their family. He is an absolute Gem, and we would like to thank him from the bottom of our hearts.

I and Richard's dad were filled with pride at the prospect of Richard getting his YTS contract, with the hope that our son would play for his hometown Cobblers one day. Richard already had a family pedigree, as his great granddad's cousin was defender Mr. Ben Collins. Ben played 222 games for Northampton over thirteen years, and his brother, Victor, also had a good career at the Cobblers. Ben earned a testimonial with Stanley Matthews agreeing to run the line as he had sustained an injury.

BEN COLLINS & STANLEY MATTHEWS
AT THE OLD COBBLERS GROUND,
NORTHAMPTON

BEN COLLINS,
RICHARD'S GREAT GRANDAD'S COUSIN,
KINDLY GAVE RICHARD BUTCHER
THIS PHOTO AS A GIFT

Both were cousins to Richard's great granddad, Thomas Collins, whom Richard helped look after for eight years. Ben was the youngest in the Collins football team that was set up in Kislingbury. Ben also ran a sports shop alongside his friend, Mr. Dave Bowen, who was a player/manager for the Cobblers. The shop formed in 1960 in Gold Street, Northampton. Dave sold out to Ben, and the shop continued for over forty years. A lot of people used the shop for all sorts of sports equipment: bowling, football, golf, everything you could think of. Richard enjoyed sharing his time with Ben as he used to call into the shop for a good old chat; he was very inspirational to Richard but also told him how difficult a footballing life can be. One of their biggest talking points was against Arsenal and Liverpool in the Cup. Ben kindly gave Richard a copy of a photo which was taken of him with Stanley Matthews. Richard was so proud of that. Neil Garret also worked in the shop, a school friend of Richard's. Their talking point was always about football boots, which were the best out at the time, and the odd football match.

There is a little story to tell about my Granddad, Tom Collins. My dad was just two years old the last time he saw his Dad. He never knew what his Dad looked like. He didn't even have a photo of him. When my Nan passed away I remember my dad over the years watching 'Surprise Surprise', always wondering what his dad was like. I decided to contact my local paper, the Northampton Chronicle. I asked them if they would put an ad in their paper which would say: "Mrs. G Butcher looking for Thomas Collins who knew of Phyllis Lyons." I noticed it was in the paper, so I just waited, not expecting to hear anything.

I set out to Billing Aquadrome in Northampton for the day with the boys. On my return, to my surprise, my husband said, "Your Granddad has phoned." I said, "Okay, I will phone him back in a minute," thinking he meant my mum's Dad. He said, "No, your Granddad, your Dad's real Dad." Well, I nearly fell through the floor. Excitedly, I picked up the phone, and for the first time ever in my life I was talking to my Dad's real dad, my Granddad, whom I had never met.

I then arranged a meeting with him over the phone. To my delight, he only lived ten minutes away; only a small drive in the car. When I arrived we sat and chatted; it was like I had always known him, he was so like my Dad. Tom, as I called him, gave me some photos to show to his son, so he could see what he looked like for the first time ever. I then phoned my dad and popped in to see him. I said, "I have found your real dad." He said, "That's impossible. I thought he had died." The shock was unbelievable. I said, "Would you like to meet him?" as I showed him the photos.

A meeting was arranged, and, for the first time in my Dad's life, he could say he had met his Dad, and he knew just what he looked like. They had so much in common, it was unreal. They were so alike; this led to a long lasting relationship between Dad and Son and great grandsons and granddaughters.

RICHARD BUTCHER'S GREAT GRANDAD THOMAS COLLINS
COUSIN TO BEN COLLINS
BACK ROW: V.H. COLLINS, V. COLLINS, W. COLLINS, T. COLLINS
2ND ROW: C. COLLINS, B. COLLINS, F. COLLINS, THOMAS COLLINS, C. COLLINS
FRONT ROW: H. COLLINS, L. COLLINS, S. COLLINS, BEN COLLINS, A. COLLINS
J. COLLINS, M. COLLINS 1938-1939
BEN COLLINS PLAYED FOR NORTHAMPTON TOWN F.C

It turns out that Granddad Tom Collins worked at Churches Shoe factory in Northampton for years, and that's where my mother had worked all her working life and we, his grandchildren, had gone to nursery there all those lost years, and he had been right under our noses all the time. I was so very proud to have known my Granddad and where our roots lay on my dad's side of the family, as my maiden name should have been Collins, so there is still a lot of family out there we never got a chance to meet, as my Granddad, Tom, was the youngest of fourteen children; but we did get to share some part of his life.

My Dad was fifty-six when he met him for the first time. Granddad Tom asked if he could move in with us when he got older and he couldn't look after himself as he didn't want to go into a home. His neighbour had said she couldn't believe the change in him after meeting us; nor could his doctor. He got so excited when we visited him. I would do his cleaning for him and change his bed. I can remember the second time I met him he asked me to wash his net curtains. Well I did, and they just fell to pieces in the water. I ended up having to buy some new ones for him; it was so funny.

After a time he became poorly and started to forget things just a little bit and would leave the cooker on; just small little things that could have become dangerous. Granddad Tom asked if he could move in with us as he was so scared of having to go into a home so I talk to my husband and he agreed Tom could move in and we would look after him. We had the loft converted at our house for Richard and Glenn, and Tom had their room, so we all supported him and looked after him. We checked with two members of his family to make sure they were ok with it, it was like he had always been in our lives.

We travelled to Kislingbury quite often to see one of my Granddad's brothers, Harold Collins. He was really nice and loved talking about football and was always keen to know how Richard was getting on. So for Richard to have met Ben Collins, whom we had met on a number of occasions, before we even knew there was a link between the two families, was amazing. My dad used the shop regularly as he was a keen bowler.

I can also remember the 1998 Easter floods when our family lost everything. We woke up that morning with the water rising. Richard's football boots were floating around the house. All photos and videos then were lost forever. Rowing boats were going up and down the street collecting and helping people out of their homes. My Granddad bless him asked me if his paper would still be delivered, not realising how bad things were. Richard had to phone Northampton Town to tell them he wouldn't be in for training that day as he could not get out of the house, and his training kit and boots were floating around the house in three to four feet of water. They thought he was joking. It really was not a joke.

We had to move out of the house for at least a year. Richard's dad and I slept at my friend's flat, and my Granddad, Richard, and Glenn moved into my mum's. It really was a nightmare running back and forth to our home, trying to work, and running between three homes to try and keep the family together. We moved back into the house with no cooker, no kitchen and no furniture downstairs. I got a table, placed a camping cooker on it, and a microwave, and brought a few plates, and a couple of deck chairs to sit on. It is amazing what you can do when you have nothing left. My Granddad was safe in his bedroom, as he had all the modern conveniences you could ask for, so he was happy. But it is the sentimental things you can't replace that you miss.

Moving back to football: Kevin Wilson was the assistant manager to Ian Atkins during Richard's time at The Cobblers.

Kevin reflects:

Richard was very unlucky and deservedly went on to prove that the Cobblers' decision to release him was wrong. It's hard as the system only gives lads two years to prove themselves due to the overriding financial constraints. Richard got two years on a Youth Training Scheme, and was cut at 18. A 3–4 year window of opportunity would give the lads a chance to realise their potential and would give lower League sides far more of an opportunity to realise a return on their investment. Inevitably, Northampton's loss was others' gain.

Richard's Mum Gail:

I have to apologise to at least one of the first-team lads who sent his kit home for me to wash. He didn't give me much washing and drying time, so I slipped it in the dryer just for one minute and it shrank. He was not happy at all.

Richard did pick up a few tricks along the way regarding his new football boots. He would always lie in the bath with them on so they would mould to his feet like slippers, but it didn't do my bath any good. Former Cobblers player Carl Heggs always liked his boots soaked in a bucket of hot water so they would mould to his feet; it certainly did the trick as he was a fantastic player for Northampton

Town. I think Richard followed in his footsteps as he so admired Carl as a player and a person.

I felt it was very harsh as a mum for all the lads, not just Richard, to be released from the Cobblers as they were on so little money. I felt some of them could have been given a chance at Northampton Town. I can remember asking one of the board members when crossing his path in town with a friend. I said, "When will the lads know if they are going to get a contract?" He replied, "Seven contracts will be given out, but not your son." I replied, "Why not?" "Richard," he said, "is not good enough." It turned out all were released, but our son had a bee in his bonnet wanting to prove them wrong. Therefore, the truth of the rumours as to why Richard and the lads were released will never truly come to light.

We were heartbroken for our son. When Richard was released from the Cobblers he found it very hard to come to terms with it. As with any job, once you get released, there is only your family to pick up the pieces. Ian Atkins always said what a fantastic player Richard was, and I think he would have been a great manager for Richard. Ian did look out for Richard on a number of occasions as we met with him frequently. Throughout Richard's career he was also the only person who contacted us to see if Richard was okay. Ian was always impressed and pleased to hear how Richard was doing. He once said to Richard, "You are one lad who I know will make it."

Great friend Andy Morrow, who landed the only deal that year, would like to share the times he had at the Cobblers. He was given a youth contract to encourage him to come over from Ireland and was on better money than his fellow YTS teammates. He had a terrific friendship with Richard.

Andy says:

I signed for the Northampton youth team when I was seventeen years of age on a two-year apprenticeship, and that is how I met Richard as he was in the same team, and we were of the same age. I had a great year and half playing for the youth team, which we all thoroughly enjoyed, but I was lucky enough to get offered a two-and-a-half-year contract with the club. As you can imagine, I was over the moon about it at the time! I enjoyed every minute of the football aspect of the club, but I found it a bit hard to settle in Northampton as I was homesick a lot.

Richard was my best friend over there, and was of great support to me, and we certainly had some laughs! He was a joker, a big character, and he certainly made my time in Northampton easier. He was always an exceptionally strong player, very fit. The only thing he lacked was a bit of confidence behind that jovial façade. His head would go down if he made a mistake, and he would really give himself a hard time over it. Having said that, he always had the ability to make a career and living from football. He was a lovely fella with a lovely family behind him. He was a real family man, and his mum and dad loved him to bits. I actually moved in with his family for a while, and they treated me extremely well and were always very good to me and made me feel at home there.

Looking on it now that I am more mature, I wish that my attitude had been better, as I would have had a good chance to make it myself with football being a professional career for me. I think you need the ability, but it needs to be backed up with hard work, determination, and dedication. Where I let myself down in certain areas, Richard excelled on the attitude side, with the necessary attributes that I lacked. I was glad to see him make it, as if any one deserved it Richard did. Richard would have been the bigger character in our age group, but, unfortunately, he didn't stay with Northampton. But, deservedly, he was lucky enough to continue with his career at other clubs.

During my time with the Cobblers they had a very strong side and enjoyed promotion to League 1 as it is now. By finishing third in the league on the last day of the season at Torquay, that was probably the most memorable match for me, as I received a promotional medal, and the celebrations were brilliant! There were a lot of good players that played for the side during my team, such as John Frain, Roy Hunter, Marco Gabbiadini, and James Hunt, but that's just to name a few. I also played under some great managers, namely: Ian Atkins, Kevin Wilson, Kevin Broadhurst, and Gary Thompson.

I began by having a couple of trials in various clubs in England before being signed by Northampton as an apprentice, then signing my pro contract half way through the second year of my apprenticeship. When I signed pro, Aston Villa contacted the club about me going down to their club for a trial. I went down for a week, and it went well, played a few games, and scored a few goals, but when I returned to Northampton they offered me a two-and-a-half-year pro contract, which I was more than happy to sign.

I made my debut then, not long after signing. I came on as a second-half sub against Torquay, which was a proud moment for me. I was unlucky not to score. I was on the subs bench quite a lot after this, and made my full starting debut against Wigan. After this, I was on the substitute bench all the time, and felt I never had the opportunity to really play. Toward the end of my contract I had a few off-field problems which led to me leaving the club when my contract expired.

After I left the club I returned home to play semi-pro football in Northern Ireland. I signed for my home town club of Bangor, which I have been with for eleven years now, and I am still extremely happy and proud to be part of the club. I don't regret coming home, but I regret not giving it my best shot when I was out there.

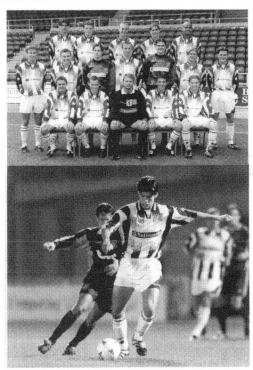

RICHARD BUTCHER NORTHAMPTON TOWN F.C
PHOTOS TAKEN BY: PETE NORTON

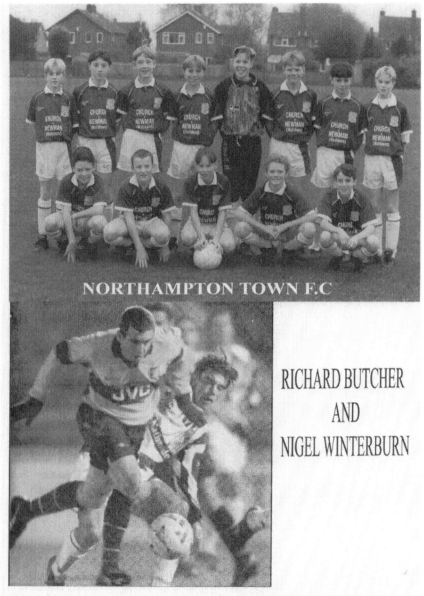

NORTHAMPTON TOWN F.C

RICHARD BUTCHER
AND
NIGEL WINTERBURN

I KINDLY THANK NORTHAMPTON CHRONICLE ECHO FOR USE OF PHOTO

Richard's Mum Gail:

In 1998–99, Richard's second year, the U18s played in the newly-formed Youth Alliance and came fourth, before competing in a secondary phase against sides from the North-East and North-West Conferences. Captained by Brad Piercewright (he and Butch would meet again at Kettering) the youngsters would excel and be crowned champions of The FL Youth Alliance Division 1. Richard would play a large part in this, but was not scoring goals, mainly due to being played on the wing or at centre-back when injuries dictated. There also appeared to be a bit of favouritism behind the scenes that kept him from his natural central box-to-box role. Everyone could see that was his natural position from a mile off.

He also played in the reserves in the Avon Insurance Combination. Richard broke into the side with an FA Youth Cup appearance against West Ham and looked set for a run. He played against Gillingham, Ipswich, Colchester & Arsenal, a 2–0 win despite Adams and Nigel Winterburn being in the side that saw 4752 turn up, but this was curtailed when Ian Atkins drafted him into the first team. The opportunity arose because of long-term injuries to sixteen players, who then came back to inspire an incredible unbeaten nine-match finale. The injury crisis gave Richard an opportunity to train with the first team along with Andy Morrow. The two made the bench for the 0–2 FA Cup defeat at Yeovil, but even though only Andy got on, Richard loved every minute of the match experience and felt his time and chance would come.

Garry Hughes was a year older, but he remembers the period vividly.

Garry says:

I first met Richard when I was seventeen and a second-year apprentice at the Cobblers. Richard was a relatively quiet sixteen-year-old when he first started in July; however, a few months down the line and he was gaining confidence in the dressing room and becoming one of the gang. Butch became one of the most popular players amongst the team on and off the pitch. I was a central defender and so was Richard when he first arrived at NTFC, but he was, however, overlooked in that position by fellow first-year apprentice Brad Piercewright. Therefore, he started a lot of games that season on the bench, if I remember correctly.

I think it was plainly obvious for everyone to see how determined Richard was to make it in the game. When he felt he hadn't played well he would really beat himself up about his performance and get himself down, but this was due to his desire to succeed. The one thing Richard needed most was a coach that would believe in him and put his arm around him, because if he had a bad game Richard was his own biggest critic. We could all see that Richard was growing into a very athletic player and was improving on a daily basis, and it wasn't long before he was moved farther up the field into a central midfield role. He loved this, and we could see it, too, as his stamina to run from box-to-box all game was unreal. At first he looked slightly alien in that new role and would often go chasing hopelessly long balls pumped over the top of the opposing defence (usually from myself) in order to get on the score sheet, and we would constantly be warning him to not go running all over the field as he wouldn't be able to last the full ninety minutes due to exhaustion. But not Richard; he could probably have kept that work rate up for another ninety-minute game if needed.

That's the one thing I remember about Butch, his amazing stamina. In pre-season on long-distance runs he would be miles ahead of the next person, and I mean miles literally. I remember we used to meet up out of season (at a field near Mereway School) and we used to ping a few balls with each other. And sometimes his old school pals would come and also his dad on occasions. I remember his dad 'Butch' and mother, Gail, was extremely proud and supporting of Richard and would travel up and down the country to watch him play. I have a lot of time for Butch's parents because during our time at Kettering Town together his parents offered to put me up at their house if I needed as I was having a few issues at home with a former girlfriend and I am truly grateful for that kind gesture. I knew Butch was really close to his parents and would often talk about them with great fondness.

Richard was a very tidy person and had an order for everything even down to his wash bag. Every bottle and moisturiser had its own place within the bag, which I found hilarious as I am the total opposite. That was still the same when we met up again at Kettering when we used to take it in turns to drive. My car was like a skip and his little black fiesta was like it had just been valeted, and I know he looked after it like he looked after everything he owned. He was really into The Backstreet Boys at the time, which a lot of the players found a little strange being into a boy band, and even though the lads would wind him up about it, Butch would stick to his guns and blast The Backstreet Boys on the ghetto blaster and dance in the middle of the dressing room or in front of the mirror singing the lyrics to himself. Absolutely hilarious, and he gained a lot of respect from the lads for being the person he wanted to be and not bowing down to peer pressure.

I know a few lads used to give him stick about it, but Butch would always give as much as he got, and some of his one-liners were legendary. He wasn't the sharpest tool in the box—he would be the first to admit he was no Einstein—but he was such a likeable character that everyone loved him, if I'm honest. He would always have time for everyone. He was not offered pro terms at NTFC, which I was slightly surprised about, even though he was still very raw, but because of his desire to succeed, willingness to learn, and his physique I thought he was always worth a pro contract. He went on to play for Raunds FC where he then got scouted by Rushden & Diamonds and offered a two-and-a-half-year professional contract. Obviously, people were starting to take note that this certain Richard Butcher could play a bit.

I stayed at the Cobblers until I was twenty-one and got released and signed for Kettering where we would meet up again a couple of months into the season. He was the catalyst for us that year, as The Poppies returned to the Conference. I stayed in contact with Butch during our time playing for different clubs and enjoyed a few nights out on the tiles with him. It was then that I noticed how much the women fancied him, and he was very much a babe magnet. Butch worked very hard on his game, but don't worry, he certainly knew how to play hard also.

Richard's Mum Gail:

Richard played for Raunds FC but found it very difficult to get into a big, physical side at times, but Adam Sandy believed in Richard and always thought he should be playing at a higher level. Adam thought a lot of Richard and was always impressed by him. Richard spent under a month at the club before moving on to Rushden and Diamonds.

Ali Gibb, who played 131 games for the Cobblers in a loan spell, and then a four-year career between 1996 and 2000, saw Richard's development at different stages of his career.

Ali says:

I first met 'Butch' when he was a trainee at Northampton Town Football Club, a tall wiry young lad who was probably lacking in self-confidence compared to some of his peers. As a trainee the young players' roles were to clean the professionals' boots, clean the changing rooms, and other odd jobs around the group. I was somewhat surprised when I signed for Northampton Town from Norwich City that the YTS players spent more time collecting balls from the shooting sessions of the older professionals, and became real life manikins for pre-match tactical play, rather than applying themselves in their own training sessions. The life of a trainee footballer at Northampton Town was a far cry from the glamour and prestige one would expect.

At this stage in Butch's playing career I had more dealings with his mum, Gail, whom I think I first met in St. James for a promotional launch of Nationwide Building Society. I later kept in touch with her as I moved clubs, receiving Christmas cards each year.

After leaving Northampton Town I went on to play for various clubs but came back in contact with Butch when we played Lincoln City in a cup game in Lincolnshire. At this stage I wasn't really aware of his development, and it was the first time our paths had crossed since Northampton Town. Richard was now an athlete. Our manager's pre-match team talk involved a number of their key players, one of whom was Butch. He had now grown a reputation as a box-to-box midfield player who would shoot from long distances and ultimately score. Our paths crossed on a number of occasions when he played for Peterborough United. Again, Butch's athletic prowess and ability to score goals from midfield was a talking point in any manager's pre-match brief.

The Cobblers were not able to repeat the play-off heroics of the previous season and were relegated at the end of the 1998–99 season, with budget cuts imminent across the board. Some say relegation was a contributing factor in the release of Richard and the rest of his title-winning teammates. However, opinion varies given that those home-grown players were ready to pay their way. Northampton Town did however prepare the young lads for a career outside of football should they fail to make the grade. A tutor came in once a week for the two years enabling Richard to gain an Intermediate Level GNVQ in Leisure and Tourism.

Richard's Mum Gail:

We can remember the endless times Richard would run around Sixfields Lake with his stopwatch on, always trying to beat his own time. He sometimes wore a black bin bag to have a good sweat. Or he would ask his brother to run with him as Glenn was a great runner; he loved having someone to chase. Come rain or shine he would not miss out on his run. I would sit and wait and watch, mind you, in the car.

Our son was the product of a caring loving family who worked hard to support his chosen career. Being a professional footballer never changed him, but he worked hard to survive and earn a good living from the game he loved. It is a very hard industry to get into. You have to smile, work hard, and keep your head down, and hope the luck will follow. Talent alone will rarely sustain a living for long. For some, the heartache of a serious injury can tear you apart, and your life can change overnight. But Richard ended up playing 26,919 precious professional minutes as a box-to-box midfielder. He played 40 or 50 games per season. His natural fitness allowed him to cover every blade of grass. He was a hero to some. His goals were vital; the fans applauded him. He was a six-foot, healthy young man, which makes it harder to understand why he died.

Richard covered more ground than most players would in a game, covering eight miles (13–14) kilometres per match and speeds up to 14–21kmh. He showed constancy throughout his career and he always prided himself on his goals; bend it like Beckham, just one of the players he so admired. I can remember writing a letter to David Beckham on Richard's twenty-first birthday to ask if he would kindly send Richard a card, and, to my delight, he did. I still have the card to this day. I really was surprised he responded.

Richard almost rejoined the Cobblers in 2007, but they were unable to meet the £50,000 fee and the deal was derailed. Incredibly, Steve Thompson stepped in and signed him for Notts County on a free transfer from Peterborough United.

I want to thank former MP Mr. Tony Clarke for his full support with the Richard Butcher Memorial Trust; he is a life-time friend, and knew Richard as a player. He would be the first one to say our son should never have been released from Northampton Town FC. But I can't express enough to parents of want-to-be footballers that it's not about what we think as parents, it's about what other professionals see in our children.

I would like to thank Northampton Chronicle Echo for all the media attention Richard had, which has enabled me to put this book together.

Northampton Town

Northampton Town Football Club is an English professional Football club based in Northampton, Northamptonshire. The club participates in football League two, the fourth tier of English football. They hold the record for the shortest time taken to be promoted from the bottom tier to the top tier and relegated back down to the bottom again, in the space of nine years.

Northampton was formed in 1897, after meetings between the town's schoolteachers and local solicitor, AJ Darnell. They play their home games at the 7,653 capacity all-seater Sixfields Stadium, having moved in 1994 from the County Ground which they shared with the owners, Northamptonshire County Cricket Club. The club's main rival is Peterborough United, a rivalry which has endured since the 1960s, although the two teams are currently separated by one division. Other recent rivals include Rushden & Diamonds and Oxford United. The club's colours have traditionally been claret and white. The club nickname is 'The Cobblers', a reference to the town's historical shoe-making industry.

Information about the club was found on en.wikipedia.org/wiki.

NORTHAMPTON TOWN F.C ; FAMILY DAY OUT AT WEMBLEY STADIUM 24TH MAY 1998 RICHARD WAS THE SILOUETTE ON THE FLAGS AND PROGRAMMES

4: Rushden & Diamonds 1999–2001

With Richard, missing out to play for his hometown Cobblers was hard for him to take, but with our support, and love, and the faith we had in him, we picked our son up and started again to help rebuild his confidence. Richard spent time with friends at Far Cotton Rec, Northampton. We knew factory life was never going to be his path. There were a few ready to twist the knife by making fun at the failure of his dreams, which had gone—for a while, anyway. I can remember Richard coming across a friend whom he once stood up for when bullied at school. He shouted to Richard across the Rec, "I will never forget the time you stood up for me, but I know you will win through and make it as a pro footballer. Don't give up!" Those words spurred our son on to keep on trying, and to keep on working hard in the profession he so wanted.

After Richard left Northampton Town we must have written to at least thirty clubs to get Richard a trial. Some replied, and some didn't. The first place Richard's dad took him for a trial was Colchester United. I thought Richard had an excellent game and even one of the other parents, standing next to me, said what a good player he was. He didn't know I was Richard's mum, and I was disappointed that we never heard anything back from them, but then you have to remember that there were lads there from a lot bigger clubs than Northampton. I got the feeling that if Richard was released by Northampton, then why would Colchester be interested in him?

Our son also went for a trial at Luton Town. His grandfather took him to that one as we were away on holiday. I remember phoning Richard up that evening and he was very upset as he had gotten injured very early on. Although he carried on playing, and felt he did okay, again the impression was that they were looking at lads from the bigger clubs who had also been released.

We travelled the earth to help Richard follow his dream. Before joining Rushden, I took Richard for a trial at Macclesfield Town, of all places. Again, he did well, but looked a little heavy-legged at times and once more we never heard anything back from them. Colchester really was disappointing for his dad, because if they had not known where these lads had come from, he is sure they would have at least had another look at him. In one respect, if the clubs didn't know where these players had been released from, and they all were judged on their ability alone, then players from lower league clubs could maybe get a look in. I know football clubs have piles of letters to get through sent from want-to-be footballers and so many miss out, but when you do get your chance, you really need to hang on to it because there will always be someone waiting in the wings to take your place.

Brian Talbot, Terry Westley and Jeff Vetere thankfully did see something in Richard, eventually offering him a two-year deal at Rushden & Diamonds. Richard gave a great display as a trial list in a 2–1 Capital League win over Aldershot. His two-year deal started on November 26th 1999. Richard also earned a further deal from 2000–2001.

Rushden & Diamonds had fantastic training facilities set up. It proved to be a confidence builder for Richard. When joining the non-league club Brian Talbot was keen to turn Richard into a box-to-box midfielder playmaker as they thought this was his natural game. This turned out to be good for Richard as during his YTS period at the Cobblers Richard had been placed in centre half.

During his time with Rushden & Diamonds he went on to appear in both the Hiller cup and F.A Trophy for Diamonds, but only made the bench as an unused substitute in the conference games. Although he signed professional forms in March 2000, he failed to make the first team.

Rushden & Diamonds were promoted in 2000-2001. Richard was then announced to the media as being one of the players to break through a very strong reserve side, but Richard sat on the bench being an unused substitute eleven times. But he had some security and was hoping his time would come. The money wasn't great, just £150 per week from May 2000–April 2001 moving up to £175 per week during 2001–2002.

Richard loved the setup at Rushden and the facilities were great. He hoped to play in front of a big crowd one day.

Manager Brian Talbot

Brian Talbot was a former English football manager and former player. Brian Talbot played for Ipswich Town, Toronto Metros (United States), Arsenal, Watford, Stoke City, West Bromwich Albion, Fulham and Aldershot. He then went into management with West Bromwich Albion, Aldershot, Hibernians (Malta), Rushden & Diamonds, Oxford United and Marsaxlokk (Malta). All players can only hope to follow the dream.

Information about the Manager's Career was found on en.wikipedia.org/wiki.

Richard had a few spectacular goals in the first half of the season at Diamonds. He scored a great goal in the 6–0 demolition of Tamworth, but his role was to be more of a defensive side to the game. He also played as a right winger for the reserves side with a more central role to his game. He was included in the first team tour of Ireland in 2001. Richard scored in the opening tour match against Home Farm in a 2–1 defeat with a superb half-volley. Diamonds reserves lost 3–1 against Kettering in the NFA Hillier cup. Richard got a 25-yard wonder goal in a 1–2 reserve defeat against Hereford. There were a lot of big egos and personalities at the club and a massive competitive edge and feel, but Richard fought on, frustrated more than ever. We just wondered if he was ever going to get his big chance. A great friend, Carl Heggs, tells us his thoughts about his friend and how when he joined Rushden & Diamonds he took Richard under his wing.

Carl Heggs says:

Brian Talbot and I didn't really get on together; although he spent £100,000 on me, breaking the Conference transfer fee record, he had spent fortunes and failed to get promotion. He was now under pressure to deliver, and so did not have time for the kids. He made me train with the reserves, and the one positive was that I got to link up with Richard again. Max Griggs did a fantastic funding job at Rushden, and the facilities were first class, but Richard would have been better off to go to Kettering first off.

Even though Richard was good enough to get into the Diamonds' side, it was all about having to win the League that year. I hardly played and eventually got a loan back into the Football League with Chester, thanks to Ian Atkins who liked me and appreciated the sort of player I was, and so I always tried my hardest not to let him down. Where Northampton was brilliant and a career highlight, Rushden was the low.

Looking back, there is always a part of you that wants to be part of football, and the soccer schools do put something back, which is important for the future of the game. But after seeing a player die on the field, and the unexplained passing of Richard, I am pleased to be in a secure career to feed my family, backed up by qualifications. Managers rarely get the financial tools to do their job, making the dreaded sacking even more of a reality. Football is like a selection box of chocolates and getting the mix right is as hard on the career of the manager as it can be on the hardworking honest player who's just trying to make his way in the game.

Ian Atkins, my former manager, now runs a soccer school in-between a full-time career as Head of Sport at Ascot College (www.footballandsports.co.uk). His philosophy on life can only be seen as a loss to football, but his values do himself and his family credit.

Richard's Mum Gail:

Richard's time at Rushden & Diamonds was a strange time for us and our son. He got the call for a trial, then he spent three weeks there with no pay, trying hard to prove he was worth a shot. It's hard for a lad who has no wages coming in at this time, but it was worth his family's support so he could follow his dream. Richard was over the moon to be given a second chance, so he worked hard to show his worth. He had kept his fitness levels up just waiting for that one more bite of the cherry. He had a good first season with Diamonds and came away for the summer break feeling great; he had been given the impression that he would get his chance as there were also other young players in the side. Richard felt Brian Talbot was the sort that would give him a chance regardless of his age. After all, he had received reserve player of the season.

But when returning after the summer break Richard soon got disheartened. One of the first reserve games of the season was against Northampton Town reserves. Richard was really up for this game, as he wanted to prove a point, and show how much he had improved since being with the great set-up at Diamonds. But this wasn't to be, as he found himself dropped from the game, which did upset him. He phoned me to tell me that's when he knew things were going to change, and you just get that feeling.

A number of the players told Richard just to work hard and keep his head down. Our son looked up to players like Carl Heggs, and Duane Darby, and Ali Gibb. They had all been through this themselves at some point in their careers. It dawned on us and Richard that this was not the club where he was going to get his calling. We went to watch Richard play regularly and felt he had done really well, but those tell-tale lines and the treatment had started. Phrases like 'One for the future', that's when you know you're on your way out. It's something we would soon learn to pick up on, and so did Richard. He soon talked to Brian Talbot who very kindly offered our son some training kit to move on with, when he left with a handshake.

I did write to Brian Talbot and ask for a meeting to speak with him, as I felt he had been unfairly treated and I didn't want him to be sat on the bench for the period of his contract, but Richard had already made his mind up to leave to join Kettering Town. He always liked to move on when he just got that feeling it wasn't going to happen for him. But Brian did send me a lovely letter saying what a great lad Richard was and that we should be very proud of him. But this didn't really help as you start to feel, *Is our son ever going to get his break?*

We always took on board what the professionals had to say and the encouragement and belief they showed in Richard also helped us carry on. Because as a parent it's so easy to have blinkered eyes, as all lads want to be a pro footballer but you do have to have talent too.

Richard was lucky to be able to move on as some clubs can make you stick to your contract; that's what I thought was going to happen at one point. Whether you're playing or not you will have to follow the rules and go into to training and work hard and do as you're told until the club allows you to move on. Richard travelled round on the open top bus after Diamonds got promoted; although he was involved in some way he never felt he could take any credit for Rushden & Diamonds gaining league status but he was proud to be a part of such a glamorous club. Diamonds had smashed the non-League transfer record three times to sign Carl Alford, Billy Turley, and Justin Jackson in pursuit of their promotion dream to claim football league status. Jackson and striker partner Duane Darby were signed for a combination fee of almost £300,000. Brian Talbot celebrated his four years in charge of Diamonds. Millionaire chairman Max Griggs had put a lot of time and money into the club. It was said in local papers that the youth lads would surely get a chance under manager Brian Talbot; he believed that the young talent coming through the ranks would provide a bright future for the club.

Richard decided to leave Rushden & Diamonds after they moved up into the football league. With the glamour of the football league being taken away, many would have thrown the towel in and thought their big chance had gone forever. The game seemed to be Richard's natural path in life so it was a question of knocking on doors and try and try again. He continued to keep fit with the help of his younger brother Glenn and focused on his diet, and the family all pulled together in support. But Kettering Town was calling with Legend manager Carl Shutt looking for some young legs in his side.

Richard was excited to be moving on but a few knives came out again with people pointing the fingerer saying if he makes it he would be found his level. But with the fantastic support from the Kettering players and club and fans and Captain Lee Howarth Richard was looking to a bright future; all his hard work and the support of others, not to mention his skill, would all pay off.

Rushden & Diamonds

Max Griggs was the R Griggs Group current owner of the Dr Marten shoe company, and one of largest shoe manufacturers in the United Kingdom. In 2002, the company ceased production in the United Kingdom and began outsourcing to China and Thailand. The Dr Martens (nicknamed DMs) boots, were manufactured in England since 1960 and were at their most popular in the 1980s, but in the following decade, their popularity started to decline. In 1992 Max Griggs bought Rushden Town and Irthingborough Diamonds football clubs. He successfully merged them into one as Rushden & Diamonds football club, which enjoyed league status for a time. One of the stands in the club's ground was called the Airwair stand (a type of DM shoe). Max Griggs sold the club to the fans in 2005 for £1. The club went into administration six years later.

Information about Max Griggs and Rushden & Diamond Football Club was found on en.wikipedia.org/wiki.

Richard's Mum Gail:

Despite Richard leaving Rushden & Diamonds, the one thing I always said to him is "look at your time at Rushden as a stepping stone; they gave you the chance to keep fit and to stay in the game until the next challenge came along." We always told our son to work hard and hopefully your time will come.

We would like to thank all the players for the support they showed to Richard for the time he spent at Rushden & Diamonds. And a special thank you to Duane Darby and his family for their support through Richard's career and after his death and thank you for your help and just being there.

There are so many players to thank who played a massive support in our son's life, like Lee Howarth, Ian Bowling, Darren Collins, and Manager Gary Simpson, Carl Heggs; just a few to mention but many many more I haven't.

I would like to thank Kettering Evening Telegraph for all the media attention Richard received which enabled me to put this book together.

RUSHDEN & DIAMONDS F.C RICHARD BUTCHER MIDDLE ROW ON YOUR RIGHT

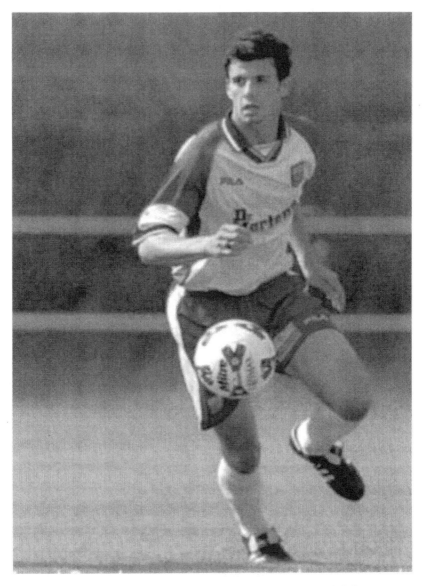

RICHARD BUTCHER RUSHDEN & DIAMONDS F.C
PHOTO TAKEN BY PAUL READING

RICHARD BUTCHER RUSHDEN & DIAMONDS F.C
PHOTO TAKEN BY: PAUL READING

5: Kettering Town 2001-2002

Richard had knuckled down once again and joined Kettering Town and had become an important member of the Poppies' squad which secured the 2001–02 Southern League Premier Division title.

Carl Shutt was going to be the right manager for Richard. Many found it hard to believe that he could not get into the Rushden & Diamonds side. He was frustrated with Brian Talbot who was stating he would be the next big thing, but if Richard wanted to get on with his career he would have to drop to the southern league. This all brought back cruel memories from Northampton Town. After being released, Richard talked this over with a number of players and they said that sometimes you have to drop to get your career off the ground again. Our son just wanted to play football and be happy with himself, and all we wanted as a mum and dad was for Richard to get on in life in his chosen career.

There were some great footballers at Kettering. Richard was a tall six foot lad with long legs and a great smile; he could also run for miles. Some say Richard was the legs Kettering needed, but Kettering was a great side. You still have to earn your place and the respect from your manager and teammates. He would always want to give a 100% for his manager and team. He was honest, hard-working, and wore his heart on his sleeve. Our son put pen to paper and signed for the Poppies for £250 a week in 2001, moving up to £300 in 2002 plus goal bonus.

Manager Carl Shutt

Carl Shutt was an English former professional football player. His league career started at the relatively late age of 23. He was spotted by Howard Wilkinson while playing for Spalding United and enjoyed two relatively successful seasons with Sheffield Wednesday. With the manager leaving for pastures new, Carl joined Bristol City and again had two relatively successful seasons. It wasn't long before Wilkinson recalled him and arranged to swap Bob Taylor and £50,000 to get his man again, right on cue for Leeds United's push to promotion.

Shutt made an instant impact at Leeds with a hat-trick in his first game. He became a fans' favorite with tireless running and unwillingness to give up any cause. Following promotion and the successful pairing of Lee Chapman and Rod Wallace, Shutt remained a popular figure and was frequently used as a substitute. At Leeds he played in fourteen games and scored twice (against Chelsea and Everton) as they won the First Division in 1992, meaning Shutt was eligible for a medal.

Perhaps the defining moment of Shutt's Leeds career came at the Nou Camp against VFB Stuttgart in 1992, in a replayed European Cup game. Within a couple of minutes of coming on as a substitute, he scored the winner with only his second touch.

After leaving Leeds in 1993 with more than 100 appearances and 25 goals, he played for Birmingham City and had a very brief spell at Manchester City before settling at Bradford City in 1994. In three seasons with the Bantams, Shutt scored 15 goals before moving on to Darlington where again he spent three seasons, scoring nine goals. *Information about the Carl Shutt and club was found on en.wikipedia.org/wiki.*

Richard's Mum Gail:

You can never expect to walk straight into a side, but then Richard never did at any club he played for. The players and manager at Kettering Town would pave the way for his future career; they would help build his confidence back up after having so many knocks.

You can't beat a good family atmosphere. It was a great club for all of us as a family, and we really enjoyed our time at Kettering Town. It was like going from home to home with great fans and great people. Richard made some fantastic friends and was playing for a team whose mates all played for each other. The bond and love of football these players had together was electric. There are too many names to mention, because our son loved them all, and so did we. His nickname at Kettering town was 'Ricky Butcher'. The girls screamed for his autograph when the bus travelled through Kettering Town to celebrate at the end of the season. Our son never minded being called Ricky, with his little blond touch at the front of his hair.

Kettering Town manager Carl Shutt was one of the most important people in Richard's life. Carl Shutt had a great personality, and the experience certainly to help him follow his dream. Lee Howarth also played a massive part in our son's career. Richard made over 341 appearances and ended up scoring fifty-four goals in his career, thirteen of them for Kettering Town—not bad for a midfielder.

Lee Howarth, captain and director of sports at Moulton College, made 394 appearances and nineteen goals. His career was at Peterborough, Mansfield, Barnet, Boston, and Kettering Town. He gives the fans a fantastic insight.

Lee says:

Butch joined us a few weeks into the 2001–2 season. I had joined six games into the season after a spectacularly crazy previous season with Steve Evans' mad reign at Boston United, before they imploded into a financial black hole from which they have yet to recover. Butch joined Kettering, a combination of hopeful youngsters and ex-pros that had been around the block and who, by this stage of their careers, were very difficult to impress. Football clubs are run by directors and chairmen, players and tactics are chosen by the managers and coaches, but the senior players dictate the culture in the dressing room and throughout the squad. Players like Ian Bowling, Steve Wilkinson, Dale Watkins, Peter Fear, Darren Collins, Craig Norman, and myself ran the place because we had all had various levels of playing success, and could all name-drop quite well. We knew that usually there was no gold at the end of the rainbow, and we just had to do the best we could for the club, our supporters, and our families before we eventually fell off the treadmill and had to get back into the real world where no one knows your name and no one wants your autograph anymore.

My immediate reaction to Butch was—'poser'—that first walk into a dressing room full of players whom you do not know is very daunting, particularly for a 'kid' as we call them (basically anyone considerably younger than yourself). The manager generally brings the player into the dressing room after contracts have been signed and reassurances given and drops them in the (often not very) capable hands of the captain who, depending on his own level of social confidence, either introduces you around the team individually to shake hands and say hello (preferable) or, once the manager has left, mumbles "These are the lads—you'll get to know them soon" (less preferable). I can't remember Butch's exact entrance, although as captain, I'm sure it was the preferable option, but I have a vague recollection of a tall, very (too) handsome young man with a bit of dyed hair, an earring, and a fantastic physique that Ian Bowling would have died for. He was going to have to be a hell of a player!

The squad was a friendly and talented bunch with a few familiar faces including Brad Piercewright and Garry Hughes who had played in the youth set-up at Northampton with Richard.

Great Mate Garry Hughes recalls:

Three months into the season at Kettering Town, now in the Dr. Martin's Premier, we were languishing in mid-table, which was not good enough for a big non-league club with a big budget, and the pressure was on manager Carl Shutt. One Thursday evening I turned up for training and Butch was there on trial. He said he was disheartened at Diamonds as he wasn't getting his chance in the first team. I think he had been there for over a year and hadn't even made his first team debut. He said he wanted first team football, even if it meant dropping down a league or two. I hadn't seen him play for a couple of years, but from that first training session, I could see a drastic improvement. He had matured into a player that was far too good to be playing reserve team football, and was desperate to be given a 'stage' upon which he could express himself and show what he could do.

Everyone at Kettering was impressed during that first training session. I think he gave everyone that little bit of hope we were all craving for, that the season may not be a disaster after all. After a few games he was literally 'man of the match' in every game and showed he was a goal-scoring midfielder by getting on the score sheet and netting a few vital goals for the team. It was then that Kettering offered him a contract, and he had a huge decision to make.

Did I say a huge decision to make? Well, not for Mr. Butcher; within minutes he was ready to sign on the dotted line. This may have been a tricky decision for most players with a year and a half still left to run on his Diamonds contract, but not for a player who wanted to make his mark on the game, even if he were to have to start with a non-league club. So Butch signed for a couple of years at

Kettering, and we went on to win the League and gain promotion to the Conference.

Richard fitted into the squad nicely. The players were easy to get on with and very ambitious. That's what Richard needed. With players like Sean Murray and Peter Fear in the midfield, Kettering had the skill, but they just needed younger legs and pace.

And players like Ian Bowling in goal who would put his life on the line later in the season. Ian knew Keith Alexander well, from their time together at Lincoln in the early nineties; he had also played for Bradford City and become a legend at Mansfield Town, before signing for Kettering in 2002.

Ian remembers:

I first came across Richard in October 2001 when this tall, dark, athletic young man turned up for training at Rockingham Road, the home of Kettering Town FC. Not only did he have all of the above, but he was good-looking and had a great sense of humour, so he could enjoy having a laugh with the lads, but also didn't mind when the lads had a laugh at his expense. 'Butch' settled in really well and was impressive in the first training session, enough for Shutty to offer him a contract. He already knew a couple of the lads, so it made it easier for him to integrate into the group.

Butch was just the kind of player we were looking for. We had lost Matt Fisher at the end of the previous season and although Butch was more technically able than 'Fish,' there were similarities with their endless stamina, running, commitment, and endeavour to work hard for their team and football club. Butch also had the knack of scoring the important goal for us as well! Butch helped us get promotion back in to the Conference, where a club the size of Kettering Town should be.

Richard's mum Gail:

Ian Bowling was right. Richard could not wait to sign on the dotted line. His debut was at Folkestone Invicta, who were level on points, behind Kettering on goal difference. The score was a 3–2, Richard came on with thirteen minutes from time to ensure the Poppies held on and moved up to eighth place. Richard again took to the bench for the visit to second place Tamworth. The excitement was great, and it only made Richard eager to deliver on the hour. Tamworth went ahead with some great chances at both ends but the Poppies hit back when Darren Collins hit home in style. A point was earned for Shutt's side now sitting in sixth.

Kettering then entertained Northwood from Ryman League 1 in the Third Qualifying Round of the FA Cup, in what was Richard's full debut for the club. It was a great first half. Darren Collins settled the nerves with a great strike. Then Richard took a touch with a great 25-yard drive in to the top corner. Dale Watkins then poached to duly set up a Fourth Qualifying Round tie at Stevenage. The fans would look forward to that with relish as Borough had effectively relegated the Poppies the previous April, a month into the tenure of Carl Shutt 'fighting fires in a caretaker role.'

Fans approached Richard as he left the ground. A lovely young man asked Richard for his autograph. Richard thought he was talking to someone else as he walked to his little white Astra. But the lad tapped him on the shoulder and said, 'Mr. Butcher, would you please sign my programme? That was a brilliant goal.' Richard chatted to the young lad for a while and signed his name. Richard thanked the fans for making him feel welcome. He said, "You can call me Butch or Richard", but they nicknamed him 'Ricky'. Richard never changed as a person and always enjoyed talking to people and was so happy at Kettering Town football club; he would treasure every little moment he could.

Kettering went to rivals Welling, but with Captain Lee Howarth out for the Poppies, Kettering had a great midfield trio with Fear, Murray, and Richard to dominate. The Poppies had a narrow defeat at their rivals. Dale Watkins curled a perfect goal into the top corner to share the points, and Richard was shaping up nicely and was going to become a great asset.

Lee Howard spoke about how his friend Richard was shaping up.

Lee Howarth says:

Out on the pitch, Butch proved our first impressions wrong, as he soon became a fabulous goal-scoring midfielder. Although maybe not always first in line for the 1980s 'ball-or-everything' style of tackling that some of us could still get away with at this time, it was obvious that he was soon our star asset and loved by the crowd. He also gave better than he got in the dressing room, which is a bear-pit of a place and not for the fainthearted. Very early on you get tested with some smart comment or other from the chief team wag . . . then the silence descends as if someone important has walked in. However, this is just so everyone can gauge your reaction, and pigeon-hole you at once. This is an incredibly important moment in a player's initiation into the new dressing room, and can dictate your place in the hierarchy— and everyone knows it. A mumbled shocker of a reply results in sympathetic "oohs," and you are dismissed as not really a 'player' or a threat, in terms of the dressing room dynamics. A snappy answer, but not an absolute classic, gets you a couple of chuckles and you are off and running. But if you can knock them out of the ground with your razor-sharp retort you are catapulted into the inner sanctum of leading 'funsters,' agenda-makers, and Mickey-takers. Butch immediately became a member of the inner sanctum.

Richard's Mum Gail:

There was an accident on the M6 which denied the team a full warm up to Stafford Rangers. The Poppies avoided a league fine, to the relief of the chairman. Once out on the pitch with Duik, Watkins, and Richard in midfield, the passing was in a different league with Richard passing a great ball to Darren Collins who scored with the opener. Then Stafford levelled when Kelly stabbed home. Kettering Town's midfielder Sean Murray passed to Cowling who crashed the ball home. Stafford refused to lie down and drew level, with a brindly header, but Craig Norman sealed the win with a great header.

The 0–0 in the FA Cup against Stevenage set up a replay with 2079 fans following the game. Richard shone from early on. This was the biggest stage so far in his career; the place was roaring with a great atmosphere. Wormal put Stevenage in front with a great header.

With Kettering legend Craig Norman weighing in with an equaliser, half-time was called, and manager Carl Shutt told his team to carry on the way they were. The midfield showed some great passing; Collins got a winner worthy of a cup final. With the roar of the crowd the roof was lifted, with Shutty punching the air with delight.

The FA cup continued at Swindon Supermarine, wingback Brad Piercewright nodded in at the far post for the opener. Supermarine took full advantage and equalised, which forced Carl Shutt to swap Lenagh to make way for Steve Wilkinson. He pounced a crisp header to restore the lead. The third was a cute chip two minutes later. Peter Fear played an exquisite ball into the box that allowed Richard Butcher to spring, and head the Poppies into the next round. Richard was amazed to see 400 Poppies' fans follow them to the next game at Havant Waterlooville. They sat second unbeaten at home.

Richard ran down the right channel and passed the ball into the path of Darren Collins who put a great drive inside the post to put them in the lead. Havant soon equalised. Ricky, as the fans called Richard, was in awe of playing a box-to-box midfielder. He soon brilliantly bagged a brace of assists. He then flicked to Dale Watkins who chipped the keeper perfectly. The third goal summed up Richard perfectly as he found Darren Collins with intent. He then sent a cross to Richard who had run seventy yards to bend it like Beckham just inside the post. Shaune Murrey and Peter Fear and Richard strutted their stuff, the midfield trio.

With Kettering who sat sixth place, Havant Waterlooville and Crawley still remained top with Weymouth second, while Tamworth and Moor Green were on 30 points by goal difference. Richard would reap the rewards with help from Manager Carl Shutt and the experience of his teammates.

Carl Shutt played in a 3–1 win over Corby, and there was the visit of Cheltenham in the FA Cup first round tie the following week. With a seventeen-match unbeaten run, which was further fuelled by the F.A Cup fever, 2942 fans saw a dream start. With Craig Norman heading home a fifth minute header just four minutes from a half-time the Poppies conceded. Howarth headed on, Naylor nipped in. And a second arrived; Victory, of all player names, routed the right flank to feed Alsop who fired in from 15 yards. Bowling was great in the second half, but full-time fitness ultimately told with 4 goals in the last 27 minutes. But the players and Richard were anything but down.

Garry Hughes reflects:

Butch was a footballer's footballer, because he relished playing regular first team football and was becoming a crowd favourite already with his honest workmanlike style, and a goal-scoring one at that. I remember once, on one of our many drives into training, him telling me a story about when he worked at a factory whilst playing for Raunds. The boss of the factory called him in to give him a warning about something or other regarding him underperforming in his daily mundane task. Apparently, Butch just shrugged his shoulders and replied, "Well, I'm going to be a footballer, anyway." I thought this was hilarious as I can only imagine the boss's response. But this goes to show the grit and determination to achieve his goal in life and proof of his defiance if anybody told him otherwise.

Richard's Mum Gail:

Kettering Town continued their league quest by beating Hinckley United 2–1. Shutty again played in the side in the Maunsell cup at Peterborough 7–1. Another Cup exit saw Kettering suffer a giant killing at Purfleet in the Trophy. A return to League action meant a trip to Bath, but thanks to a box-to-box Richard Butcher's belter as he bounded onto Dale Watkins' squared ball, Ricky swept the ball into the empty net 1–0. It was victory well earned. But a fourth win lifted Kettering to fourth. Make that five with visiting Merthyr Tydfil thumped 3–0.

Richard was really coming into his own as his confidence continued to take shape with the Poppies. In the fourth minute Richard skipped round three men to tee up with Dale Watkins, the ball soon burying itself into the top corner. Murray floated a free-kick to Darren Collins who then nodded home. A rather quickly taken Matthews set-piece picked out Collins who then headed home to finish.

With Kettering now in joint place with Tamworth and just four points behind Crawley, where they would play next, Richard—still only 20 years old—was showing what a fantastic modern midfielder he could be to his manager and pro teammates who were teaching him the tricks of the trade. With Richard shaping up nicely into a box-to-box midfielder, he was now starting to get a foot in with some great tackles; he often chased lost causes to break down the opposition to support his teammates. He made vital tackles and used his height well, which had led to four goals and 10 assists. He provided the perfect cover and energy to be everywhere on the pitch.

His true professional friends could only appreciate the ground a midfielder like Richard could cover. Fans noticed goals and crunching tackles or clearances, but shadowing and closing down often went unnoticed. He covered 8 to 9 miles, and he delivered a 70% pass rate, in each game. He played over 40–53 matches each year, but it was pleasing to the eye when you saw those 30-yard goals pop in. He certainly felt privileged to be able to play the game he so loved and to be able to pay his way in life.

Back to Crawley. Some say there were 600–700 fans that day. The crowds swelled to 2133 at the Broadfield Stadium. The match got on the way. Richard came close twice, then 13 minutes from time, Murray won a corner and Lee Hughes' header carried the day. While Crawley threw in everything they had, the Poppies broke with speed and passion with some great passing work. With Richard bombing forward back from 90 yards, he then coolly side-footed into the top corner only to send the Poppies' fans wild. While Boxing Day saw a home defeat to Cambridge City, it just wasn't their day due to a frozen pitch. Kettering went on to destroy Chelmsford on the 29th December. It ended up with a six-goal thriller. Richard scored a great goal with his teammates congratulating him.

The weather forced the game at Kings Lynn to be postponed, but the players got a run out over Wellingborough with the score line ending with a win 10–1. On the 19th January the Poppies went to struggling Salisbury. Having weathered their luck and the storm, they found themselves in the top spot. The 3–1 of Welling at Rockingham Road went as smooth as silk. The Poppies then received a wake-up call against Weymouth. Lee Howarth, however, got a consolation in the 3–1 defeat. Kettering now needed a vital win over Moor Green, which they did.

The Poppies then went into the home game against Hednesford with the top spot back on the cards. Tamworth got the rub of the green by beating Stafford with a last-minute goal to leapfrog Kettering and Crawley to top spot. With the Poppies on 56 points with a game in hand, and Crawley sat 2 points behind, Richard scored an eleventh-minute opener away at Newport County only for a deflection to send Bowling the wrong way to even things. A brilliant rearguard action from the defence and two truly world-class saves from Ian Bowling kept Kettering in it, so that a late corner could win the day. Piercewright delivered, Richard went up for it and couldn't quite get a decent touch, but composed Wayne Duik did, curling the ball home: Kettering 2 Newport County 1.

It was a disappointing 0–0 draw at home to Tiverton that caused a horrific injury to Ian Bowling. The St John's Ambulance came racing on to see to him, with blood pouring from his head wound. The ambulance journey to The John Radcliff in Oxford was a lengthy one and proved to be very much touch and go. No one's thoughts were on the game, but in a double dose of ill-fortune Darren Collins also got a concussion for his own heroics between the sticks. Richard was shaken and stunned, but the game was allowed to continue.

Ian would undergo an emergency operation to remove blood clots from the brain and sustain a double fracture of the skull for keeping that clean sheet. It would alter his life and cost him his marriage. Kettering drafted in keeper Paul Pettinger from Lincoln, Havant forced the game early on, but Fear turned the game with a through ball to Watkins, and Collins volleyed home. Havant hit back, but the second goal came from Craig Norman with an outstanding strike to gain the winner.

With Merthyr holding Tamworth, the Poppies were now just a point behind.

The Poppies then travelled to Ilkeston. The game got on the way a minute later. Darren Collins nodded down a free-kick from Lee Howarth to Dale Watkins who teamed up Shaun Murray, who finished from fifteen yards with a classy goal. Just before the hour a neat one-two with Richard Butcher saw Murray clip a second. This 2–0 victory meant that a win on the Tuesday against Hednesford could put the Poppies on top at last. It would be Captain Lee Howarth who would do it. Hednesford were 6 from bottom but 4 points clear from the drop zone. Watkins went close, and Richard began to shine. Dale Watkins headed a lovely inviting ball from Richard Butcher which was headed past the post and then on the fourth hour Peter Fear turned and touched to Watkins. He drove a fantastic 25-yarder shot into the top corner with 90 minutes on the clock. Kettering won another corner. Shaun Murray passed to Darren Collins and flicked on to Captain Lee Howarth for him to hook home to claim top spot. The Kettering fans were dancing with joy— they were two points clear. A great win at Kings Lynn, 3–0. Richard rounded off a great performance on the hour. Dale Watkins slipped a lovely ball into the path of Richard Butcher and he took aim and nestled the ball into the top corner. Richard had covered every blade of grass. The final whistle went and the 1842 fans were doing the promotion song with Rockingham Road rocking.

Then moving on to a 2–1 defeat by Ilkeston that didn't go down too well. Tamworth had won and gone top which set the 1456 Poppies fans praying at Rockingham Road. A hearty 500 went to Hinckley and saw a second 2–1 defeat after Richard had forced an equaliser from close range. This made the game at home to Folkestone Invicta, the club Richard had made his debut against, simply vital, with the Poppies now trailing Tamworth by 4 points and fading fast. With injuries blooming Kettering conceded a soft corner which allowed James to head home. Roy then put a cute ball to Richard, who split the defence with a ball to Dale Watkins. The Poppies were level. Turner then teamed up with Chris Perkins who headed into the top corner. The pitch was invaded. The heroes had restored the faith. It was a standing ovation at full time. Richard, known to the fans as Ricky, was overwhelmed with the fans' response, and was full of excitement for himself and his teammates.

With just six games left to play, Carl Shutt started himself away at Chelmsford. Carl Shutt had delayed his introduction against Folkestone to see if Murray's hamstring would hold out. He simply had to lead from the pitch with a 20-yarder midway through the first half. The side clicked; Lee Cowling scored just inside the top post 2–0. A 2–1 home defeat to Newport Isle of Wight left everyone in limbo. Almost 400 fans made the trip to Moor Green. It was still 0–0 in the first half. Shaun Murray threaded the wall to Darren Collins. Richard Butcher latched on to the rebound and buried it in a flash, a perfect shot from Shaun Fear from 30 yards out split the defence and Dale Watkins slotted home full time Moore Green 0 Kettering Town 2.

The dream was still alive. Kettering were off to Kings Lynn with 600 travelling fans. It was still goalless at half time but the supporters were roaring with pride and excitement. With just six minutes before time the midfield trio had the control and pace. Richard Butcher released Darren Collins down the right-hand channel, again aware that his partner's eye was in; he passed to Dale Watkins, who made a confident first time effort. Peter Fear found Lee Cowling who fired coolly into the bottom corner; just one more goal and Kettering could have gone top on the number of goals scored. Dale Watkins two, Lee Cowling one. The car horns blared and voices were raised;

excitement and hugs and handshakes were all around. Kettering Town–3 Kings Lynn–0.

Kettering then went on to beat Weymouth 4–1 with 2420 Poppies fans in tow, with Richard Butcher having efforts saved and Dale Watkins having to come off in the last 15 minutes. Lenagh came on and Darren Collin cushioned the ball back to Lenagh who sent a 30-yarder into the roof of the net with seven minutes to half time. Peter Fear released the ball to Richard Butcher who squared it to Darren Collins to tap the ball home. With Fear and Richard again Lenagh nodded past the post; a penalty decision allowed Weymouth to change the goal difference before Lee Cowling's cross in injury time allowed Collins to head home.

The final day came at Tiverton. It boiled down to Tamworth's results; Kettering's away record was good to that of the lambs that were away at Folkestone Invicta. Fear's free kick struck Saunders and Norman sent the keeper the wrong way. The 1,500 Poppies fans roared with excitement at the news Tamworth had gone a goal down. But Tiverton had an equaliser from a free kick which rewrote things once again. Turner's cross found Lenagh to restore the Poppies' lead. The dancing and singing sounded through the roof tops. Further good news was to follow. Folkestone led Tamworth 3–2 the drama continued. Richard Butcher beat four players, but Peters blocked the shot of the line. The whistle blew, the Poppies fans invaded the pitch and the celebrations started.

Richard had a great career at Kettering Town. His teammates were a great bunch of lads; they took him under their wing and shared their experience with him. He was very proud to be a Kettering player and teammate.

Garry Hughes recalls:

So in Butch signing for Kettering, we went on to win the league and gain promotion to the Conference. So much of that success had to be put down to the introduction of Butch. He brought a lot to the team in terms of energy, creativity, goals, and general positivity, and I would go as far as saying he made the place more exciting and enjoyable. This was reflected in the end of season awards when he cleaned up. Butch was on a high and I know deep down he was getting the recognition he felt he deserved and was certainly heading in the right direction.

On a personal note it was not a bad first season for the 21-year-old team player, with ten goals (eight League and two Cup) plus fourteen assists from twenty-eight League & six Cup starts plus the two substitute appearances early on. But Richard recognised that another big part of that Championship side perhaps gave more than any other to both the cause of the team and Butch's career.

Ian Bowling is a great professional, and a lovely lad who had kept a heroic clean sheet in the early games against Tiverton 0–0 where he sustained that horrific double fracture of the skull in the process.

Ian recalled in a recent conversation:

Yes, the head injury changed my life. My ex-wife (it cost me my marriage) said I changed as a person, but I don't really believe that. I have since gone on to work with people who have also suffered brain injuries, and let me tell you, I was so lucky to be alive, but also to go on and do the things I do every day. When you look back at that time, and it is only an afterthought, I think we were lucky to do it. I can tell you it wasn't Shutty's introduction in those games that did it! I was down at Tiverton on the last day and it could have gone either way, but you need luck in anything you do, and respect is earned not given, and overall, I think we deserved the respect we received and proved the doubters wrong. We were a great bunch of lads who were in a thankless position where we were damned if we didn't win the league and damned if we did, because it was expected but nobody has the right to just turn up and expect to win. All credit to the lads, club, and supporters for getting over the finishing line.

The return to the Conference was tough. The Poppies drew their opening two games, but won two, drew five and lost eleven from the opening eighteen games of the season. Carl Shutt could not fill the departures of key players, let alone strengthen the side to compete, as the club had taken the main sponsors' money early to keep them going during the promotion run in the previous season. Finances worsened and crowds fell along with team morale.

Richard scored against Hereford, Telford, in a rare win at Farnborough and at Leigh, but it was tough for a young lad struggling to make his way in the game. The humorous moments became few and far between and the threat of a pay cut made him question whether even a part-time career in football was beyond his ability and means. Pessimism quickly envelopes optimism when you have bills to pay, and you are continually requiring your parents to bail you out. Was it wise? Was it even fair?

RICHARD BUTCHER KETTERING TOWN F.C
PHOTO BY: www.kappasport.co.uk

Lee Howarth as captain and mentor lent another helping hand as the club lurched into a testing financial period, to say the least.

Lee Howarth says:

After a fantastic first season Butch decided to get a bit more serious and asked me about returning to education. He was a part-time player, and we trained in the evenings, so he thought he should do something more constructive than the traditional bookies/snooker hall pastimes that footballers tended to drift into (to keep them out of the pub!). I had done something similar by returning to university after I packed in playing full-time football and now had a job as a Sports Science Lecturer at Moulton College located about 20 minutes from Kettering off the A43 towards Northampton. I brought him a prospectus and he decided to join the college as a mature student (!) on a HND in Sports Management. I was now one of his lecturers as well as a team-mate—a difficult balance in the classroom as they are distinctly different environments. I had to gently warn him that what goes on in the dressing room, coach, hotel, etc. stays there, and does not get transferred to the classroom where I obviously needed to maintain some semblance of a reputation and respect. He was as good as gold and never leaked anything apart from when I had not really troubled the Man-of-the-Match deliberations on the preceding Saturday.

He joined the college on the 30th September 2002 and was just as big a hit in the classroom, soon becoming the life and soul—and as popular with the gents as he was with the ladies. As I was writing this I typed his name into our student management system (yes—I still work there) to see if we still had any record of his brief time at the college—and we do. Unfortunately, the academic career of student S0012014 soon ended (although probably for the best!) when his move to Lincoln City materialized, as he became accustomed to the pace of the Conference game, and he officially left the college on 8th November 2002 classed as a 'withdrawal.' I had a small part in Butch's move into professional football with Lincoln City as it came out of a now sadly familiar Kettering Town financial crisis, although I had not realized that Ian Bowling effectively set the whole thing up— I hope he got a cut! After promotion back to the Conference, we had an underwhelming start to the season and after a couple of months Shutty told me that the club was struggling to pay the wage bill, and things were not looking good going forward. After a couple of weeks of rumours, the chairman Peter Mallinger called a meeting after training one night and informed us the club was going through a cash-flow problem and that they could only afford to pay us 85% of our wages that week; this would also be reviewed on a weekly basis and would be by cheque rather than going straight into our bank accounts—an even worse sign! I remember some heated player meetings over the next few weeks, but I was always adamant that we should back the chairman.

Peter also gave us a quick financial breakdown of the club's finances and how dependent it was on attendances—which may seem obvious—but I had never considered the impact that season tickets and child/OAP discounts had on the weekly cash flow of a football club. Apparently, a crowd of 1000 was probably made up of 200 season ticket holders (where the income has already been collected and presumably spent) and 150 discounted tickets, leaving only 650 paying full price. Hence, when the previous season's crowds of 1200–1500 had dwindled to 800–1200 with a similar wage bill, but still reliant on the bigger break-even attendance figure, we were clearly headed for trouble. Obviously, a football crowd wants to watch a winning team, and our poor results were not helping the situation—we suddenly seemed a million miles away from those 1500 fans that made the 400-mile round trip to Tiverton for our promotion back to the Conference!

A financial crisis at a football club has a different impact on different players—for some it is a disaster; for others an opportunity. As a senior player I was less reliant on my football income at this stage—ten years earlier this certainly would not have been the case. However, for Butch, the financial impact would have been felt more keenly as a greater overall percentage of his income was to be reduced.

As soon as a football club defaults on your contractual wages they are in breach of their side of the contract, and after 14 days without resolution, you become technically a free agent—great if your twenty-one-year-old talents are in demand; not great if your thirty-five-year-old talents are not! Soon the vultures were circling, and Butch was approached by Keith Alexander (a friend, former coach, and teammate of mine) who was then manager of Lincoln City, and Butch was thrust immediately into the typical footballer's dilemma. You do not want to desert your teammates, especially in a time of need, but equally, you owe it to yourself and your family to do the best you can, play at the highest level you can and—yes—earn as much money as you can in a very short career (PFA figures demonstrate that the average professional footballer's career lasts just eight years from age sixteen). So when the opportunity that he had been yearning for since he was a kid presented itself, he had no choice.

As I was captain of the team (and his academic course manager at college), Butch came to see me for some advice on this situation, just as I had done on several occasions over the years when I spoke to senior players who have been in these positions before, and who know what it is like to negotiate with managers and chairmen—an experience that is very intimidating for a young player. I imagine in his later years as a player he would have had similar conversations with younger players given his own experiences. I told Butch that it was too good an opportunity to miss out on (although this would affect my course figures, and possibly bonus at college!) and we went to see the manager to spell out the situation and get the ball rolling. Carl was gutted as his best player leaving the club was not going to help his cause of hauling us up the league. My idea was to get the chairman to pay Butch what he was owed (presumably by paying the rest of us less), thus removing Kettering from the breach of contract technicality, then get onto Keith and squeeze £5-10k out of Lincoln, effectively throwing the rest of us a lifeline for a few weeks.

I outlined my idea about trying to get a small fee from Lincoln to the chairman but he was so much more experienced in these matters, he did not really consider it. Basically, he had to let Butch go on a free, or Lincoln would have just hung on until matters had gotten worse, and he had an unhappy player on his hands whom he would have to let go eventually. I think as a football club director and chairman who is well used to dealing with a turnover of hundreds of thousands of pounds it was probably just a drop in the ocean. Peter was a fantastic man and chairman who paid every penny that was owed from this situation over several years—I was owed about £7,000 when I left Kettering and, frankly, was not hopeful once I had left the club, but I got a cheque and an update regularly until it was cleared after about 2 years—not many football chairmen are that honourable. I think the respective recent fortunes of KTFC and Corby Town FC say everything about him since he sold Kettering and bought Corby, and every Kettering fan and ex-player wishes he was still in charge. Sadly, I was at his funeral a couple of years ago but it was also attended by hundreds of well-wishers there to pay their respect to a great football man.

The few days or weeks that these transfers take are nervous times for the player who, in those days before everyone had an agent, is usually the last to know what is going on. A bad call on either side as they try to wring the last penny out of the deal can lead to one party pulling out leaving you exactly as you were a week ago, but now disappointed, disillusioned, and demotivated. You normally get a call saying yes or no and not much else after you have agreed your personal terms, which, to be honest, did not take that long in the early 2000s Conference era. The rule is basically still sound, but with a few more zeros involved—negotiate as big a basic wage and signing on fee as possible for a starter, as goal bonuses, clean-sheet bonuses, finishing position bonuses, promotion bonuses, staying-up bonuses are nice if they kick in, but are not guaranteed and if your season turns out to be a shocker, as this one was, are effectively worthless.

They managed not to mess this one up, and Butch was off! It was a sad day for us as we were now a weaker team, as well as losing one of the characters that made going to training worthwhile—he used to get a little cheer from us all when he walked in the dressing room as we knew the fun would get funnier—a bit like Norm on Cheers! But we also knew that he was too good for a team bouncing around at the bottom of the Conference.

Keeper Ian Bowling, who would be instrumental in the transfer, recalls:

When we turned up for pre-season that summer, Butch was still on holiday. When he returned, we had been two weeks into our training programme. We trained at Wicksteed Park and used to go on long runs around the perimeter of the park. The first training session that Butch was back, Shutty sent us on the long run around the park. Off we went! All the quick runners were up at the front. I took up my usual place at the back, so nobody got lost lol! Butch absolutely hammered it. He came first in the best time yet. Shutty then said to Butch, "Butch, seeing that you have missed two weeks training, you have got to go again!" Without a murmur, Butch set off again at a blistering pace. Butch had gotten about 100 yards away when Shutty shouted him back and told him he was joking! That typified Butch. Whatever you asked him to do he would do it with great enthusiasm.

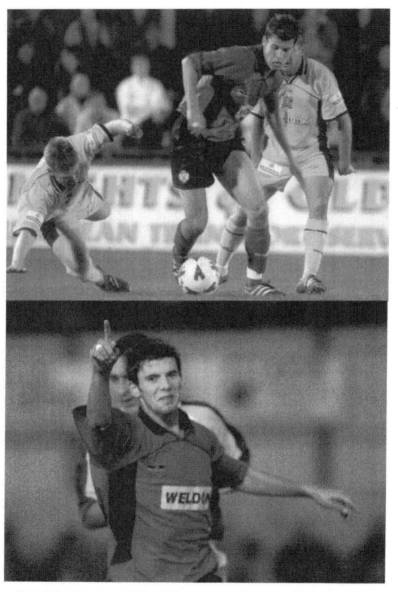

RICHARD BUTCHER KETTERING TOWN F.C
PHOTOS TAKEN BY : www.kappasport.co.uk

Whilst we had been away playing in the Southern Premier the Conference had changed. It had gotten a lot more professional and there were more and more clubs turning full time. We were struggling in the league and couldn't seem to get a win anywhere. Attendance had dropped, and the chairman Peter Mallinger was finding it hard to find the money to pay the wages. We were called in to a meeting one training night at the ground. The chairman informed us about the dire situation and that he could only afford to pay us a percentage of our wages.

I was on non-contract which basically meant I didn't have a leg to stand on in terms of getting my money, but, true to his word, Peter Mallinger paid me every penny that he owed me, and, even though it took four years in part-payments, I will be forever grateful to the man for doing so. He really did have Kettering Town in his heart, and I know how painful it was for him to have to tell us that he couldn't commit to agreements he had with players. He also looked after me and my family when I had my serious head injury, which I will be also grateful for, along with every supporter of Kettering Town Football Club.

Back to Butch! We came out of the meeting and had a meeting of our own. The lads were expressing their concerns about what was going to happen. I could see it had affected Butch. When the meeting had finished, I pulled Butch to one side and asked him what the matter was. With tears in his eyes Butch said he had just taken out a loan to buy a car (a Black Ford Fiesta Zetec) and it meant that he couldn't afford to repay the loan. I told him not to worry and not to do anything until I had spoken to him later in the week.

We had played Lincoln City pre-season and their manager Keith Alexander, who was an ex-teammate and friend, had asked me about Butch after the game. The next day I phoned Keith to tell him about the situation and that Butch was available if he still fancied him, and that, because the club was in breach of contract with Butch, they could have him for nothing. Keith took Butch's number off me and said he would phone him. I phoned Butch straight away to tell him Keith was going to phone him, and whilst I was on the phone with him he was trying to get through. Keith and Butch went on to form a great friendship and appreciate each other, and, even though both of them are sadly not with us anymore, you can be sure that they will still be in contact somehow.

Garry Hughes was chuffed to hear the news:

At this point I had been released by Kettering and had signed for Moor Green. I had already accepted that my playing career was heading in one direction which is what made me different from Butch. I was pipe-fitting and working on a warehouse in Northampton. I remember one afternoon when I was working away about 60 feet up on a scissor-lift that I noticed Butch was calling me. I answered it and noticed straight away that Butch was excited. He blurted out "Guess where I've been, Hughes?" He never gave me the chance to reply with a simple, "where mate?"; he just bounded in, in true box-to-box fashion, with, "I've been up Lincoln City Football Club all afternoon." I asked him why, but I kind of knew in my heart that it was to sign for them as a professional. I knew this as there were lots of rumours of interest from League clubs, but none had taken the plunge of signing him. So when he told me his awesome news I was totally buzzing for him for the fact that he was finally getting recognised for his talent, and that he told me that I was the first person he told after his family members. I felt totally honoured that he wanted to share his fantastic news with me, and that he was asking advice from me on how he should go about things, as I had played for Northampton at a similar level. I just said, "You're easily good enough to be playing regularly at that level, and just keep doing what you've been doing during your time with Kettering, and you will be flying, son."

Butch was a big success as soon as he started his first season with Lincoln and ended up playing at The Millennium Stadium in the playoff final. It was a game I watched in a pub in Northampton and, as I was sinking my fifth pint, I realised how our career paths had become worlds apart. I was never envious or jealous of Butch, of what he went on to achieve; in fact, I would say the opposite. I was proud to tell people of our relationship together, and wanted him to get as high as he possibly could up the football ladder. As our career paths drifted apart, and with me returning back to my parents in Birmingham, we didn't make contact with one another often, but I always kept a close eye on his career.

I remember Lincoln was drawn against my beloved Birmingham City in the League Cup the one season and me and a friend went to watch; I remember Butch having banter with Robbie Savage on the pitch and would say that Butch got the better of him that day. I'm not even sure if Butch knew I was in the crowd that evening but I was proud to be witnessing his career blossoming. I followed his career game by game and would always look out for his team's match write up in the national papers and would often see his name pop up on soccer Saturday on Sky Sports when he bagged himself a goal. I will never forget our experiences together and I'm truly honoured and proud to have played alongside him, and he was someone I would call a real friend and true gentleman. RIP Butch.

Richard's Mum Gail:

The Poppies would play such a perfect part in Richard finding his footballing feet. When he signed for Kettering Town he had chipped a bone in his wrist so he was in plaster for a limited time. When signing, he told manager Carl Shutt that he would not be in plaster for much longer, only a matter of a couple of weeks. The story he told was that he had tripped over the dog. I went off shopping as I would normally do on a Friday only to come home and to find Richard had cut his plaster off his wrist himself. I said, "You will have to go straight to the hospital and have one put back on." He refused point blank, and said, "Mum, the team needs me tomorrow, and I am not missing out for all the money in the world. I am playing, so this is my chance." And so he did play. I shut my eyes at every run he made, and at every twist and turn, with worry, thinking someone was going to kick it or fall on it. How he got through that game and survived to play another day, I will never know.

My son was so strong-willed he would never have let this one big chance slip away. He always had his own mind. Kettering Town was a fantastic club right in the heart of the community. When arriving for the match on a Saturday, the Town was buzzing come rain or shine. Spirits were high, the club house was filled, the staff and fans were so friendly, and you would so look forward to a game. The smell of burgers, hot dogs, onions, and chips was like no other, and the friendly banter was shared by fans and friends alike. The terraces seemed filled with laughter and singing, whether they won or lost.

This club was the heart of a community and should not be lost forever. I often sent Christmas cards to the girls in the club shop to say hello, just to let them know we had not forgotten them. The club girls were always interested to know how Richard was doing, and they also looked out for him with great delight. A young Kettering fan, Sarah, used to follow Richard wherever he was. She would be there cheering him on and would send Christmas and Birthday cards, even little presents, too.

The memories we have with the proud Poppies, right through the team to the staff and fans, will never be forgotten. The council should really put the heart back into Kettering Town and help give them their little club back, and let them sing again. My dad has a second cousin, Joan Streather, who lives in Kettering, and they all say how much they miss their Saturday afternoons, walking up to their club to watch their team play. Clearly, there is still a lot to be said and done before Kettering is allowed to die.

Carl Shutt finished the season with a double celebration. The Kettering Town boss was named the 'Dr. Marten's Southern League Manager of the Year'. He also picked up the premier Davison's final monthly award following his championship-clinching 2–1 win at Tiverton. The Poppies' squad had an open-top bus trip round the town from the Rockingham Road ground to the council. 2,000 fans lined the streets, and there was a great presentation night to follow with 300 guests. Wayne Duke was named as the Concorde Printers' player of the year, while Richard Butcher took the Executive Members and supporters' player of the year award, and Sean Murray was voted the players' player of the year, and Dale Watkins took top scorer.

After the bus had travelled through the town, it then travelled back to Rockingham Road where the fans packed the main stand to see club and team captain Lee Howarth and Darren Collins hold the shield over their heads while the rest of the team collected their medals. Shutt paid tribute to Richard. He said, "He has been a revelation this season and that has been recognised by the awards which he fully deserves. It was nice to see the young supporters have spotted what a great talent he has."

The reception to the players and myself was magnificent and it was a fitting end to the season. Mr. Peter Mallinger said, "I have been a chairman of this club for nine years and it's the first time we have won anything major." Richard was so proud to be a part of a great season at Kettering Town. He got to know Mr. Peter Mallinger very well. He was such a great person who really cared a lot for Kettering Town and who will always be remembered.

RICHARD BUTCHER AND TEAM MATES AT KETTERING TOWN F.C
PHOTOS BY: www.kappasport.co.uk

Lee Howarth, a Poppy legend, who was such a huge part of Richard being able to survive and thrive in football, says:

I bumped into Butch a couple of times over the years on the pre-season circuit, and it was like you had been with him the day before, not several years previously, as the old jokes would immediately be recycled. It was good to see him forge a successful career as a pro for many years before I heard the devastating news of his sudden death. I was at Sincil Bank for his memorial service with several ex-Kettering players, and the fact that it had to be held in a football stadium says more about what Butch meant to so many people than any of us ever can. Butch—not the greatest student I have ever met, but an unforgettable player, teammate and friend.

Former Kettering Town Legend Craig Norman paid an emotional tribute to his teammate and friend. Norman was a key player in the famous Poppies' team and he struggled to find the words.

Craig Norman says:

I was, like everyone else, shocked when I heard, and I still am now. Butch was the sort of player who would get goals, and he had a great engine. He was a box-to-box midfielder who would be a nightmare to mark.

I can't speak highly enough of him as a footballer and a man. But there was never any doubt in my mind that he would go on and have a good career. He was the complete player and a fantastic friend. I am still close to his mum and dad and they doted on him. My heart goes out to them.

Richard's Mum Gail:

The Poppies held a minute's silence for Richard Butcher and Former Kettering Town chairman Peter Malinger, who was at the helm at Corby Town. Richard knew Peter very well, just as we did, his mum and dad. We send our love to his family. And thank you Kettering Town, and the fantastic team and fans for giving us such great memories to keep forever in our hearts. The parting of the ways at The Poppies—we can remember the last game Richard played for

Kettering Town. We told him we would see him at the game, but he said that he didn't want us to come. He said it would be too difficult for him on that very day. The emotions ran high for Richard and for us. He really did get so attached to the clubs he played for, especially when he was so well liked. Myself and Richard's dad sat and listened to the game on the radio. It really is heartbreaking when you have to leave a club so dear—one that he appreciated and that had given him his big break. But he knew he had to chase his dream to become a full professional.

Mr Dave Dunham sent Richard a book the Story of the Season Kettering Town 2001–2002; this is where I found some information about the games. He wrote in the book 'Congratulation on a fantastic season, Richard you did keep smiling! And you made a difference, with best wishes Dave Dunham.' The book had been signed by all the players and sent to me. I am so proud to have all these memories.

I also found it a great help with the Kettering Telegraph after collecting all the media attention Richard had over the years at Kettering Town. I am so proud and feel so lucky that I have all these precious paper cuttings to keep forever.

Kettering Town

Between 1897 and 2011 they played at Rockingham Road, after spells at North Park and Eldred's Field. Chairman Imraan Ladak had stated the club's intention to return to a new ground in Kettering. In June 2011, it was announced that Kettering had reached an agreement with the owners of Nene Park, the home of former local rivals Rushden & Diamonds, to secure a lease on the ground that would potentially secure the club's future. The club was forced to move to Steel Park, Corby Steel Park, in late 2012, as the club could no longer afford to pay for electricity at Nene Park. For the 2013/14 season the club will play their home games at Latimer Park, Burton Latimer, and Kettering.

Information about the club was found on en.wikipedia.org/wiki.

RICHARD BUTCHER KETTERING TOWN F.C
PHOTOS TAKEN BY: www.kappasport.co.uk

RICHARD BUTCHER'S SHIRTS AND MEDALS OVER THE YEARS

www.kappasport.co.uk took photos above

6: Lincoln City FC 2002–2003

Richard's great granddad, Bill, would have been particularly proud of his grandson when he put pen to paper at Lincoln City. Bill served his time as a mechanic in the RAF within the county during the war in the early 1940s, and around 1942 he watched the Lancashire bombers take off when they bombed the Dams. He was stationed at Wickerby near Market Rasen, but, sadly, he died before Richard got his move to the Imps. He would have been very proud of his great grandson.

RICHARD BUTCHER WITH GREAT GRANDAD WILLIAM WRIGHT
WHO WAS STATIONED AT WICKENBY AIRFIELD
AS AN AIRCRAFT MECHANIC

Keith Oakes remembers the day Gary Simpson made his case for Richard, who soon became known as Butch, like his dad, and brother, and his ancestors before him. Gary knew the Imps had a tight budget. Keith was always eager to unearth a gem. He had just been to see Halifax v. Kettering 4–0. Richard was on the losing side, but he continued to go box-to-box throughout the 90 minutes. He was a tall six-footer and was certainly worth a gamble.

Richard approached manager Carl Shutt who had given him a chance in the game, to see if he would allow him to leave. Our son always felt he owed Carl so much. Kettering was struggling to pay the wages and was going to cut the squad down to a third. That meant Richard's wages would have been less, and this meant that his contract had been broken, and he could give a 14-day notice for breach of contract. Carl Shutt would never have stood in his way. Carl needed money to pay Richard to get a fee, and also to pay the outstanding wages for the rest of the team. He made 56 appearances and scored 14 goals. Carl was disappointed to lose him, but he knew it was Richard's chance at league football.

We can remember driving Richard up to Lincoln City the day he got the call. The car was filled with great excitement, not knowing what was going to be said. When we arrived, we dropped Richard off at Sincil Bank. It looked big, modern, and professional, but there was still that personal, homey feel of a caring club sitting in the middle of those terraced streets, right in the heart of the community. Off we went for a coffee with girlfriend Anna, with everything crossed, waiting for his interview to be over.

We finally got the call to pick him up, and his face was just glowing from ear to ear. We sat and talked for a while with so much excitement. He told us what a great meeting he had with Keith and that he would like to offer him a contract. Richard's first contract was to be £350 per week 2002–2003 moving up to £400 a week 2003–2004 plus £100 goal bonus. But he was worried that he would have to move to Lincoln; his first move away from home. Our son was a very homey person but he soon got his head around things with a big hug from us. The thought of leaving your friends and family to start a new life was a big deal to start with, but he soon settled in.

Lincoln would become our second home, too. The understandable butterflies began to flutter. *Would things go well or would they not?* You never know what is going to happen, as Richard always said, "Life is like a box of chocolates; you never know what you might get."

On the gift front, according to Richard, in a discussion a small payment was made by the Imps' board helping with Kettering's financial plight. After he left Kettering, we also made a small payment to help with wages as a 'thank you' for their support. We also attended an auction at Kettering Town football club to help raise money towards players' wages. The whole family went along. I still have the items to this day. His dream had finally come true—to play professional League football with a two-year deal with the Imps.

Richard turned out to be one of the great signings that Keith Alexander took under his wing. His personality fitted the bill, not to mention his feet, and being six-feet-tall, with dark hair and having a lovely Chinese tattoo on his arm.

I can explain the oriental lettering. When Richard first had his tattoo done, I was a bit mad with him but he was so proud of what it stood for, it meant family, something he said was even closer to his heart. And that's what Keith was—a loving family man. Our son saw that in Keith the moment he met him.

Manager Keith Alexander

Keith Alexander was a footballer as well as a manager. He was the manager of League Two side Macclesfield Town at the time of his death, in a career that included international appearances for Saint Lucia. Alexander played for a whole host of lower league football teams. His main success, however, came from football management, managing in both Non-League and the Football League. He took League Two side Lincoln City to four consecutive play-offs, taking them to two finals at the Millennium Stadium. His eldest son, Matt, is a FIFA licensed Football agent and works with many top flight players. He was the first full-time black professional manager in the Football League, and is considered by many to be a pioneer of the modern game. Richard thought the world of Keith Alexander, and he was highly respected by our family.

Information about the club and Manager was found on en.wikipedia.org/wiki.

RICHARD BUTCHER WITH MANAGER KEITH ALEXANDER
TOGETHER FOREVER ALWAYS IN OUR HEARTS
LINCOLN CITY F.C & RICHARD'S FAMILY

In his own words: Richard was quoted in the Lincolnshire Echo in 2002 when first joining the Imps. "Play-Off place is possible, says Sincil Bank newcomer, Richard Butcher. Who would believe it?"

He couldn't have been further from the truth at the time when he said this, when he joined the Imps in 2002. He completed his transfer from the conference side Kettering Town. He spoke to Keith Alexander. "Basically," Keith said, "What you see is what you get," and he told Richard straight what he expected from him after training with the lads just twice. Our son's words were, "I've already noticed the team spirit—there's loads of banter, no-one is down, everyone is chirpy, and I think we will get to the play-offs. I know it's a bit early to say things like that, but from what I've seen so far, I think we will."

These are just a few of the games our son played in and goals he scored which will help you experience a little bit about Richard's football life: a story within the games:

23/11/ 2002 Home Debut – Attendance 3,198. Richard's first game of the season was against former club Rushden & Diamonds–2 Bell 27 Wardley 56 Lincoln City–1 83 minutes Gain. There was good build-up play from the Imps' 4-4-2 formation. It was a scrappy affair with the Imps up against a quick Rushden side who looked threatening on the break. Their pressure eventually paid off on 26 minutes when new boy Richard Butcher conceded a free kick 30 yards from goal. The kick was taken short to Bell who then unleashed a low effort on goal. A swift break down the right by Duffy who carved out the opportunity. His excellent out-swinging cross was met by the head of the onrushing Wardley, who planted a net effort. A glimmer of hope with seven minutes on the clock, Peter Gain danced his way past two defenders and buried a superb drive.

14/12/2002 Home Attendance 2,845. Cambridge United–2 Guttridge 4 Waneless 78 Lincoln City–2 Butcher 34, Weaver 67 minutes. The Imps were made to pay early doors; a break down on the right saw tall striker David Kitson fire a low effort towards goal with Allen Marriot only able to parry the ball into the path of the onrushing Luke Guttridge who blasted the loose ball into the roof of the net. That changed, though, as, in the 34th minute, the Imps drew level. City's seventh corner of the half, taken by Stuart Bimson, was only half-cleared by Cambridge defence with Ben Sedgemoor drilling a low effort back towards target with Richard Butcher on hand to grab his first goal since joining the club. Good work from Cornelly. Down the left saw the former Ashton United man send a dangerous ball into the box which was palmed away by Marshall. On hand to smash the loose ball home was Simon Weaver, which resulted in some superb celebrations by his teammates. This was capped on 78 minutes when some dreadful hesitation in the City defence allowed Paul Wanless, who had only been on the pitch for a matter of seconds, to nip in to slot the ball past Allan Marriot.

18/01/2003 – Home Attendance 2,885. Lincoln City–1 Butcher 33, Shrewsbury Town–1 Jagielka 73 minutes. The Imps found their breakthrough after thirty-two minutes of play in which they had presented themselves as the livelier of the two teams. Sedgemore's corner to the far post hit the stanchion and fell to Richard Butcher on the edge of the box who hit a powerful drive straight down the middle to thrust his side into a—some would say deserving—1–0 lead. Shrewsbury then levelled matters around the twenty-minutes from time through Steven Jagielka as City was caught napping on the edge of the box. The ball broke to Jagielka who fired a low drive past Marriott into the bottom right-hand corner.

26/4/2003 – Away Attendance 7,578. AFC Bournemouth–0 Lincoln City–1 Butcher 28 minutes. Bailey became the recipient of the game's first yellow card on the quarter-hour mark when he clattered into Thomas for a second time, whilst three minutes later, a quick break down the right saw City win a corner of the afternoon when Richard Butcher's cross was headed behind by Carl Fletcher. Another corner followed midway through the half, but Gain's centre was easily cleared with the home side breaking away to earn themselves their first flag-free kick of the afternoon which was headed over by Derek Holmes.

The play once again switched to the other end with Dene Cropper winning a 28th minute free-kick after being bundled over by two home defenders. Peter Gain took the kick with the ball falling to Richard Butcher on the edge of the box. The former Kettering midfielder took a touch to wrong-foot his marker before curling a superb right-foot effort past the outstretched arm of Neil Moss for his third of the season. The Imps' Dream of the Play-Offs Match winner, Richard Butcher, admits a place in the play-offs would be beyond his wildest dreams.

Butcher's priceless strike at Bournemouth on Saturday means the Imps now need just a point at home to Torquay United this weekend to secure a place in the Division's top seven. City Boss, Keith Alexander: "It was a big result. We've worked hard all season to earn a little bit of luck. They've given effort and commitment all season. Sometimes they've lacked a bit of quality, but it was a magnificent goal from Richard Butcher that won the game, and I thought we deserved to win it. I'm very pleased. They've worked hard together all season on and off the pitch. You look at the likes of Ben Futcher, Simon Weaver, Richard Butcher, and Simon Yeo who were all playing non-league football last season. Some of them were in the Unibond First division so it's an amazing achievement. I can't stress how hard these players have worked. They want to play for the club and they have given the supporters something to cheer about.

03/05/2003 Attendance 7,906. Home Lincoln City–1 Yeo 86 Torquay United–1 Gritten 31. City boss Keith Alexander named an unchanged starting XI for the crucial Division Three encounter against Torquay United at Sincil Bank. The first goal came from Gritten firing the ball into the unguarded net for the opener, but with less than four minutes on the clock, Sincil Bank exploded. A long ball forward from Richard Butcher bounced in the path of Simon Yeo who unleashed a powerful volley past Van Heusden. What a time for the former postman to deliver his first goal in seven months. The whistle went, thousands invaded the pitch. The Imps were in the play-offs.

10/05/2003(P/O) Home Attendance 8,902. Lincoln City–5 Weaver 15, Mayo 18, Smith 55, Yeo 82, 90 Scunthorpe United–3 Calvo-Garcia 26, 69, Stanton 70. Play-Off Semi-final first-leg against Scunthorpe United at Sincil Bank. A rousing rendition of the Dambusters Theme, complete with a flypast in the distance by the battle of Britain memorial flight, got everyone in the party mood as the team emerged from the tunnel. With both sets of supporters in a near-capacity Sincil Bank's was in good voice. The Imps got the game underway. The first goal came with good work from Paul Smith on the opposite flank just before the quarter-hour mark saw him win a free-kick for obstruction and from that resultant free-kick, the Imps grabbed the lead. Stuart Bimson was the man who swung the ball into the danger area and on the back post was Simon Weaver who made room for himself before heading home to send the City contingent wild. It was all City now with their tails well and truly up as they pushed the Irons back, and three minutes later the roof was lifted off the stadium as the Imps doubled their advantage.

The second came when a City attack was only half cleared with Richard Butcher hooking the ball back into the danger area where Paul Mayo had escaped the offside trap and brilliantly lifted the ball over Evans for the first of the season. The Irons pulled one back after they forced their first corner of the game on the left-hand side. Peter Beagrie took the kick with Spaniard Alex Calvo-Garcia looking as though he got the final touch with the ball over the line despite the efforts of Mark Bailey on the goal line. It was certainly an electric start to the game with the Irons, with Paul Mayo going on the attack for the Imps six minutes later only for Mark Jackson to sweep up and hammer the ball out for a throw-in. Before the throw-in could take place, referee Walton had words with Ben Futcher and Martin Carruthers following consultation with the assistant, and once Bimson hurled the ball in the area, it was headed behind by a United defender.

The flag-kick came to an abrupt halt, before Richard Butcher found the net with a header; the whistle went for a foul to the visitors.

In the second half the break came on the left with an excellent control from Paul Mayo seeing him feed Dene Cropper who ran at the visiting defence. Cropper did well to shrug off his marker before pulling back the ball from the by-line, and on hand it was Paul Smith who neatly rolled the ball into the net, to once again turn Sincil Bank into a cacophony of noise. So much for 'long ball' football, eh? It was nonstop action. United pulled it back to 3–2, Calvo-Garcia finding the loose ball falling to his feet, and he hammered the ball into the roof of the net from six yards. Two minutes later, the Irons were on the attack again through Hayes. He held the ball up to find the onrushing Nathan Stanton. He took a couple of touches to get the ball under control before drilling an effort past the arms of Allan Marriot to bring the game three apiece. City brought on Simon Yeo within eight minutes on the clock; the city crowd were on their feet. Yeo latched onto a clever ball forward from Stuart Bimson to pull the trigger for the second time in two games with a pinpoint volley nestling in the back of the net. The game now in the first of two minutes' added time; City won a throw-in on the right—could this lead to a fifth? Well, yes! Although the flag was cleared by the visiting defence, a lovely ball down the left by Stuart Bimson found Richard Butcher who did equally as well to keep the ball in play before squaring the ball into the path of Simon Yeo who spectacularly volleyed the ball into the roof of the net.

14/05/2003(P/O) Away Attendance 8,295. Scunthorpe United–0 Lincoln City–1 Yeo 88th minute. City named an unchanged squad for this crucial Nationwide League Division Three Play-offs Semi-final Second leg against Scunthorpe United at Granford Park with the Imps going into the game with a two-goal advantage with a 5–3 victory at Sincil Bank. Steady rain was falling as the team walked out onto the pitch with a massive roar from the 2,000 fans who had made the journey to North Lincolnshire. Steve Bennett got the game on the way with the Imps kicking off, defending the end behind which housed their travelling band supporters. The Imps just in the third minute saw Paul Smith beat his marker before sending it across, which just evaded the head of Dene Cropper before the hosts scrambled the ball clear. The Irons then broke quickly with Paul Dalglish seeing a shot deflect off Stuart Bimson for a corner and when Dalglish's flag-kick was headed clear by Simon Weaver, Andy Dawson blazed a low effort wide.

It was evident from the opening stages a number of players were having a job to stay on their feet; persistent rain and greasy surfaces were not helping. Dean Cooper did well in the 12th minute but shot tamely at the Scunthorpe 'keeper Tom Evans a quick break down the left, Dalglish saw his low centre fell to Greg Strong who saw his 20-yarder effort pushed wide by Allan Marriott. City keeper Allan Marriott had to be at his best on 21 minutes to tip over a Matt Sparrows effort after the ball had bounced kindly for the United player.

The Imps replied with Richard Butcher testing Evans but the Scunthorpe keeper easily held the midfielder's strike. Scunthorpe's Ian Kilford needed treatment after some neat footwork from Peter Gain with the United midfielder being forced to leave the field on a stretcher following his attempted block on the City man.

Wayne Graves replaced Kilford. Paul Mayo was inches away from getting on the end of a Dene Cropper flick as the imps went on a foray forward shortly after this switch before Richard Butcher disposed Alex Calvo-Garcia before seeing his run towards goal halted by the outstretched leg of Mark Jackson. Meanwhile, Mr. Bennett told Steve Torpey to calm down following a physical aerial challenge on Simon Weaver whilst a late challenge from behind on Mark Bailey saw Matt Sparrow receive a similar lecture from Kent-based official when it look as though he would receive the game's first card.

The flag denied the Imps a goal when Paul Mayo was deemed to be in an off-side position before he knocked the ball down for Richard Butcher to fire home. As the fourth official indicated that two minutes were to be added at the end of the half, Alan Marriott bravely saved at the feet of Hayes whilst a minute into added time Ben Futcher was forced to clear the ball behind with the resultant corner eventually seeing Sparrow fire well wide. For the last of the action the Imps fans were making most of the noise as the team went off for a breather.

Second half both sides emerged, the Imps quickly on the attack with Stuart Bimson's cross appearing to strike the arms of the Iron man defender only for the ref Bennett to wave away the protests from the City camp. The home side were soon pressing the Imps back through roared on by their fans who were packed into the all-standing Don Cass Community stand, with an Andy Dawson cross forcing Ben Futcher to leap high to clear the danger. Dean Cropper saw Paul Smith break down the right five minutes after the restart and when Cropper returned to his feet after requiring treatment after being bundled over in the incident he received a hostile reception from the noisy home crowd. And that's not including Brian Lew's reaction on the bench on the home bench...Cropper was in the wars again in 56th minute when he was crudely up-ended by Mark Jackson with the home skipper picking up the game's first booking for his troubles. Mark Bailey sent the resultant free-kick inches wide as the on looking Imps tried to suck the ball into the net.

The Irons were left holding their heads when Sparrow fired wide after getting on the end of a Hayes flick before Dawson saw his 25 yard free kick clip the City wall before going behind for a corner. City dealt with a flag kick before forcing one of their own when Stuart Bimson's subsequent centre fell to Richard Butcher on the edge of the box; he drilled a left-footer wide of the right-hand upright. In a dig to get themselves back into the tie, Scunthorpe went all-out attack with Martin Carruthers replacing Matt Sparrow in the 66th minute and before Carruthers had time to touch the ball, Bimson won the Imps a second corner of the half following an excellent break into the box. Scunthorpe boss made his final change in 72 minutes with Jamie McCombe coming on for Andy Dawson and seconds later Imps' chief Keith Alexander made his first switch with Simon Yeo replacing Dene Cropper.

A couple of goalmouth scrambles in the Imps' box did nothing to calm the nerves, although things were calmed down a bit 13 minutes from time when utility man Matt Bloomer replaced Paul Smith on the right. With there now being less than 10 minutes on the clock it continued to be backs-to-the-wall stuff with a superb block by Simon Weaver denying Dalglish from the edge of the box. Then, with just two minutes on the clock, the Imps' fans were dancing with delight as, with Scunthorpe pushing forward, Peter Gain fed a great ball through to Simon Yeo and the in-form front man came up with the goods; he neatly slid the ball past Tom Evans to clinch a place at the Millennium Stadium Cardiff. Play was halted as the game entered stoppage time following a scuffle in the Scunthorpe end and with ref Bennett bringing the players to the centre of the pitch, on came the police horses and dogs to restore order. THE IMPS WIN 6-3 ON AGGREGATE, what a great day.

24/5/2003 (P/O) League 2 Play-Off Finals Away Bournemouth–5 Lincoln City–2 saw 15,000 travelling fans queuing up at the Millennium Stadium. Richard would savour that moment for the rest of his life, just to be a part of a great team, and to have the experience of playing at the Millennium Stadium was a great privilege to Richard. However this was to be a game you didn't want to pass you by, and sometimes teams can get so overwhelmed and star-struck; it is possible for that to happen. The family had a fantastic day. I can remember our son calling us when he first arrived with the team at the Millennium Stadium. He was so proud to be there, he said, "Mum, Dad, I am sitting in your seats for when you arrive. You have got a good view of the game; they're great seats." We had 36 members of the family travel to watch the game. It was the Butcher family coach. We even had posters on the coach, and some of the kids wore T-shirts with his name on, we were all so very proud. The coach driver remembered Richard from his Kettering days and he even videoed the match. What a brilliant day out for all of us. His dad did sulk at the result a bit on the way home—like father like son—but Richard was not very good when losing a match.

The biggest day in Lincoln City's history ended in defeat with dignity at the Third Division Play-Offs Final in Cardiff. The Imps met a quality Bournemouth side who now took their place in division two, and leaving City wondering what might happen. A record crowd from a third division play-off, 32,148 were inside the Millennium Stadium to produce a magnificent atmosphere. City's 15,000 followers played their part in creating deafening sounds throughout the 90 minutes. The game burst into life on 25 minutes when the Cherries' Stephen Purches shot narrowly wide. Only four minutes later Bournemouth went ahead when Steven Fletcher fired a volley past the outstretched hands of Marriot's dive. City hit back on 35 minutes when Bimson swung in a corner from the right and Ben Futcher rose above two defenders and the keeper to head into the net. As half time approached Elliott sent a shot wide before City's Weaver received the first yellow card of the game. From the resulting free kick the ball fell to O'Connor on the left and his cross was met by Carl Fletcher's header, which restored Bournemouth's lead in the first half added time. The Cherries added to their lead on 56 minutes. Moss punched out a city throw-in and a swift four-man move ended with a right wing cross into the net. Three minutes later it was all over, Conner outpaced the city defence and finished with a crisp left foot shot into the far corner. The Imps reduced the deficit with 15 minutes to go when Mark Bailey scored for the first time this season. But Bournemouth were not yet finished and added a fifth when Purches' free kick was headed in by Carl Fletcher. City kept going with dignity and Mayo hit the bar when it looked easier to score. After the game City boss Keith Alexander acknowledged the Cherries had been the better side and that his defence had saved their worst performance of the season for their biggest day. The people of Lincoln turned out in their thousands to pay tribute to their fallen heroes. Lincoln City had lost their play-off final 5–2 against Bournemouth but that didn't bother the thousands of fans who turned out for an open-top bus tour that welcomed the Imps home. Chairman Rob Brady said, "It was a wonderful day, and not many more people could have turned out, even if we had won. It really did show the great unity in the club. It was a wonderful final chapter in our season, as we begin preparations to start all over again."

When Richard lost a game I tried to make him feel a bit better. He really did have a sulk on. I would phone him and, as mums do, I would say, "Sounds like you had a good game." But Rich, he would say, "We lost, Mum." So there was no talking to him. He showed great passion in his football career, so losing was not on the menu, but a few days later he would be fine, striving for the next match.

I can remember once when he asked his Lincoln teammates if they could spare their old football boots because his brother's team could do with some. At the end of the season, several Lincoln players were good to their word. He collected a few pairs of football boots and sent them down for his brother's team as money was tight for some of them and, to this day, they are still wearing some of the boots that were given to them by Richard and the team. It is strange, though, because I don't have a pair of his football boots myself.

Paul Morgan, one of the Lincoln City players, continues:

As a group, we had a fantastic team, not just on the pitch, but off it! I remember some great times we all had out, and those memories will never leave me. The ones that stick in mind are the ones when I and Butch would meet up in Starbucks for a coffee and cake on a Wednesday afternoon and just people-watch. It was our weekly routine. Sometimes, we would talk about football, girlfriend problems, and money! But sometimes, we would just sit and stare out the window, watching the people all rush by without saying much to each other. That's when you know you're comfortable in someone else's company, when you don't have to make an effort.

Richard's Mum Gail:

Richard made his debut against Rushden, the very side that failed to give him his opportunity. He was allowed to leave on a free in 2001. He didn't let it worry him; he thought it was brilliant. Lincoln was his new home and the biggest club in the world to him, and all he wanted to do was show his worth, and thank Gary and Keith in style.

It was Gary Simpson who scouted Richard, and both ended up being very good friends, a 'like father, like son' in the football world.

The teacher's pet as some would say, but our son was never under any illusions that if he wasn't pulling his weight he would be dropped from the side, because you can't win games on friendship alone. Managers are not in the job for long enough to let friendships get in the way. They need points on the board, or your job will pass you by. Richard used to say that when you were called into the office Keith and Gary had such a good way about them that the players never came out disheartened, even when dropped from the side.

There was a belief that some players at times would be happy to sit on the bench and count their cash from their contracts, but this wasn't Richard. To be injured or to be dropped was difficult for him. He would watch from the stands very frustrated his teammates were losing. Not that he thought he could do any better, but just not being out there with his teammates and being unable to help them was enough for him. Come Saturday at 3 o'clock you're itching for the game to start. Win or lose, he just wanted to be out there. He would train all week not knowing if he was in the starting line. When Saturday morning arrived, he would phone home to let us know if he had made the team or if he would be on the bench, or he would phone us while driving up to the game—using hands-free, mind.

Injured or not, Richard would still keep to his diet and work on his upper body strength to keep himself fit. He was always a good target for banter from his teammates, but he gave as good as he got. His confidence came from an organised routine and his hard work and determination in his fitness and pre-match diet.

Moving on to friend Andy Pearson:

I have been the football intelligence officer for over twenty years and crossed paths with Richard on numerous occasions whilst working the games.

I always found him to be a lively character and so full of life. The club had such a good ethos and close-knit bunch of lads during those special years instilled by the great KA. I was fortunate to have been on a night-out with a colleague and bumped into Pam whom we knew through work, now married to Paul Morgan. We had such a laugh that night in the Revolution Bar, such a great evening. All the lads present were great company that evening, including Simon Yeo, Ben Futcher, Peter Gain, Paul Morgan, and, of course, Richard. Very fond memories, gone but not forgotten.

Big Ben Futcher talks about his best friend and teammate:

There were so many stories from the time, but finding clean ones are difficult, as you can imagine, when we were all so young. The team spirit was unbelievable, and every time someone had a birthday they used to get all their clothes cut and put in the shower, and they were tied to a chair, and covered head-to-toe in black boot polish. What Butch did was he told us the wrong birthday date, so it was close to mine, because he thought if there were two of us the punishment would be less. This little white lie continued for years, but the thing was, we even used to go out and celebrate our birthdays and he managed to keep it going for years.

Richard's Mum Gail:

Our son was not on a great wage at the time when playing for Northampton Town YTS, Rushden Diamonds and Kettering Town; with his move to Lincoln City football club his wages slightly improved but he called upon us, his parents, for help. I remember that Richard was so looking forward to buying his first house with our support. Myself and his dad spent so much time at Lincoln, it was like a second home, but having to spend so much time in hotels was no fun for us. A lovely little two-bed house turned up that Richard fell in love with. We had a look round it and helped him sort the mortgage out. Once sorted, and everything had gone through, he jumped for joy when collecting the keys. His dad laid the flooring, I hung the curtains, and it was great being able to spend so much time with him instead of stopping in hotels on our visits.

I can remember he didn't have a Christmas tree, so I gave him a small optic tree, but when it was switched off it didn't look very Christmassy so, when he was out for a bit, I found some kitchen towel paper on a roll that had snowmen on it. I sat down and made some bows and pinned them on the tree. He said, "Do you know, Mum, the lads are really going to rib me over that." It did look nice, though.

A game to remember as Gary Simpson puts it:

Keith and I were delighted for the young and rising star. Richard's goal at Bournemouth was massively important as it proved to be the difference between the two sides and virtually guaranteed us a play-off spot. It was an unbelievable strike at one of our high-flying rivals, and, best of all, it had come from the boot of one of the ten non-league players we had plucked from nowhere. Those lads delivered time and time again as the club battled its way from admin. to the play-offs, backed by some of the most fantastic supporters in the game.

Good friend, physiotherapist Keith Oakes, remembers:

Butch, still only 22, had been the first in and the last out in training. Sometimes I had to kick him out so that we could lock up. But on a baking day, not helped by a delay due to the crowd congestion, he was focused and went box-to-box for 90 minutes and got a fantastic 20-yarder to confirm our play-off place. An honest lad had given the most honest and hardworking bunch I have ever worked with the chance of a play-off shot. Whenever they went on a pitch they gave everything for Keith and Gary and the club and fans they were proud to play for.

Richard Mum's Gail:

We knew the admiration Richard had for Keith Oakes, the physio at Lincoln City.

He loved his meetings with Keith Oakes; he always said he was the best physio money could buy. Not that he paid him, but there was no question in his mind that Keith was fantastic at his job. These days you seem to need paperwork to run alongside everything you do in life, but I really don't think you can beat the experience Keith Oakes carried about with him. There was nothing he could not do to help players when injured. He even came up with his own ideas which he thought may help some of the injured to heal that bit quicker—the man with the magic sponge whom all the lads had great respect for.

Richard took all his coaching badges right up to managerial level. He trained and coached with the best, but whether he would have gone down that road I really don't know. When some managers apply the tricks of the trade when having to move players on by sending them to Coventry—no offence meant, just something that comes with the trade—this means having to ignore them and blot them out of the first team; this normally happens when you are still under contract, mind, as the club needs to save money and they want to let up your wages for new playing staff.

I could never really imagine Richard being able to be so unkind, or even to be able to tell a player he's just not good enough, and knock his confidence back. After all, this is only said to the player to make him feel unhappy, so he leaves with no payoff. Some players use this experience to make a point at their next club, playing wise if they are lucky enough to have one, but some give up because mentally they can't take any more, and it can force their career to be cut short.

Normally, when a new manager moves in he likes to have his own players that he has brought in himself. It's nothing personal. They just like to create their own winning side. This is where, if you do have an agent, he can come in handy to help take the pressure off a bit, so you don't have to deal with this by yourself from a personal point of view. I was pleased our son had a great agent in Richard Cody, which allowed us and Richard to have someone to talk to who could help deal with any problems that may occur.

I really would like to say to you young want-to-be footballers, you have to realise that you can follow your dream, but school work and education is very important for life after football, as there are no guarantees. And the higher you get in the league, the tougher it gets. The only good thing is——you may get paid ridiculous wages.

As a family, we have to say what a great lifetime experience we shared with Richard and all the players and fans and managerial staff at Lincoln City football club. We will never forget the special times we had at the club. This book may not be for the real diehard fans, but I feel it tells Richard's story and ours, and some of the things he felt and we did while following his dream.

Finishing on a lighter note, there was one holiday that comes to mind that we shared with Richard in Ibiza. He always seemed to make great friends whilst away, with his charming personality. I can remember people asking him what he did for a living and he always told them he was a plumber as he wanted people to like him for who he was and not because he was a footballer. Well, he made this secret last all week. Until he was dragged onto a stage along with the lads he had made friends with. They were made to take off their shirts and then asked once again what he did for a living he replied, "I am a plumber," and the drag artist said, "Not with a six pack like that you ain't." Well, he had to own up then and there. The secret that he had kept all week was out. And all of a sudden, he was handed more phone numbers from the girls around him and the photo shoots started.

I would like to thank Lincolnshire Echo for all the media attention Richard received, which has enabled me to put this book together.

PHOTOS WERE KINDLY DONATED BY MR GRAHAM BURRELL
RICHARD IS HOLDING MR BURRELL'S SON, ELLIOTT

Lincoln City Games 2002–2003

Year 2002

23rd November	Home Rushden & Diamonds	(D3) 1–2 Debut
30th November	Away Oxford United	(D3) 0–1
14th December	Home Cambridge United	(D3) 2–2 SCORED
20th December	Away York City	(D3) 0–0
26th December	Home Macclesfield Town	(D3) 1–0
28th December	Home Swansea City	(D3) 1–0

Year 2003

1st January	Home Boston United	(D3) 1–1
18th January	Home Shrewsbury Town	(D3) 1–1 SCORED
21st January	Home Rochdale	(D3) 0–0
25th January	Away Swansea City	(D3) 0–2
4th February	Away Carlisle United	(D3) 4–1
8th February	Away Hull City	(D3) 1–0
15th February	Home Darlington	(D3) 1–1
4th March	Home Hartlepool United	(D3) 1–0 Substitute
8th March	Away Southend United	(D3) 1–0 Substitute
15th March	Home Wrexham	(D3) 1–1 Substitute
18th March	Away Exeter City	(D3) 0–2
22nd March	Away Bury	(D3) 0–2
25th March	Home Kidderminster	(D3) 1–0
29th March	Home Bristol Rovers	(D3) 2–1
5th April	Home Oxford United	(D3) 0–1
12th April	Away Rushden & Diamonds	(D3) 0–1
19th April	Home York City	(D3) 1–0
22nd April	Away Cambridge United	(D3) 0–0
26th April	Away Bournemouth	(D3) 1–0 SCORED
3rd May	Home Torquay	(D3) 1–1
10th May	Home Scunthorpe United	(P/O) 5–3
14th May	Away Scunthorpe United	(P/O) 1–0
24th May	Away Bournemouth	(P/O) 2–5

7: Lincoln City FC 2003-2004-2005

Richard always worked hard to make sure he was ready for the new season to start. He spent time in the gym and went running regularly with his little dog, Charlie. He always made sure he was fitter and stronger than before, as there was always competition waiting in the wings.

Our son hated being away from football. Once his summer holiday was over, he couldn't wait to get back and for pre-season training to start. His approach to pre-season training was always impressive. Keith Alexander and Gary Simpson always promoted the club well. Richard always wanted to learn and earn his place. Every player had a chance to play; there was always a healthy bond shown amongst the player and management team.

Keith Alexander and Gary Simpson had been together since their days at Ilkeston and Northwich Victoria. They had been given an improved budget thanks to better crowds. The support from the fans is so important to ensure any club's survival.

Richard's new contract at Lincoln took him from £450 per week 2003–2004 to £500 per week in 2004–2005 plus £100 goal bonus, which would give Richard the security he needed. He was quite happy with his first deal with Lincoln City. Richard Cody soon became his agent.

Before going to Lincoln, his wages weren't great at Kettering in his first year, 2001–2002. At Kettering he started on just £250 a week. After fifteen appearances it moved up to £275, with £300 per week after making twenty-five appearances. It may sound a lot, and it was to our son at the time, but all the travelling soon eats into your money when you have to pay petrol, clothes and of course football boots.

With Richard driving between Northampton and Lincoln we didn't feel his first car was very reliable for long distance, so Richard changed his little run-down car from a white Astra to a black Ford Fiesta; he took a loan out to upgrade. With having to travel, and needing a good car to get around in, it never left much in the saving department, so we agreed with our son to help him buy his first home.

He was always very careful with his money, and the digs that were provided for him were very good. He was looked after very well indeed. He so enjoyed his time at Lincoln but started to need his own space.

One thing that was great for us is we got free tickets to the game, a little perk for mums and dads. Staying in a hotel on our regular visits was no fun for us so Richard started looking for his little house. He found a perfect little two-bed house, a new build. We supplied the deposit and helped him out with all the essentials you need for a new home when just starting out in life. We then helped sort the mortgage out. His dad and I would sleep on an air bed while we helped our son do his first house up. His father was a trained chippy, which came in handy when laying the new laminated flooring in his living room, while I set out to sort curtains and bedding and furniture, right down to the toilet rolls.

One of Richard's close friends, Chris Connelly, decided to move in with him. The pair would share some great times. Chris suffered a bad knee injury with his time at Lincoln City, which really made our son realise how short your career could be.

Another big shock that came to Richard is when manager Keith Alexander was taken ill, only to find out later that Keith's life was hanging in the balance and the best surgeons were working to save his life in trying to repair a ruptured cerebral aneurism. While trying to do this they found a second but bigger aneurism, which was serious and rare; very few people survive this but Keith fought back to full fitness. Richard was so pleased for Keith and his family. Gary Simpsons and players were so happy to have him back and grateful he was back to his old self.

We all empathised at the time when the shocking news came through that Keith had been taken ill and we saw how sad our son felt about the whole situation. Richard also knew Keith's boys quite well and was really feeling the sadness for the family at that time. We were all willing Keith to get better and sent a card to be passed on to Keith and his family, hoping he would have a smile when he came round. The card had photos on the front of Keith and Gary together, and the players of course.

It was a very worrying, frightening time, especially for his wife and family. It was great news to hear when he was finally on the mend and the worst was over. Richard really did love Keith's attitude and zest for life and his man management skills were second to none; he was loved by all at the club.

Looking back at just one of the injuries Richard suffered in his career along with Keith Oakes, he suffered a medial ligament injury on the 5th February. He was gutted; he was told he might have to miss the rest of the season. However, he was reassured by his great lifelong friend Keith, the physio, that it was a grade two medial collateral ligament in his left knee, and Keith soon cheered him up and told him they would work together to get things right and he would be back playing before he knew it. They both worked out a plan together with the hope he would be back playing between eight to ten weeks, which would give him time to return for the play-offs and allow our son to end the season with a good goal spell.

Chris Connelly was a great friend who was also suffering a knee injury himself; he unselfishly set about cheering him up and got the play station out and ordered pizzas. Chris was a great friend. Richard always enjoyed his company; and he was brilliant at DIY, and our son liked that. I think this might have been where the electrician came out in him. Although Richard was injured for a long period he was very concerned about Chris, whom we got to know very well. He was a lovely young man; he never seemed to let anything get him down.

Keith Oakes remembers the healing process was a question of heat treatment, ultrasound, massage and straight leg work to ensure that the muscles wouldn't waste away.

Richard always listened and learned, determined to get back as quickly as possible despite the frustration of not overdoing things. With great work and good advice and sound therapy he was back fighting fit and playing again in just two months.

He found it frustrating when not playing. His goals were amazing, but he was always chasing and harrying to help support his team mates. He was a hero to his fellow pros but sometimes the fans didn't realise the work that he did off the ball to help support a fantastic winning side.

A few highlights:

Richard played fifty-three league, cup and play-off games. We want to share some of the important games with you that tell their own story, and the experiences Richard shared alongside his team mates and great manager Keith Alexander and Gary Simpson, not to mention Keith Oakes with his magic sponge.

Our son made an emotional return to Kettering in the Conference North; a full strength Lincoln side beat the Poppies in a friendly, with Richard scoring the fourth goal. The Poppies gave our son a standing ovation alongside Lincoln City fans. In the pre-season friendly, the Imps scored a 5–2 victory over Kettering Town at Rockingham Road, Marcus Richardson opening from the off, scoring with six minutes on the clock. Simon Yeo made it two on the quarter-hour mark when he tapped in a great cross by Gary Taylor Fletcher; just 10 mins later Richardson grabbed his second. New boy Michael Blackwood added a third on 49 mins before Kevin Wilson's side got themselves on the score sheet through Wayne Diuk, but the ex-Kettering star Richard Butcher restored the Imps with a four goal advantage when he unleashed a 25-yard blockbuster which gave the Poppies' keeper Steve Corry no chance. In the 77th minute Kettering's substitute Simon Underwood added the seventh goal of the game.

30/8/2003 Home Attendance 3,892 ref Kevin Friend. Lincoln City–3 Fletcher 21, Butcher 72, Mayo 88 York City–0. Alexander's faith in his squad was indicated with some aplomb as they clicked into gear and knocked huge holes of doubt into the new-found confidence of York City. The Minster-men kicked off boasting the 100 percent record in the football league, but by the time the final whistle had blown that record was in tatters and Brass confessed he had suffered his bad day at the office. The vital ingredient which had been missing was a second goal when Lincoln was on top. For all the time they were dominating against York, there was Gary Fletcher's 21st minute opener separating the sides. And that being the case going into the last 10 minutes, then there would have undoubtedly been flashbacks to the Bury game. As it was, Richard Butcher's goal 18 minutes from the end crucially came at the right time for City. After he had failed in an attempt to get over a cross which was charged down, Richard Butcher whipped the ball off the York defender's toes, looked up and curled a shot into the far corner from outside the box. For Richard Butcher, it capped what was his best display of the season. The midfielder engineered Lincoln's best move and was a tireless worker at both ends of the pitch. Then just five minutes from time, Bailey again went on the outside of him to the by-line, but just as he was about to cross Dunning took his legs away. Ref Kevin Friend pointed to the spot. Paul Mayo stepped up and drilled home a penalty sending Mark Ovendale the wrong way. It was fitting that Richard received man of the match.

Ben Futcher talks about his best friend:

As young lads we used to like a day/night out. We would always arrange a time to meet and get the first round in—Bobby (Butch's nickname) was always about ten minutes late. He would come into the bar, see all the boys with a half-full beer and ask if anyone wanted a drink—knowing everyone would say no. Then one day in Varsity we all got there on time, got the round in and Butch wasn't there. We knew he'd pulled his usual trick and agreed that when he asked if anyone wanted a drink, we would all say yeah! So as he walked in and came to say hello, he asked if anyone wanted a drink—to his horror the lads one by one said yeah go on then. The lads burst into laughter. We're all still waiting for that drink to this day!

16/9/2003 Away Attendance 2,874 ref M Thorpe Southend United–0 Lincoln City–2 Richardson 10, Butcher 78 minutes. Leading 1–0 with 15 minutes to go, Imps' left-back Paul Mayo swung a cross into the Shrimpers' box and Dene Cropper challenged unsteady United keeper Ryan Robinson and defender Leon Cort. The ball ran loose to substitute Simon Yeo, 20 yards out facing an unguarded goal. But whereas at the end of last season he would have buried the chance with his eyes shut, a lacking in confidence Yeo put it over the bar. Seconds later Marriott was punching the air in delight. Southend had already missed two penalty kicks this season; Jupp became the third man to try his luck. He connected well and placed the ball into the corner, but Marriot dived to his right and made a save. It was Southend's seventh miss out of eight games from the spot. The resulting corner was swung over Kevin Maher; Cort met it but his header was cleared. The ball was brought clear by Richard Butcher who found Gary Fletcher before Yeo received possession on the touch line, midway inside the Southend half. A return pass to Richard Butcher, a couple of strides and the midfielder rocketed home a 25 yarder blockbuster with his left foot.

20/9/2003 Away Attendance 2,462 ref S. Mathieson. Kidderminster–1 Dyer 11 Lincoln City–2 Richardson 32, Butcher 43 minutes. A nail-biting affair—the Imps fought back from a one goal deficit to win. Goal scoring had been cured; Richard Butcher and Richardson were on target again. However, Richard Liburd had an afternoon in front of goal he will want to forget in a hurry. City's tasks had been made difficult as early as the 11th minute when the Harriers took the lead. Simon Weaver wanted too much time on the ball; Lloyd Dyer dispossessed him, powered into the box and lashed home a low drive. Falling behind was arguably the best thing that could have happened, because the Imps threw off their shackles and started to move the ball about with precision and assurance. Soon after, Richardson took just four minutes to atone for his error, meeting Richard Butcher's cross with a brilliant overhead kick to draw the Imps level. And two minutes before the break Lincoln took the lead when a Mayo corner fell to Richard Butcher on the edge of the box and he cleverly looped home a header.

30/9/2003 Richard would come back while playing for Lincoln City to play against his home town the Cobblers but it would end in a 0–0 draw. Our family followed him with pride. He received the man of the match award from his home town club.

4/10/2003 Away Attendance 7,914 Ref Mr Evans. Swansea–2 Robinson 17, Trundle 74 Lincoln City–2 Butcher 11, Mayo 15 minutes. Almost 8,000 were silenced inside 15 minutes as Lincoln surged into a two-goal lead. After just 11 minutes a weak goal-kick fell to Marcus Richardson; he powered into the area before slipping the ball to Gary Fletcher's chip over the keeper. Freeston was blocked, and Richard Butcher played a cool one-two with Richardson before slamming the ball low into the bottom corner for his fourth goal of the season. The small band of Lincoln fans were on their feet again four minutes later as the Imps were awarded a penalty. The ball was played back in by Paul Mayo and Fletcher tried an overhead-kick which struck Richard Duffy on the hand. Mayo stepped up and lashed the ball low to Freestone's left. The keeper got a hand to it, but the pace of the shot still took a corner. Swansea pulled one back just two minutes later after Mayo's successful penalty kick. The impressive Britton broke down the Swansea right and played the ball to Andy Robinson who thundered in a left-shot from the edge of the box, which gave Marriott no chance. Lincoln had to hang on for five minutes, and a turn and a shot by Trundle inside the area was tipped away by Marriott, but the unlucky Futcher was unable to react quickly enough and the ball hit his foot before trickling over the line.

21/10/2003 Home Attendance 3,441 Ref P Prosser. Lincoln City–3 Gain 24, Butcher 56, Green 90 minutes Macclesfield–2 Tipton 55, 79 minutes. Macclesfield Town stretched the Imps' unbeaten run to 12 games. It had looked as though plucky Macclesfield, who had been reduced to 10 men after 69 minutes, were going to hold out for a point after Mathew Tipton had twice levelled. But it wasn't to be: the Imps broke the deadlock on 23 minutes when a long ball lick up field by the keeper was contested by Green. Defender Karl Munroe made a hash of his clearance and the ball fell to Gain who hammered home a volley from the edge of the box for his first goal of the season. After 55 minutes it was no real surprise the visitors drew level when the dangerous Tipton met a cross from George Abbey and glanced home a header via the post. Their joy was short lived as Lincoln regained the lead a minute later. Yeo got free down the left and flashed a low centre across the face of goal. Richard Butcher, arriving from deep, latched onto it and hammered the ball into the top corner from 15 yards. But Macclesfield began to battle back and Tipton was not to be denied. He drew his side level only for Lincoln to get the winner soon after.

13/12/2003 Away Attendance 5,797 Ref C Webster. Mansfield–1 Lawrence 34 Lincoln City–2 Butcher 3, Gain 50 minutes. Tenacious work by Richard Butcher saw him dispossess Lee Williamson and let fly from all of 25 yards, with the ball arrowing into the corner; Marriott saved well from Liam Lawrence, and excelled himself soon after as he flew to his left to clew away a thunderbolt from Tom Curtis. Just when it looked as though the Imps had weathered what had been a raging storm, the hosts got back on level terms with more than a little tinge of controversy. Skipper Paul Morgan tussled with Williams close to the corner flag. The Stags midfielder clearly pulled Morgan's shirt as they battled; this should have been a free-kick, but the City player still emerged with the ball. He elected to run across his own box, hesitated when it looked as though Ben Futcher was going clear and that was all the invitation Iyseden Christie needed. He nipped in between the two defenders and Futcher had little option but to bring him down, giving away a penalty. Lawrence stepped up and placed the penalty high to Marriott's right. The goal visibly lifted the home side. The Imps regained the lead just five minutes into the second period in a move involving short passes between Butcher, Bailey, and Richardson and finally Peter Gain who rifled the ball home from the edge of the box.

15/5/2004 Home (P/O) Attendance 9,202 Ref G Lews. Lincoln City–1 Fletcher, 51 Huddersfield–2 Onuora, 5 Mirfin 72 minutes. Keith Alexander was sacked by Lincoln City, to bring to an end his first stint in charge at Sincil Bank almost 10 years previously; he was certainly making the most of his second spell in charge. Huddersfield goals were disappointing as they came from set pieces. Keeper Alan Marriot came out. Veteran striker Iffy Onuora glanced the ball in from no more than two yards; it was the wakeup call Lincoln needed, and they responded. The ball broke to Futcher who stabbed it goalwards and Fletcher was able to tap home from virtually the goal line for his 19th goal of the season. A corner from Andy Holdsworth was met by a towering header from Andy Booth. It seemed destined for the corner until Alan Marriott flung himself to his right to make a fingertip save. But the ball broke to David Mirfin who somehow squeezed the ball home from the angle, despite the close attention of both Allan Marriott and Mark Bailey. Unfortunately we lost the game.

19/5/2004 (P/O) Away Attendance 19,467 Ref M Pike. Huddersfield–2 Schofield 60, Edwards 83 minutes Lincoln City–2 Butcher 38, Bailey 39 minutes. Lincoln City learned lightning could strike twice at Huddersfield Town's McAlpine Stadium. After narrowly losing Saturday's first leg 2–1 at Sincil Bank, City knew they had to win by two clear goals. It was a tall order but the Imps were buoyed by the knowledge their away form had been far better than at Sincil Bank. That was underlined by an exhilarating first 45 minutes from Keith Alexander's well-disciplined troops, who tore huge holes in the Huddersfield rearguard. Two goals in 66 seconds, from Richard Butcher and a collector's item from Mark Bailey, overturned the home side's advantage and put Lincoln firmly in the driving seat to the delight of their travelling army of more than 3,000 supporters.

Huddersfield appeared bereft of ideas, and the only real surprise was that City's lead was just 2–0 at the break. The home fans were restless, and their anxiety grew into the second period until one controversial moment flipped the game completely on its head. A hopeful punt into the Lincoln box by Danny Schofield was too far ahead of striker Andy Booth. The ball bounced out of play as Booth collided with Jamie McCombe. Ref Mike Pike was well placed, no more than 10 yards from the incident, and quite rightly waved play on. But after a quiet glance at assistant Barry Sygmuta, he inexplicably pointed to the penalty spot. Lincoln's immediate reaction was one of sheer disbelief, and it was several seconds before they launched their protest appeals. But Mr Pike was convinced to allow Schofield to slot home the kick from the spot. The goal galvanised Huddersfield's efforts, and they swarmed forward to put the Imps under sustained pressure for the first time in the match. And it paid off seven minutes from time when Rob Edwards rifled home an unstoppable drive from the edge of the box. That sent the Terriers into a final meeting with Mansfield or Northampton on May 31st, in Cardiff.

Former Lincoln City Midfielder Peter Gain shares his post-football life from a player's point of view and the shock after:

I played for twenty years so it's like starting a new life, which is difficult in this current economic climate. At the moment I am grafting away in construction. Lincoln City was the best years of my life and I would love to thank the Lincoln supporters for their incredible support over the years. I will always have Lincoln City in my heart.

We were a family on and off the pitch and Keith had a special way of making his players form special bonds, which carried onto the pitch. But the Lincoln fans were the ones that really cemented this with their incredible support during the bad and good times.

It is easy for a pro to say, but the camaraderie under Keith Alexander and Simmo was just that great with Butch, Futch and Yeo all seeing that Lincoln era as the highlight of their careers.

We would like to say what a fantastic time we shared with Richard and Lincoln football club and its fans. While our son was at Lincoln the place became our second home. We spent most weekends coming up for the games. Our son always called us on the phone on our drive up, to let us know if he was playing or not, because he never knew until the day. He never took it for granted that he was playing and nor did we. We shared some great times, and we always loved to come to the match and mingle with the fans. No-one knew who we were, which was great as his Dad could have a good old chat with fans about football. He enjoyed every minute of it. Although nerves got the better of Richard's Dad, who at times spent half his time on the loo. You always hope your son's going to have a good game most of all, and to top it all a great win into the mix. Richard never cared who scored as long as the team won, but it was great to see some of his 25-yarders.

One of the games our son particularly enjoyed with his time at Lincoln City football Club featured Paul Gascoigne.

11/09/ 2004 Home Attendance 7,142 ref Nigel Miller. Boston United–2 Pitt 82, Lee 88, Lincoln City–2 McCombe 33, Green 59 minutes. Sincil Bank was rocking in the build up to kick-off with supporters pouring through the turnstiles, eager to see England Legend Paul Gascoigne in action; 'Gaza' was named on the Pilgrims' sub bench for this afternoon's Derby clash, so supporters would have to wait a while. Gascoigne took regular breaks from his warm-up to sign autographs for City supporters, young and old, by the Co-op Community stand. Imps were two–nil up second half; Matt Bloomer's long throw-in found Jamie McCombe in the box and his flick on header was met on the half-volley by Green whose instinctive shot-on-the-turn nestled in the bottom left hand corner to send the home fans wild with joy. Boston needed some inspiration and if there was a player to do it, it was Paul Gascoigne. Gaza, wearing the number 19, replaced Tom Bennett in the centre of midfield on 61 minutes. The former England player international entered the field to a huge round of applause-and a cheeky chant 'Who Are Ya?' from some section of the home crowd. Two goals ahead, the game really began to open up for City. A lovely bit of skill in the midfield by Richard Butcher delighted the crowd—the Imps' midfielder was no doubt determined not to let Gascoigne's flair overshadow him. Minutes later, Richard Butcher was involved again as his long-range strike crashed against the advertising boards behind the Pilgrims' goal. Gazza tried a trick of his own, but it almost proved to be costly for Boston as Jamie McCombe dispossessed the bleach-blond midfielder outside his own box, before trying a cheeky chip over Abbey. And in 83 minutes Boston pulled one back. Courtney Pitt stepped up and dispatched a penalty into the bottom corner with keeper Alan Marriott going the other way. Three minutes later Jason Lee came back to haunt Sincil Bank as he latched onto Paul Gascoigne's free-kick, glancing his head past Allan Marriott and into the back of the net to make it 2–2 when the match looked beyond the Pilgrims. The goal deflated the home side, although it was the Imps who looked more likely to grab a winner in the closing stages. City forced three corners in quick succession as three minutes of added time were held up by the fourth official. Richard Butcher saw a volley sail agonisingly over Abbey's upright as time ticked on.

THIS PHOTO WAS KINDLY DONATED BY MR GRAHAM BURRELL

What a great tribute for our son to get the chance to play against such a great star and an ex-England player. It gave him a massive lift; he played so well, and what a great memory to have. We were so proud that he had the chance to play against Gazza, he was really pleased to get his autograph for me, his mum. Gazza wrote and signed, "To Gail, Best wishes, Paul Gascoigne." I have it in a frame on my wall with a photo of Richard and Gazza playing against each other. Our son said what a fantastic man he was; he was so pleased to have met him. "Gascoigne is a Legend and certainly was a boyhood hero of mine," said Butcher as his friends call him.

Our son said he remembers watching him in the 1990 World Cup, and his tears in the semi-finals against Germany. That was a long time ago, but I'm sure Gascoigne is still a quality player who will have flair, skill and a great footballing brain. These days Steven Gerrard and Frank Lampard are England's key midfielders, but for me Gascoigne is the best of them all—he was top drawer at his peak.

Richard met some of the Liverpool players at one of the hotels he stayed in pre-match and he got a few of the players to sign their autographs for his brother, as Glenn supports Liverpool, which never went down too well in our house as Richard supported Everton. I did even things out a bit in having to side with Glenn.

Journalist Michael Horton BBC Lincoln Radio talks of his time with Richard:

Having covered for the best part of fifteen years I have met hundreds of players who have played for the club. Amongst the many Richard was one of the few I got to know a little bit. He was very down to earth and just a nice guy. I don't think he ever realised how good he was, I always felt he should have played at a much higher level than he did.

Two things stick in my mind about him. The first was after Lincoln City had drawn against Boston United in a local derby. Ex-England player Paul Gascoigne had come off the bench to inspire a Boston comeback. After that match I interviewed Gazza; halfway through our chat I realised that a couple of the Imps players, including Butch, were waiting for me to finish. After I did they went up to him to ask for an autograph. The second was when he returned on loan to the Imps from Oldham and scored away at Leyton Orient.

Just before we went live with a post-match I asked him if it was good to be back. He just grinned; for him the Imps was home.

Moving on to a great match against Birmingham City where Richard would meet another hero of his, Robbie Savage.

21/09/ 2004 (CC) Away 14,500 (2,500 Visitors) Birmingham City–3 Lincoln City–1. They say fortune favours the brave, but the brave didn't get what they deserved. A battling performance by the Imps kept out star-studded Birmingham City for more than an hour but in the end, Premiership class and guile was made to count. Blues manager Steve Bruce—a good friend of Keith Alexander—paid the Imps and the Carling Cup the ultimate compliment by fielding a near full-strength side. It's a competition which has become maligned in some people's eyes in recent years, with the so-called big guns such as Arsenal and Manchester United fielding weakened sides. Last night's fielding Birmingham City side cost more than £20m to assemble. The Birmingham side fairly tripped off the tongue—Mario Melchiot, Mathew Upson, Darren Anderson, Robbie Savage, Emile Heskey, Jasper Gronkjaer and Dwight Yorke and on the bench Muzzy Izzet, Clinton Morrison and David Dunn. The game may have ended in defeat, but it was a memorable night in the history of Lincoln City. A standing ovation at the end was testament to what a spirited display it had been. Against the premiership rivals it was a good performance. Lincoln were in a crowd of 15,363. Richard Butcher had a few run-ins with Robbie Savage who was centre stage; he was a really nice person. He had asked Robbie for his shirt but he was substituted and Richard thought he had lost his chance. But after the game Robbie Savage waited for him outside the dressing room and stuck to his word and kindly gave his shirt to him. Our son then had it proudly framed with a photo and team sheet inside. It now hangs proudly in Richard's brother's house. He also had the chance to have a drink and a chat with Robbie Savage after the game; he said what a great person he was.

THIS PHOTO WAS KINDLY DONATED BY MR GRAHAM BURRELL

Our son always had a soft spot for the 'Cobblers', Northampton Town, although politics got in the way and he had always felt the director's favouritism had led to him being released from the club. The Imps were 13th; the Cobblers brought a crowd of 774 in a crowd of 4,808, which was a dream for Richard, just one of the games against his home Town. He would always follow score lines of other Clubs he shared his career with; whether you have a good or bad experience at any club at the time you still carry on looking out for them. That bond is always with you when you move on. He did dream of playing for the Cobblers, his home Town, at some point in his career.

20/11/2004 Away Attendance 4,035 Ref Paul Simpson. Darlington–0 Lincoln City–3 Yeo 36, Richardson, 45, Butcher 70 minutes. City boss Keith Alexander was able to bring Peter Gain back into his side for this Coca-Cola Football League Two encounter against Darlington at the Williamson Motors stadium. They were quickly on the attack with Paul Morgan forced to clear a dangerous cross from Neil Wainwright. Seconds later, the Imps had a glorious chance to open the deadlock when the ball was played forward for Richard Butcher to run on to. Butcher again took a couple of touches to compose himself as Quakers' keeper Sam Russell advanced off the line but the final product was disappointing: Richard Butcher's effort was easily claimed by the Darlington stopper. The Imps were certainly enjoying the better of things as the clock ticked past the half hour mark with the hosts' first-half chance seeing former Middlesbrough striker Alan Armstrong send a weak drive past the post. City eventually got their rewards for their first-half pressure when, on 36 minutes, they grabbed the lead. The move started from defence when Paul Morgan broke up a Darlington move and, after he brought the ball forward, he fed Peter Gain on the left. Gain did well to get the ball under control and a neat back-heel saw him lay the ball into the path of Gareth McAuley who swung a cross into the danger area. A combination of great communication and excellent finishing then saw Marcus Richardson dummy the ball and then it was left for Simon Yeo to finish things off as his superb first-time shot with the outside of his left boot sailed into the top corner of the Darlington net. Seconds before the break, Marcus Richardson made it 2–0. Peter Gain was again the architect as his through ball saw Richardson break clear of the offside trap and, after taking time to compose himself, he pulled a cool finish as he drilled the ball across Russell for his second of the season.

In the second half Richard Butcher tried his luck from range as the game entered its final quarter but his effort was always rising. Butcher went on one better shortly afterwards though when good work from Taylor Fletcher who won possession in his own half before breaking forward at pace saw the Imps' midfielder receive the ball in space before he showed a cool head to slot the ball past the advancing Russell to put City three up. The day belonged to the Imps and it was the men in red and white, together with their terrific band of travelling fans and supporters, who travelled home with smiles on their faces.

Gary Simpson—what a great assistant manager; he always had the ability to get the best out of his players, specially our son. He would always show great faith in Richard and was a genuine person; he always knew what buttons to press to get the players going. Gary said the kid was a scorer and Butch had a trademark and a great strike and a spectacular finish.

16/4/2005 Home Attendance 5,289 Ref Mike Thorpe. Lincoln City–2 Butcher 33, Green 69 Macclesfield Town–0. Macclesfield got the game underway. The Silkmen had the first chances of the match in the opening stages when Tipton sent a glancing header into the arms of City keeper Allan Marriot. The Imps had a half-chance of their own at the other end a minute later, as the ball fell out by Jamie McCombe on the edge of the box but his effort sailed wide. City carved open a good chance in the fourth minute when a neat, sweeping move between Derek Asamoah and Gary Taylor-Fletcher down the right flank saw the latter pull the ball back to Richard Butcher whose shot from 12 yards was saved by Wilson. After an evenly balanced opening half an hour, the game tilted Lincoln's way when they went 1–0 ahead on 32 minutes. A lovely bit of skill by Peter Gain near the dugouts saw him dink the ball down the line to Simon Yeo. His blistering pace took him past Barras, to the by-line, before firing the ball across goal. Gary Taylor-Fletcher missed it, but Richard Butcher didn't: the ball hammed home past Wilson. Butcher wheeled away to the home dugout and celebrated his second goal of the season. City, buzzing with confidence after their goal, had a ball in the back of the net again on 37 minutes but the effort was ruled out for offside against Simon Yeo. A ten man pass move ended in Simon Yeo beating the keeper with a crisp finish, but the linesman had his flag up. City won another corner as one minute of added time was given. Gary Taylor Fletcher whipped it in, the ball fell to Richard Butcher on the edge of the area but his powerful drive was blocked. 57 minutes into the second half Macclesfield had a good chance to level matters when Mark Bailey sneaked in at the far post, latching on to a deep cross by Morley. But the keeper Alan Marriot stood tall and stopped it with his body to divert the ball high. The Imps were enjoying a spell of pressure as they won two corners, which the visitors sent clear, before Butcher tried his luck from distance. Six minutes after coming on as substitute, Francis Green was to play a major part in City's quest for three points when he put Lincoln into a 2–0 lead after 69 minutes; a two-goal lead was the cushion City craved, with just over 20 minutes plus injury time remaining. Macclesfield still posed a threat and the game was far from over. But the ball remained in the visitors' half as Richard Butcher again tried a long-ball effort, which caught a wicked deflection and gave City a corner. With two minutes of normal time left, Imps boss Keith Alexander made a double substitution to eat up the time; five minutes of added time were announced but with a two goal lead, there was too much for Macclesfield to do, and City had three points in the bag in their race for promotion.

14/05/2005 Home Attendance 7,032. Play offs first leg Lincoln City–1 McAuley 11 Minutes Macclesfield Town–0. The sun was shining on a sea of red and white; the scene is for City's most important game of the season. Football's national anthem, 'You'll Never Walk Alone', was sung before today's match in memory of the Bradford Fire Disaster in which Lincoln fans Stacey and Jim West lost their lives. The two teams emerged from the tunnel to a rousing reception from the crowd, which was dominated by Lincoln supporters, with 600 Macclesfield fans playing their part. The Sky sports cameras were in position. Lincoln kicked off attacking the Stacey west end, and they won a corner after 38 minutes. Kevin Sandwith whipped the corner in, Jamie McCombe met it with a header but Town keeper Fettis gathered the ball easily. City bounced back from an earlier scare in the best possible fashion when they raced into a 1–0 lead after 11 minutes. City won a free-kick around 25 yards from goal, Kevin Sandwith floated the ball in and Gareth McAuley rose high to send a deft header into the bottom corner of the net from 15 yards out. It was McAuley's fourth goal of the season and no doubt the most important goal of the campaign. Macclesfield won a corner on the 19th minute when Ben Futcher was forced to head the ball behind; the corner caused City a problem, Jamie McCombe having to make a vital block to keep the visitors out. On thirty minutes, Macclesfield were awarded a free kick wide on the right, and Bailey's delivery was hacked to safety by Richard Butcher. Macclesfield came agonisingly close to making it 1–1 with two minutes left in the first half. Tipton's striker staying out was a little bit of City's luck to triumph in the play-off.

Second half the Imps had a first attempt at goal when Simon Yeo tried his luck on goal from distance, a second chance game from Gary Taylor-Fletcher who saw his effort sail over the bar. City were surging forward in search of a second goal, with Richard Butcher's speculative long range drive catching a deflection and running through to Fettis as Kevin Sandwith closed the goalkeeper down. City were on top now as Gary Taylor-Fletcher weaved his way into the Silkmen's 18 yard box, played the ball into Jamie McCombe's feet, he played it out to Richard Butcher but his strike from the edge of the box was blocked out by Barras. Macclesfield Mcintyre tried his luck with a long-range drive. Three minutes of added time were given but Lincoln held on until the final whistle was blown to leave the Imps with a 1–0 lead to go into the second leg at Moss Rose for the play of Semi-Final second leg.

21/05/2005 Away Attendance 5,223 Ref Phil Crossley. Macclesfield–1 Harsley 76, Lincoln City–1 McAuley 15 minutes League 2 Play-Off Semi-Final second leg.

City roared on by 2,000 supporters, it was the Imps who enjoyed the opening stages with a deflected effort from Gary Taylor-Fletcher for the game's first corner on the 90 second mark. Kevin Sandwith floated the flag-kick in with Jamie McCombe unlucky to see his flick hammered off the line by David Morley as a number of Lincoln players looked to get hold of the loose ball. It was end to end stuff and, a couple of minutes later, Bailey sent a blocked Jon Parkin effort well over the open terraces. This time in the 15th minute, Taylor-Fletcher was the man with the flag-kick and his deep centre was met by the towing head Gareth McAuley—whose goal at Sincil Bank separated the sides at the kick off. McAuley's header had too much pace on it as it powered its way to the target and despite the efforts of the town defenders, the ref assistant was quick to indicate that the ball had indeed crossed the line. Gary Taylor-Fletcher wasted a good chance at the other end on 29 minutes when he volleyed over from just inside the box. 37 minutes later a great move from the Imps shortly after saw them come close to adding a second with Simon Yeo's break into the box ending up with his blocked shot falling to Richard Butcher on the edge of the box. Butcher took a touch to get the ball under control and had it not been for a brave deflected block by Morley, the ball would have nestled in the bottom corner of the net.

Second half Richard Butcher was well positioned to block a goal-bound free-kick from Jon Parking after the Imps' midfielder pulled back Mark Bailey 25 yards from goal and before the resultant throw-in could take place, Town boss Brian Horton replaced Kevin Townson with John Miles with an hour on the clock. With Lincoln's supporters in full voice, City looked to stamp their authority on the second half with some lively build-up play seeing them enjoy the better of things after weathering the early Macclesfield storm. City defence had stood firm for 76 minutes but a rare lapse in concentration allowed Paul Harsley space to turn just inside the box and he sent a fine curling effort past Allan Marriott to make it 1–1 on the day, 2–1 City on aggregate.

The home side piled the pressure on as the game entered the final five minutes. On the 87th minute, Matthew Bloomer replaced Simon Yeo in a bid to eat up some valuable seconds.

There was one medal our son never gave to us, his mum and dad; this one always hung on the end of his bed. It was the Powerade man of the match from the Lincoln v Macclesfield playoff semi-final second leg game. This was one medal Richard was very proud of and he always kept it. This is the only one we have missing from his collection of medals. It meant so much to him. I am sure he would have given it to me in time for safe keeping. I collected everything I could through our son's career: every paper cutting, every programme. I have mugs and scarves from every club he played at as well as his track suits starting with Northampton Town. I was hoping one day to give them all to him so he could look back at what a great career he had and he could have shared this with his children, but sadly he didn't have any.

Keith Alexander and Gary Simpson would only choose a player on current merit. Richard's personality shone through once he had got to know people well, he so loved having a laugh with team mates. He would always phone us after an interview and say "Mum, Dad, did I sound ok? I didn't make a fool of myself, did I?"

Richard's lifestyle was a very private one. On and off the field his career was at the forefront of his mind. He was teased at times from players who said he was a bit of a mummy's boy, something he denied to his friends, but in truth our son loved his family. We were the most important people in his life; he could always approach us and ask our opinion on anything. Whether he took our advice was clearly up to him.

I remember the strict diet and the personal discipline it took: Richard would often have bananas before a match for energy. Jaffa cakes were his favourite biscuit but he was also into sweet potatoes and beans and chicken and rice. He loved his fish too. He had a book right from when he was a youngster that would cover all the vegetables possible. In this book it would tell you what every vegetable was used for and how you can protect your body for the future and why you would eat certain greens for energy.

Even at Christmas time Richard would never overeat; he would have lots of vegetables and plenty of chicken or turkey with just a couple of roast potatoes. After the Boxing Day match he would then have a treat but his diet was so strict. For his little treats, he liked melted chocolate gateaux and banoffee pie.

Just one thing his Nan always brought him that he loved from a young age and he still enjoyed was baby's rusks; every Christmas she would wrap a box up and give them to him for a present. He loved her doing that. Richard sent her a CD with 'Grandma I love you'. He used to sing it to her over the phone; this just showed the caring side our son had. Just because you are a pro footballer it really doesn't mean you have to lose yourself by getting too big for your boots. I think that's why Richard liked Gazza; he did show that soft side to him at times.

Just a little story a close friend of Richard's remembers. When they were away at Torquay they stole Gary Simpson's room keys at the hotel and removed all the furniture out of the room into the lobby Gary Simpson wasn't happy but did laugh later! This is just one of the many jokes I am sure friend Peter Gain is willing to share with us.

Back to football; another great friend of Richard's, Simon Yeo, remembers:

Sedge (Ben Sedgemore) did Sedge's Sermon in the programme that lifted the lid on some of the antics that went on in the dressing room. But Lincoln had a closeness and camaraderie that many teams would envy. We lacked the divide that many teams have due to the in and out nature of the first team. It is always hard if you are not on that pitch come 3 o'clock, but the Gaffer, Simmo and Oaksey had an honesty and a humour that made the hard work rewarding. You always knew you had a role even from the bench so the banter was healthy, none of the darker edges you can get in the game.

It's a long old season, ups, downs, frustration, elation, so you need a laugh to get you through the cold and dark winters, until the spring grass or your next chance comes along. Richard was an easy target and the pink pants and the slippers when he came out of the car did not help either. He was always five minutes late, yet Oakes and Simmo had to throw him out at the end of a session so they could lock up. You may find it hard to believe but I'm a natural victim myself (gesturing to his nose) so I was able to advise him to give as good as he got. Butch was quieter than some of the lads, that was all, he let his feet do the talking on the training ground and the pitch. The respect there got him the acceptance. He would be able to get there and keep the ball in for the full 90 minutes. Those are the lost causes that give forwards the chances to get a draw or a win late in the game against tiring legs. Many of my goals came from him doing that and though the fans give the scorer the credit, we players know the true score.

He was prepared to the point of precise. You know he once put £4.97 in the car, for petrol—paid on a card too! It was on his day to ferry Futch, myself and Gainy to and from Posh; we had to fold Futch to fit him in and out of the car. On the way home he pulled into a petrol station. Futch folds out like, to stretch his legs (Ben is 6' 9") and we race in for some snacks before the man-mountain eats everything. Well he is the size of a horse so he is going to eat like one. When we asked Butch what he was doing he said—using the scientific approach mind—"a fiver will do to get us home and then I will fill up when I get home. You see, your weight and that of a full tank combine to use more petrol." He was probably right, but lucky to not get showered in crisps.

Richard's Mum Gail:

We can always remember as a family how nervous Richard was about his career coming to an end as you may only have a contract for a year or two; it all depends on how well you have done through your last season to whether someone may come in for you. Your agent sets about contacting other clubs and bands your name about to see if there's any interest, or you may be lucky enough that a club has been watching you, but with so many players out of contract you never know what might happen. During the season Richard went on an electrician's course. He paid for the course, and only lasted one day and realised it wasn't for him. We asked him why he would want to do that when his career was over. He said he just thought he would try it. I think he did this because at the time a lot of his friends were electricians in Northampton and he thought he might like it. But the lads at Lincoln thought it was so funny; they brought Richard a boiler suit and on the back they put 'fully qualified electrician 1 day experience'. I think he had seen so many players out of contract and struggling to find other clubs, it just got him thinking what if.

He was a private person; he loved his own company and was happy within his own skin. He had a true friend in his dog, called Roger. A Japanese chintz, Roger was his running partner right from a young age. The poor thing was worn out by the time Richard had finished with him. Right from when he was little he loved that dog and missed him when he moved to Lincoln. I can remember one weekend he was meant to come home but because they had lost the game that weekend, they had to be in on the Sunday. Our son phoned me and said that he could not come home. Well that night the poor little thing died; the dog suffered with fits and because the fireworks were going off he seemed to have a massive fit that evening and died in my arms. I was heartbroken; when I phoned Richard he was so upset it broke his heart.

The lads at Lincoln really got into him. I can remember him telling me the lads had left a lead and dog bowl by his peg and some dog food. He was not impressed at all.

His next little running partner was his little dog Charlie, a Yorkie Poo. He would run for miles with him. The poor little thing was found to have an illness when he was born and could not eat very well. Richard ended up saving his life by paying a fortune out on a heart and throat operation. It was touch and go but the little dog made it, much to our son's delight. They were best pals and no one came before his little friend Charlie.

I can recall Richard showing us around Lincoln many times. He really enjoyed that; he took us up to the cathedral and said he wanted to show us where the little Imp was. He used to say "can't you see it, there it is," then he would put his money in the box to light him up. The cathedral is an amazing place; he always loved it in there.

Gary Simpson and Keith were so funny. Richard so enjoyed their company and the excitement they gave to the team. Some players will never have the chance to play at the Millennium Stadium, so what a great memory, especially getting to play there twice. This is a memory the players and their families and fans will have to keep for the rest of their lives and what a story to tell the grandchildren.

Thank you Lincoln, for the memories you have given us and for the great times Richard was able to share with us.

Moving on to the Millennium Stadium:

Saturday 28/5/2005 Millennium stadium Cardiff Attendance 19,653 Referee Martin Atkinson. Lincoln City–0 Southend United–2 Goals Eastwood 105, Jupp 110. Both teams had unhappy memories of the Millennium Stadium; Lincoln had lost to Bournemouth in the play offs two years previously. Southend on the other hand lost two LDV vans finals at the stadium in consecutive seasons. The game proved to be even with both sides having their chances but not converting them into goals. Southend felt they should have had a penalty in the dying minutes of the game when Bentley went in the box but the referee waved play on.

The match went into extra time and midway through the first half Southend scored twice in quick succession. The first goal came via Freddy Eastwood who smashed the ball from a poor clearance by the Lincoln defence. He turned provider for the second goal setting up Duncan Jupp to score his first goal for the club.

Richard had played every minute of every game for the Imps this season and his action ended at the Millennium Stadium. He chalked up a total of 122 appearances for Lincoln City since joining from Kettering in the 2002–2003 season.

2003–2004 one goal will live in memory for the Lincoln fans: a mammoth 35-yard effort against Mansfield Town just before Christmas in 2003. That was just one of the 12 stunning goals Richard scored for the Imps.

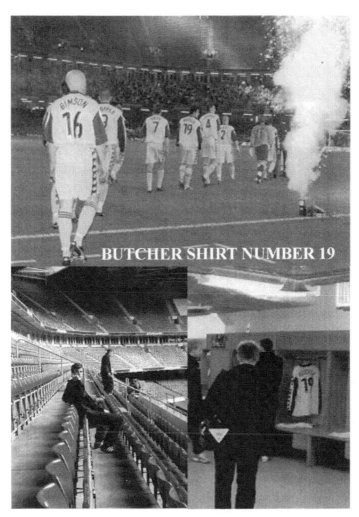

LINCOLN CITY F.C AT CARDIFF STADIUM
RICHARD BUTCHER PHONES HIS PARENTS TO TELL THEM
WHAT A GOOD VIEW THEY WILL HAVE

Richard and his friend Peter Gain complemented each other.

Peter explains:

Everyone will remember Richard as a great athlete with a fierce and accurate shot. But the midfield at Lincoln was very hard work. With Butch being such an incredible athlete, he gave me the opportunities to express myself more on the ball. It's a shame as I didn't play a lot with Butch at Peterborough due to my hernia op on his arrival and then Fergie opting to leaving him out. Mansfield away had to be the best midfield performance for me. We won 2–1 and Butch scored the best goal that season, a thirty yarder right in the top corner. We conceded a penalty shortly afterwards to level the score but second half I scored the winner and ran to the opposite end of the pitch to celebrate in front of the massive travelling Imp supporters—great memory.

Richard's Mum Gail:

Agent Richard Cody never pushed Richard to move on; he knew he wanted to stay at Lincoln City. They knocked back the £750 a week deal in 2005 and then another for £900 hoping Richard would be offered a thousand pounds a week to bring him up to the same level as some of the Lincoln players. If this had been agreed he would have stayed even though he still would have been on less than some of the other players. But Richard Cody did have a few firm offers set up for Richard; he was aware our son had his own mind. Meanwhile he packed his suitcase for his summer holidays still not knowing where he was going to be on his return. He set off for Manchester Airport. Phone calls were coming in thick and fast. Oldham Athletic's Ronnie Moore was offering £1400 a week; Richard couldn't turn it down. He signed at the airport before shooting off on holiday. If he had waited till he got back, a better offer was on the table waiting for him: Dave Penny was offering £1600, not to mention Colin Todd at Bradford and Billy Davies who was offering to top that with an extra £150 a week. Ronnie Moore had a file on Richard as he admired him. Mick Harford, his successor at Rotherham, was interested to as part of a rebuild after relegation from the championship.

I remember the move and the moment well. Richard's head was buzzing at the time; he didn't know which way to turn. There must have been at least ten clubs come in for him, which made us feel so proud. I can remember writing them all down just to keep count. The trouble is you are chased to hurry to make a decision not knowing which way to turn; you have to make your mind up quick because the clubs soon track down the next player they want. The players are made to feel they have to hurry even though they have a few clubs to choose from, because the bills have to be paid and you can't risk missing out and waiting too long to make your mind up or you could end up with nowhere to go.

Richard decided to take the jump and give it a go in League one. I can remember driving up to Oldham with our son to take a look at the ground and to see where he would be living. We were taken to a house where a few of the lads were staying. His room was no bigger than a small box-room. What awaited him was a far cry from his lovely little two bed house he so loved in Lincoln. He would be back to living out of a suitcase again.

Whatever club you choose to move to you, will not know if it was the right one until the season starts. Richard always missed Lincoln, there was no doubt about that, and so did we. As parents we were back to travelling at least three hours to get to see him for a weekend; sometimes we would do this all in one day, six hours of travelling, just to get to see our son for a few hours. It was always worth it.

A further offer was made from Lincoln City but Richard had already signed for Oldham so he made the jump and gave it a go. Our son had more money, and his lifetime relationship with Gary Simpson and Keith would keep forever. The fans of Lincoln City filled a massive dream for him that came true. All his hard work had paid off. Our son had learned to look after his finances really well and learnt to budget his money, always looking ahead for the future in mind. But you have to grab your chances with both hands as they can be few and far between.

I would like to thank the Lincolnshire Echo for all the media attention Richard received, which has enabled me to put this book together.

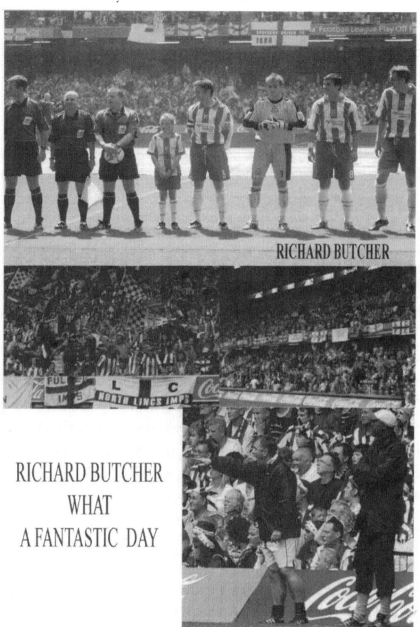

RICHARD BUTCHER

RICHARD BUTCHER
WHAT
A FANTASTIC DAY

WE KINDLY THANK LINCOLN'S MEDIA TEAM AND JOHN VICKERS FOR USE OF PHOTOS

RICHARD BUTCHER AND GREAT FRIEND KEITH OAKES HAVING A CHAT
A "BRILLIANT" PHYSIO, RICHARD WOULD SAY ONE OF THE BEST
LINCOLN CITY F.C

Lincoln City Games 2003–2004

Year 2003

9th August	Home Oxford United	(D3) 0–1
12th August	Away Stockport County	(CC) 0–1
16th August	Away Torquay United	(D3) 0–1
23rd August	Home Doncaster Rovers	(D3) 0–0
25th August	Away Bury	(D3) 1–2
30th August	Home York City	(D3) 3–0 SCORED
3rd September	Away Cambridge United	(D3) 0–0
13th September	Home Leyton Orient	(D3) 0–0
16th September	Away Southend United	(D3) 2–0 SCORED
20th September	Away Kidderminster	(D3) 2–1 SCORED
27th September	Home Rochdale	(D3) 1–1
30th September	Home Northampton Town	(D3) 0–0
4th October	Away Swansea City	(D3) 2–2 SCORED
11th October	Away Scunthorpe United	(D3) 3–1
14th October	Home Telford United	(LDV) 3–1
18th October	Home Huddersfield Town	(D3) 3–1
21st October	Home Macclesfield Town	(D3) 3–2 SCORED
25th October	Away Hull City	(D3) 0–3
1st November	Home Carlisle United	(D3) 2–0
3rd November	Home Chesterfield	(LDV) 4–3
8th November	Home Brighton & Hove A.	(FAC) 3–1
15th November	Away Darlington	(D3) 0–0
22nd November	Home Bristol Rovers	(D3) 3–1
29th November	Away Yeovil	(D3) 1–3
6th December	Away Southend United	(FAC) 0–3
13th December	Away Mansfield Town	(D3) 2–1 SCORED
16th December	Away Halifax Town	(LDV) 0–1
26th December	Away Boston United	(D3) 1–0
28th December	Home Cambridge United	(D3) 2–2

Year 2004

10th January	Away Oxford United	(D3) 0–0 Substitute
23rd January	Away Doncaster Rovers	(D3) 2–0

3rd April	Away Rochdale	(D3) 3–0 Substitute
10th April	Home Swansea City	(D3) 2–1 Substitute
12th April	Away Northampton Town	(D3) 1–1 Substitute
17th April	Away Carlisle United	(D3) 2–0 Substitute
24th April	Home Darlington	(D3) 1–1
1st May	Away Bristol Rovers	(D3) 1–3
8th May	Home Yeovil	(D3) 2–3 Substitute
15th May	Home Huddersfield Town	(P/O) 1–2
19th May	Away Huddersfield Town	(P/O) 2–2 SCORED

Lincoln City Games 2004–2005

Year 2004

7th August	Away Shrewsbury Town	(L2) 1–0
10th August	Home Southend United	(L2) 1–1
14th August	Home Rushden & Diamonds	(L2) 1–3
21st August	Away Scunthorpe United	(L2) 2–3
24th August	Home Darby County	(CC) 3–1
28th August	Home Notts County	(L2) 1–2
30th August	Away Swansea City	(L2) 0–1
4th September	Away Bury	(L2) 1–0
11th September	Home Boston United	(L2) 2–2
18th September	Away Bristol Rovers	(L2) 0–0
21st September	Away Birmingham City	(CC) 1–3
25th September	Home Chester City	(L2) 1–1
28th September	Home Doncaster Rovers	(LDV) 0–1
2nd October	Away Mansfield Town	(L2) 2–2
9th October	Home Kidderminster Harriers	(L2) 3–0
16th October	Away Oxford United	(L2) 1–0
19th October	Home Rochdale	(L2) 1–1
23rd October	Home Leyton Orient	(L2) 3–4
30th October	Away Cambridge United	(L2) 1–0

6th November	Home Northampton Town	(L2) 3–2
13th November	Away Hartlepool United	(FAC) 0–3
20th November	Away Darlington	(L2) 3–0 SCORED
27th November	Home Yeovil	(L2) 3–1
7th December	Away Macclesfield Town	(L2) 1–2
11th December	Home Cheltenham	(L2) 0–0
18th December	Away Wycombe Wanderers	(L2) 0–1
29th December	Home Grimsby Town	(L2) 0–0

Year 2005

1st January	Home Bury	(L2) 1–0
3rd January	Away Chester City	(L2) 1–0
8th January	Away Kidderminster Harriers	(L2) 1–2
15th January	Home Bristol Rovers	(L2) 1–1
22nd January	Away Grimsby Town	(L2) 4–2
29th January	Home Mansfield Town	(L2) 2–0
5th February	Home Oxford United	(L2) 3–0
12th February	Away Rochdale	(L2) 1–3
16th February	Away Boston United	(L2) 2–0
19th February	Home Cambridge United	(L2) 2–1
22nd February	Away Leyton Orient	(L2) 1–1
26th February	Away Cheltenham	(L2) 0–1
5th March	Home Wycombe Wanderers	(L2) 2–3
12th March	Away Southend United	(L2) 1–1
19th March	Home Shrewsbury Town	(L2) 2–0
25th March	Away Rushden & Diamonds	(L2) 4–1
28th March	Home Scunthorpe United	(L2) 2–0
2nd April	Away Nott's County	(L2) 0–1
9th April	Home Swansea City	(L2) 1–0
16th April	Home Macclesfield Town	(L2) 2–0 SCORED
23rd April	Away Northampton Town	(L2) 0–1
30th April	Home Darlington	(L2) 0–0

7th April	Away Yeovil Town	(L2) 0–3
14th May	Home Macclesfield Town	(P/O) 1–0
21st May	Away Macclesfield Town	(P/O) 1–1
28th May	Away Southend United	(P/O) 0–2

8: Oldham Athletic 2005-2006

Ronnie Moore signed Richard for Oldham Athletic in August 2005 on a two-year deal. Although there was interest from Preston in the championship and league one, Doncaster, Rotherham, and Bradford, three other clubs in league one, showed interest in our son. Sitting in limbo just wasn't his style—waiting. And hanging around, and not knowing where he was going to be, and what wages he would receive. He was always keen to get started, so he knew where he stood. Richard needed security. He always knew that his profession could be taken away from him at any time.

The stress that is caused by the waiting and not knowing is, to some players, 'too much to handle', not only for them, but for the families as well, as they also have to uproot. He actually signed at Manchester airport; his wage was to be £1400 plus goal bonuses. If our son had waited a bit longer, Dave Penny was offering £1650, and Ronnie would have offered him more. Collin Todd at Bradford and Billy Davis at Preston verbally offered to top it. So sometimes by rushing in too quick you can also lose out.

The day came when I was driving up to Oldham with Richard to check out the digs he would be moving into. It was a lovely house not far from the ground, but our son had drawn the short straw—a small box room awaited him—back to living out of a suitcase. While Richard was sorting his career out, we would be packing up his Lincoln home to move his belongings, which were stored in a garage that the club provided, up to Oldham.

It wasn't long before our son started house-hunting. He found a lovely four-bed house with a garage. I thought it was too big, and he should go for a one-bed flat, just till he knew how things were going to pan out for him, but Richard loved the house, and a good few of the Oldham players had bought one in the same area, and it wasn't long before he moved in. No more hotels for Mum and Dad. We helped him decorate and arrange the house. His dad set his tools out once again to do all the handy work. I would enjoy shopping in Manchester with our son to put a colour scheme together.

Manager Ronnie Moore

Ronnie Moore is an English former footballer who is the current manager of Tranmere Rovers (2014). He played for many different clubs in a career spanning almost two decades, including Tranmere Rovers, Cardiff City, Charlton Athletic, Charlton, and Rotherham United. He is widely considered to be one of the greatest Rotherham players of all time. Beginning his career in management at Southport in 1997, he went on to manage Rotherham, guiding them to two successive promotions from Division Three to Division One. He moved to Oldham Athletic in 2005, before becoming manager of former club Tranmere Rovers one year later. He returned to Rotherham for a second time in 2009, before returning to Tranmere Rovers for a second time in 2012.

Oldham Athletic Manager, Ronnie Moore, said when signing Richard:

Butcher is a ball winner who shows leadership qualities, but he can also play a bit. He's a very fit lad, which is important when looking for new signings. I like people who can run for 90 minutes. He's hungry to step up to our level. The midfielder summer signing from Lincoln City under the Bosman ruling, Richard is a busy instrumental player who covers every blade of grass during the game. His 116 games for the Imps brought 15 goals, but, more importantly, the energy Richard supplies is priceless.

Agent Richard Cody always put Richard's feelings first, and tried to get the best deal he could. He was always willing to listen to our son from a football point of view and from the financial side of things. Richard never expected to be in the starting line-up, but he would work hard and would weigh up his options, trusting us, his parents, his close football friends, and, of course, his agent, Richard Cody. It must be so difficult for the players who have wives and children. Every club they go to, their families have to follow. Their wives have to leave their jobs, and the children change schools and leave their friends behind, maybe just for a year or two, and then only to move on again. Our son didn't have children, but he could sympathise with other players and their families.

Richard believed in Ronnie Moore, and the players had a fair chance of promotion under Ronnie, who had inspired Oldham to survival the season before, despite being thrown in at the deep end in March, after parting company with Rotherham in January. Ronnie Moore, who could always lift the spirits of his players, had joined Rotherham in 1997 and rebuilt them after relegation to Division 3 (now League 2) but he also got the best out of his players and comparably poor resources to ensure the Millers survived and thrived for a time. In 1999 Ronnie inspired the Millers to two successive promotions and kept them up, in what is now the Championship, for four seasons, where they punched well above their financial weight.

He also has the flair and inspiration to bounce back. After just a season at Oldham, he would brush off being sacked for 'poor season ticket sales' by joining Tranmere Rovers. His sense of humour is legendary within the game. Our son had a lot of time for Ronnie Moore, another manager he enjoyed working under.

Richard Butcher talks about his career at Oldham in his own words:

"My Oldham career didn't exactly get off to the start I wanted, but," he insisted, "I can promise everyone that I will be doing my best and giving 110 percent." Butcher added, "I knew of Ronnie Moore's reputation for getting the best out of players and teams. Oldham was one of the clubs that stood out. It was just one of those instincts."

Ronnie Moore turned out to be a fantastic manager, and our son had a lot of time for him, but I don't think Ronnie understood Richard to start with, even though he soon did. I can remember seeing what had been put on the internet chat sites about Ronnie and our son after certain games, and I really could not believe what was said on there. Richard hated us seeing it, but people loved to tell us about it, and our son, too. A few of my family members soon stuck up for Ronnie and Richard. It turned out, so I have been told, that some people use a number of different names on these sites and they actually write replies to their own nasty piece of work that they have written to make it look like people are agreeing with them—when, in actual fact, they are agreeing with themselves.

It really was the worst I had ever seen, and that was the first time I had ever felt like I needed to have my say on a chat site. No one deserves to be talked about in the manner they both were. It was disgraceful. People always thought Richard lacked confidence because he was quiet and shy at times, but it is the manager's job to produce confidence in his players. I do feel that Ronnie Moore 'sticking' with our son helped lift him and gave him his confidence back, but I feel the fans also play a big part in giving their players confidence when they are on the ball, even when things are not going as well as they would like.

It is always a certain section of the fans that start this sort of thing off. Even if players seem to come across as tough, underneath they really are not. They are 'seething' when the fans get on their backs. But Richard just showed his feelings when things weren't going right. Our son then looked to his manager and teammates and lifetime friend and manager, Gary Simpson, to ask for support because he always wanted to improve his game and give his best. Sometimes he could not understand what he was doing wrong to warrant such bad behaviour by a section of the fans.

Richard was a shy hardworking professional. He had not done much wrong in his career at Oldham. Our son bought a house in Swinton and was looking to settle down. A section of the home fans turned on him, which followed onto the forums. This was a shock to Richard and to us. Many fans have the right to an opinion as they pay their admission, but what was posted on the forum was so shocking and caused far more damage than people realise. It's there for players and fans to see. However, someone with a bottle in one hand and a keyboard in the other can set out to destroy a player's career, before they have even had the chance to show their true worth.

What many don't realise is that some of the abuse was at the level where threats against Richard were to the degree that he should be hung, drawn, and quartered. The abuse was so bad this caused our son to rethink. He had just bought a house and had a mortgage to think of, as living out of a suitcase was not his scene. He also wanted somewhere for us his parents and brother to stay on our visits to see him.

Richard made daily calls to us, his parents, feeling very down and low and not understanding why this was happening to him, and nor could we; and we couldn't understand why the site allowed it to go on.

I really do hope something can change, and this is not allowed to carry on. Abuse has to stop, whether it is on the football forums or in the terraces. We should start to make football more about a family day out, or our future generation of children will follow suit, and nothing will change. We know this is only a small section of fans, but they are destructive. No one should be allowed to post on any forum without using their real name. The law should change to stop any abuse happening to anyone. I agree with freedom of speech on all forums, but only if it is put in the right context and used in a constructive manner.

We recall the match against Oldham and Barnsley. That game was heart-breaking for us, Richard's parents. Our son called us after the game and said he just felt he needed a break. A quick call between agent Richard Cody and Gary Simpson, and a heart-to-heart with Ronnie Moore, paved the way for a loan, and a shock return to Lincoln.

When we were listening to the Barnsley game on the internet, the commentary was so bad, you just wanted to crawl in the computer and lift him out. As his parents we were heartbroken, and Richard had stopped us coming to the games to shield us from it so as not to upset us.

We have to thank those lovely Lincoln City fans for welcoming our son back with open arms and giving him his confidence back. They were the ones who made him strong so that he was ready to face the music on his return to Oldham.

Somehow his white boots seemed to be the focus of the problem. I heard them mentioned so many times on the radio commentary by one certain person who really didn't seem to like Richard at all. I noticed straight after the game these so-called internet boo boys jumped straight on to air their views on these websites. They obviously weren't even at the game; they were just following the running commentary. The Oldham boo boys had nearly killed Richard's career off. A section of the crowd slaughtered him when he was booked against Barnsley; some fans were shouting for him to be sent off. I don't agree with abuse in this manner in any shape or form. Other players suffered too; whatever colour or race we all are, no one deserves it.

Ronnie recalls:

Richard did not do much wrong, but at Oldham the crowd gets on your back quickly and easily. We had a heart-to-heart and agreed that a month out on loan would be the confidence booster he needed, with Lincoln the best option, as he knew them, and it would bring the player I knew was in there back quicker. That Oldham side had nothing missing, full of quality players who just needed the luck. The crowd turned quickly at Oldham, and we were accused of long-ball football, with some injuries to some key players not helping.

With most of League 1 having to compete against ex-Championship sides with £1.1-£1.3 million budgets to help you—if the Rolls Royce is at the mender's, you are going to struggle to replace it with the less stylish but more reliable mini, aren't you? You couldn't say as that 4–0 thumping early doors at Rovers helped the cause much either! I and the Latics' fans still have a love–hate relationship to this day—I love them, and they hate me. The dugouts are really close to the banter at Boundary Park, and the manager has to be careful—because he's the one that gets banned and fined. Now manager of rivals Tranmere, as soon as the fixtures come out I always want to get Oldham away out of the way.

Richard's Mum Gail:

Ronnie rated our son, and felt he would have the quality to prove the doubters wrong. A one month loan deal for Richard to return to Lincoln City would help him regain his confidence. Ronnie's hunch was right.

With Richard back to Lincoln on loan from Oldham, our son, Keith and Gary were reunited once again. While at Oldham, Richard wrongly put his two fingers up to the fans. He knew himself that it was the worst thing he could have done. I have never seen our son react in this way. His confidence was fragile; he needed a lift and Gary and Keith were just the tonic he needed.

Lincoln City proved to be a breath of fresh air to our son. The fans welcomed him back and showed a massive support to him and to us, his mum and dad. It is true that during Richard's time back at Sincil Bank he was quoted in the local press as wanting a permanent return. Agent Richard Cody was frustrated at the Oldham fans.

Ronnie Moore, in a typical fashion, made light of it, calling him a 'rather silly boy' in the press.

Ronnie kept the loan to a month, but he wanted our son to give it another go. He felt he had more in the locker, particularly goals. Ronnie pulled Richard back, sat him down, and played to his strengths and weaknesses, not to mention dealing with the adverse newspaper PR perfectly.

On our son's return to Oldham he changed his white boots, and he got 'man of the match'. One fan asked where his white boots were, and Richard politely told him that they were in the bin.

Ronnie Moore talks of our son:

It was surprising how such a good-looking six-foot lad could lack the confidence that so many others have, but you have got to be able to take the banter on and off the pitch, and Richie couldn't at Oldham for a while. If he had that, he would have gone to the top. But when he got on the ball, the quiet and shy lad went out and proved what a fantastic footballer he could be. That's why I signed him. He was so full on in training when he was up, what a player! But you knew he was one who needed to be lifted through the downs, and there are plenty of them in this game.

Richard's Mum Gail:

Just a few memories of Richards's goals to take a look at: his first was back on loan to Lincoln City.

15/10/2005 Leyton Orient–1 Lincoln City–1. Butcher on loan after abuse from Oldham fans. The hosts went ahead in the 18th minute when Captain Gary Alexander headed in after keeper Marriott's parry. But Lincoln levelled through Richard Butcher's 70th-minute volley from the edge of the box. The fans roared and showed fantastic support on his return to Sincil Bank.

Our son was happy again and his nerves were settled once again. It wasn't long before our son had to return to Oldham.

Just a few highlights to share with you:

26/12/2005 Home Oldham–2 Bradford–1. Oldham opened the scoring after seven minutes when defender Danny Hall crossed for Richard Butcher, who calmly dispatched his first goal since arriving from Lincoln in the summer. And the hosts punished Bradford in the 12th minute when Paul Edwards sent Andy Liddell racing away and Luke Becket followed up with a close range finish.

15/02/2006 Home Oldham–3 Notts Forest–0. Oldham closed in on the act on a play-off place with a second-half show. Gary Megson's Forest had no answers as the Latics cruised to a comfortable victory. Richie Wellens gave Oldham the lead in the 53rd minute when he cracked home a first-time shot following a Richard Butcher cross into the area. Butcher then got in on the act with 17 minutes left; he beat two defenders on the edge of the box and drilled his shot into the corner of the net.

11/03/2006 Home Oldham–1 Colchester United–0. Richard Butcher hits an injury-time winner for Athletics against Colchester at Boundary Park and runs off in celebration. Victory maintained Athletics' momentum in the push for promotion play-offs and the score line made it five games without conceding a goal.

18/03/2006 away Bradford City–1 Oldham–4. Luke Becket fired Oldham back into the play-off hunt with a double-strike. Oldham took the lead through Paul Warner after a mistake by keeper Donovan Ricketts. Within a minute they were two up after Beckett finished a Wellens through ball. Richard Butcher added a third before Bradford's Aran Wilbraham scored but Beckett wrapped up the points eight minutes from time with a classy finish.

Ronnie Moore revamped the Oldham side with twelve new signings; Butch was one of the new faces, and so was striker Captain Andy Liddell.

Andy Liddell says:

I first met Richard in 2005 when we both signed for Oldham in pre-season. I remember instantly liking his manner as a friendly, always smiling, and laughing person. After our first few pre-season runs, he pulled me to one side and asked how I had gotten my fitness to such a high level. I think he was a bit miffed, as I was way out in front of him! He was a very fit and athletic player, but typical of him, he wanted to know how he could improve, asking questions and discussing training routines to better himself. Unfortunately for Frank, he could never get up to my fitness level, which I let him know about on many occasions! The nickname 'Frank' came about through calling him 'Pat' initially. He took a dislike to being called 'Pat' Butcher from 'Eastenders' for some reason! So I said I would call him 'Frank' instead then.

RICHARD BUTCHER : OLDHAM ATHLETIC F.C
PERMISSION WAS KINDLY GIVEN TO USE PHOTOS BY : GORDON LAWTON

Chris Porter, now at Sheffield United, has bagged a hundred League goals, taking in Bury, Oldham, Motherwell and Derby County. Ronnie signed the 6'1" striker from Bury for £150,000 after a tribunal was required to agree on the fee. Chris would go on to be a good friend of Richard's after first meeting that summer.

Chris Porter says:

I met Richard in July 2005 on the first day of our Oldham careers. We both signed under the management of Ronnie Moore. Both being new signings and of similar age, we instantly got to know each other. Butch, as we used to call him, was an instant hit with the lads. As well as being a great footballer, he had a very funny and infectious character. Due to his great work ethic and ability to get a goal from midfield, he quickly established himself in the team.

Although I have many football memories of Butch, I also have a lot of memories from our time outside of football. Playing for Oldham we were living very close to Manchester, so we were often tempted after a Saturday game to have a night out in Manchester. I can definitely say that when out with Butch we never had a dull night.

A lot of players will say that once a player moves on, they don't keep in touch with many players, so you know that when you are still in touch four years after, that you were truly good friends.

Next-door-neighbour and midfield team-mate Mark Hughes remembers it was not all downs:

Butch and I became friends straight away when he signed for Oldham. I had been searching for a house for a few months before the end of the season, so I knew the area I wanted to live in and told Butch about it. He ended up buying the house next door, and made sure he paid the exact price I had done. He showed moments of class during his time at Oldham and always gave 100 per cent with his brilliant fitness levels. We had many nights out, and quite a few bets on the horses watching the TV in his living room, both filled with laughter and competitive banter. He was such a loving person, and this is the main reason for me he is so sadly missed.

Captain Andy Liddell gives his thoughts on Richard Butcher:

I was immediately impressed with his all-round ability and found it strange that he had never actually played at a higher level than he had previously done. Getting to know him a lot better in the coming months, it became a bit clearer to me why that was. He struggled at times to just accept mistakes and get on with the game, instead of dwelling on the mistakes he had made.

As captain at the time, I tried to tell him that mistakes are part of the game, and that he could easily deal with them because he was such a good player, but he really struggled with this part of football in our time together. He had doubts about his own ability to play with the players he was playing with, and it was here that I could see the reason why he hadn't played at a higher level before.

It certainly wasn't his ability that was holding him back, because he was a fantastic midfield player. 'Frank' had two good passing feet and a strong shot with either foot. He was a strong runner and a fearless tackler, which all made him a potentially fantastic player. The mental side of the game, though, was not his strong point. Self-doubt played too large a part in his makeup.

Although he played a lot of games for his clubs, there is no doubt in my mind that if he could have just dealt a bit better with his self-doubt issues, and had a bit more self-confidence, he would have played at a lot higher level for many years.

Richard's Mum Gail:

It is true that Richard always strived for perfection, and that he never liked making a mistake. It was intrinsic to his makeup as a person and football was very much the focus of his life.

Andy continues:

When he left at the end of the season, I was annoyed with him and told him so. I thought he should have stayed at Oldham because League 1 football was the lowest level he should be playing at and League 2 was beneath a player of his talents. He said that he would be much happier going to play for a club where he felt more at home and where he would enjoy his football much more.

I always kept in touch with Richard through phone calls or texts, congratulating him on goals I had seen him score, or performances I had seen him produce, or generally to take the **** out of him on numerous occasions! We became lifelong friends; he was a man few could have a bad word to say against. The last time I saw Richard was when Rotherham played at Macclesfield, and I had a great chat with him. It was great to see him laughing and smiling, enjoying his football. This is how I will always remember 'Frank'; as a smiling, friendly, fantastic human being.

RICHARD BUTCHER ; OLDHAM ATHLETIC F.C
PERMISSION WAS KINDLY GIVEN TO USE PHOTOS BY : GORDON LAWTON

Chris Porter remembers:

A fond memory of Butch was when we were playing at Brentford away, in the cup. Butch was always someone who took a lot of pride in how he looked, so when he went up for an aerial challenge, he was devastated when he came out with a broken nose. Being injured at the time I was in the dressing room with him, trying not to laugh. I told him it didn't look that bad, as he hurled verbal abuse at myself, and cursed his guilty opponent. A week or two later we both managed to have a good laugh about it, and the opponent in question was, in fact, his team-mate Garry Hughes.

Richard's Mum Gail:

We can well believe what Chris Porter is saying. Richard phoned us while lying on the treatment table—not very happy at all—but we had been worried. We were so pleased to get his call. We had just watched Mark Hughes and Richard smash heads as they had gone up for the same ball as it had happened on TV. The reason why that happened was that he was worried about the fans getting on his back again, so, without thinking, he went up for the ball not realising that Mark would go for it, too. Richard was worried about making any mistakes.

But when our son broke his nose the second time at the end of the season, well, that just took the biscuit, as he was off on holiday a few weeks later. Twice in one season was a bit of bad luck. You can be tough, rough, and ready, but Richard always showed his true colours as a person. He never hid his true self from anyone, and with the right mentor behind you, it just shows you can go far. Carl Shutt and Gary Simpson and Keith Alexander fulfilled that for our son. They saw that he always wanted to learn, always wanted to improve, and was always willing to give it his best shot. It is about never giving up when the going gets tough, but you do have to be happy in your job. But more than ever it was so important that Ronnie Moore had the belief in Richard; and he did.

Ronnie Moore looks back:

At least when I got the boot it wasn't by text—it's always a good way to get it confirmed in writing like that. We had finished 9th, so it was a bit of a surprise to get a phone call on my sun bed by the pool in

Tenerife. I was told of the decision to release me, but did not get too much time to chew on it before a phone call arrived from Tranmere—news certainly travels fast in football. They kindly pre-booked a flight from the airport to Liverpool. We struck a deal, and then they did the same two days later, so that I could sign on the dotted line and get cracking with the summer recruitment drive. The Tranmere Chairman has always generously maintained the budget here so you know where you stand year on year. Last year we were top for 31 games, but injuries to the two strikers, a centre-half and centre-midfielder, does you, and we finished 11th. It was almost the same thing that had happened at Oldham, although the luck there had run out earlier than it should have started.

In football, especially at our level, it's about quality and compromise. You have to go for players on frees, with other lads needing to be moved on to free up the wages. We all want to go shopping at Marks & Sparks, but Aldi (should I say that as they are supermarket of the year?) is more the place. You find the usual suspects haring around with their trolleys stampeding through the doors as soon as the window opens in the summer. The faces may change, but the style and ability does not, because you have got the pot you have got, and so you can only afford so many Rolls, even though the minis are the ones that meet the budget, and make the whole thing work. That is why, for so many teams, anything above 50 points is a bonus.

I became a butcher at 16 after my mum had died when I was 14. I had fallen from Everton's books, blown my GCEs, and ended up in Sunday League, showing you can't drink and play, even if you think you can. But someone at Tranmere saw something; so I grabbed the trial with both hands and feet at 17, and was rewarded with amateur forms for two years before earning a deal at 19. I will always have a loyalty to Tranmere, but perhaps it took a Butcher to know a Butcher, and he came back to prove what a fantastic player he was, and to turn that crowd around. As a dad I would not want my daughter to go anywhere near a footballer, but if she had brought Richard home, I would be pleased. He was brought up right, had rare values, and was a credit to mum, Gail, and Richard, his dad. He was a model pro, too.

RICHARD BUTCHER : OLDHAM ATHELETIC F.C
PERMISSION WAS KINDLY GIVEN TO USE PHOTOS BY : GORDON LAWTON

Richard's Mum Gail:

Ronnie would go on to spend three years at Tranmere, whilst John Sheridan would come in and clear the decks and start all over again, including neighbour Mark Hughes who dropped down to Thurrock for a season before returning to Chester City in 2007. Richard was not supposed to be one of them, so it was of some surprise to see him ask for a pay-off. Sheridan said to our son, "Why would the club want to pay you off, when you are a player we want to keep?" John quickly realised our son's head had been turned, and that his heart lay elsewhere. Richard would get a free transfer, but he would always regret not giving Oldham another season. It was one that would have seen him catch the eye of some Championship clubs, as the Latics missed out on promotion via the play-offs, after losing to Blackpool 5–2 on aggregate.

John Sheridan knew Richard's heart had been dwelling in Lincoln. The October loan had been good for him, even if the January transfer had not, but the three-day events put paid to that, along with a fourth play-off failure, which ensured things were continuing to unfold at Sincil Bank. Our son would be reunited with Keith Alexander and Gary Simpson, but it would be at Peterborough United and not the Imps.

Manager Gary Simpson and a great mentor to Richard:

Football-wise I was closer to Butch than anyone throughout his whole career. He used to call me at other clubs and I even went to watch him when he left Lincoln, Oldham being one of them, and I gave him a rollicking after one game. He was playing too much of a supporting role to Richie Wellens; almost worshipping him he was at times, because he was winning the ball and then giving it straight to him, when he had the ability to go on himself and finish the job he'd started. He was too nice sometimes, but as Ronnie says he was a great footballer, definitely the sort you would want a daughter to bring home on her arm.

Richard's Mum Gail:

We tried to persuade Richard to stay at Oldham to prove a point at least, as we felt the worst was over. But our son felt he needed to move on. He locked the door at his house and called it a day. It was a beautiful house; we had all worked so hard on it to make it nice. Our son so enjoyed taking us into Manchester shopping, but most of all he enjoyed just a good old chat and catch-up about the family. Richard off the pitch had always loved settling in for the night. He would go shopping and get a few treats in and watch 'the footie' with his dad.

He was certainly not short of suitors clambering for his signature, but he was honest enough to admit he made the wrong choice when joining Oldham in league 1; but he did say a year down the line he should have stuck it out to prove the doubters wrong. He explained that after three good years with Lincoln he was flattered to have a lot of interest in him, and right or wrong, he rushed into the decision because Oldham was offering him a much higher wage than anything he was used to. He agreed to join Oldham without even seeing their ground. Looking back, he regretted doing that, because he couldn't settle, and after the abuse he suffered he soon wanted to leave. It was quite lonely at the time for him. To top it all, he broke his nose for the second time on the last game of the season 2005–06 with then 10 minutes from time; it was the last straw. Nothing was going right for him. The final whistle came and he jumped into his car, still in full kit with blood all over him, and drove off.

He did return to say his goodbyes, as it wasn't the club who wanted him to leave. We have to thank the playing staff and manager Ronnie Moore for showing fantastic support towards our son at a time in his career when he most needed it.

Oldham Athletic

In 1895 Pine Villa Football Club was formed. The club changed its appearance and name in 1899 to Oldham Athletic Football Club. The club immediately gained professional status and played in both the Lancashire Combination Lancashire and Lancashire League. Unlike many clubs, Oldham Athletic gained quick success and gained acceptance into the Football League, as it was called then, in 1907–08. After three years in the Second Division, Latics gained promotion to the First Division.

Within a couple of seasons, Oldham had announced themselves serious contenders, finishing 4th in the league in 1912–13, and reaching the F.A. Cup semi-finals the same season, losing out 1–0 versus Aston Villa. In 1914–15, Latics reached the quarter-finals of the FA Cup but were knocked out once again after a 0–3 replay against Sheffield United. In the league that season they almost won it all; Latics lost the league by one point, as close as they have ever come to winning the league. Latics' early success was only halted by the First World War.

Oldham Athletic Association Football Club is a professional football club based at Boundary Park, on Furtherwood Road off Sheepfoot Lane in Oldham, Greater Manchester, England. The club currently competes in the football League one, the third tier in the English football league system. They have been in this league since their relegation from the old football league first division in 1997. It is incorporated as Oldham Athletic (2004) Association Football Club Limited, but is more commonly known as Oldham Athletic or by its nickname Latics.

Information about the club was found on en.wikipedia.org/wiki.

RICHARD BUTCHER : OLDHAM ATHLETIC F.C
PERMISSION WAS KINDLY GIVEN TO USE PHOTOS BY : GORDON LAWTON

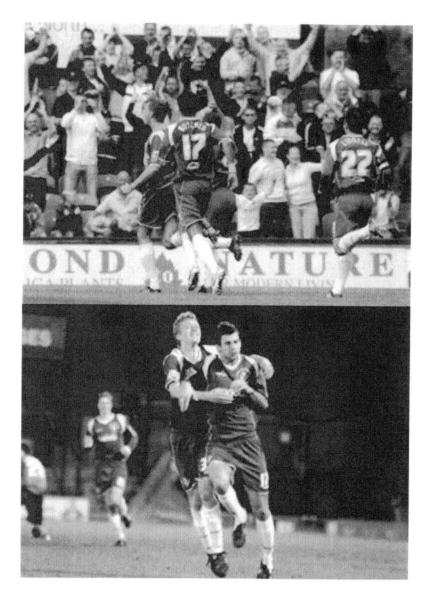

RICHARD BUTCHER : OLDHAM ATHELTIC F.C
PERMISSION WAS KINDLY GIVEN TO USE PHOTOS BY: GORDON LAWTON

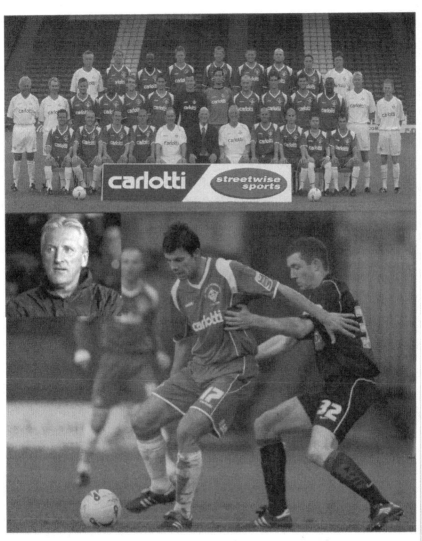

WE KINDLY THANK OLDHAM EVENING CHRONICLE FOR USE OF PHOTOS

Oldham Athletic Games 2005–2006

Year 2005

6th August	Home Yeovil Town	(L1) 2–0
9th August	Away Swindon Town	(L1) 3–2
12th August	Away Tranmere Rovers	(L1) 0–4
20th August	Home Chesterfield	(L1) 4–1
27th August	Away Colchester United	(L1) 0–0
29th August	Home Rotherham United	(L1) 0–1
4th September	Away Southend United	(L1) 1–2 Substitute
10th September	Home Huddersfield Town	(L1) 0–3
28th September	Away Port Vale	(L1) 2–2 Substitute
1st October	Away Barnsley	(L1) 0–4

Lincoln City Games 2005–2006

Year 2005

7th October	Home Cheltenham	(L2) 0–1
15th October	Away Leyton Orient	(L2) 1–1 SCORED
22nd October	Home Wycombe Wanderers	(L2) 1–2
29th October	Away Rochdale	(L2) 2–1

Oldham Athletic Games 2005–2006

Year 2005

16th November	Home Chasetown	(FAC) 4–0
19th November	Away Brentford	(L1) 3–3
26th November	Away Yeovil Town	(L1) 2–0
3rd December	Home Brentford	(FAC) 1–1
6th December	Home Walsall	(L1) 2–1
10th December	Home Swindon	(L1) 2–0
13th December	Away Brentford	(FAC) 0–1
26th December	Home Bradford City	(L1) 2–1 SCORED
31st December	Home Hartlepool United	(L1) 2–1

Year 2006

2nd January	Away MK Dons	(L1) 1–0
7th January	Home Southend United	(L1) 0–0
10th January	Away Blackpool	(L1) 0–1

28th January	Away Huddersfield Town	(L1) 2–3
4th February	Home Port Vale	(L1) 0–1
11th February	Away Bournemouth	(L1) 0–0
15th February	Home Nottingham Forest	(L1) 3–0 SCORED
18th February	Away Walsall	(L1) 0–2
25th February	Home Tranmere Rovers	(L1) 1–0
11th March	Home Colchester United	(L1) 1–0 SCORED
14th March	Away Rotherham United	(L1) 0–2
18th March	Away Bradford City	(L1) 4–1 SCORED
25th March	Home Blackpool	(L1) 3–1
31st March	Away Hartlepool United	(L1) 1–1
8th April	Home M.K.Dons	(L1) 1–2
15th April	Home Barnsley	(L1) 0–3
17th April	Away Bristol City	(L1) 1–2 Substitute
22nd April	Home Swansea City	(L1) 1–1 Substitute
29th April	Away Doncaster Rovers	(L1) 0–1
6th May	Home Scunthorpe United	(L1) 1–1

9: Peterborough United 2006–2007

Richard still had a house in Lincoln, but our son, along with many of Keith's players, realised that Manager Keith Alexander would be joining up with his old mate Barry Fry. Our son had always kept in regular contact with existing and ex-members of the squad. He was looking forward to meeting up with Keith and Gary again. Richard had heard rumours in the past that Barry Fry had put his house and everything on the line for Posh. It just shows the love that Barry Fry showed for his club Peterborough United.

Keith Alexander was delighted with the 25-year-old. He said, "Butcher is a player I know well. A few clubs are chasing him, but the fact is I know Butcher has worked in my favour. I'm very pleased to have signed him. He's a fantastic footballer."

Richard signed on a free transfer from Oldham and was given a three-year deal at Peterborough on around £1200 a week plus bonuses and, given the familiar faces, he slotted straight in.

I felt I needed to include words that came directly from Richard, so you can get the feel of what he was thinking with his time at the club. Richard's words: "I am really enjoying myself at Peterborough United at the moment because we have made a good start, and the manager can't really change the side, well I hope he doesn't. It is going to be tough to keep our places, especially in midfield, because Peter Gain and Paul are such good players."

Our son never took for granted that he would be playing, he just worked hard on and off the field. Peterborough played 54 games during the season, and Richard appeared in every one of the team selections. Once again he was standing out in the middle of the park netting five goals during the season.

There was one big game our son would look forward to playing in, being a supporter himself: the premiership side. Everton was a reward for Keith Alexander's Peterborough United after they progressed into the second round of the Carling Cup by knocking out fit Ipswich Town on penalty kicks at London Road. It was a great night for a sizable crowd and Mark Tyler turned out to be a hero after a string of fantastic saves. It's not very often you get a chance to have a premiership team or club like Everton, particularly a side that is highflying. It was a great occasion at London Road.

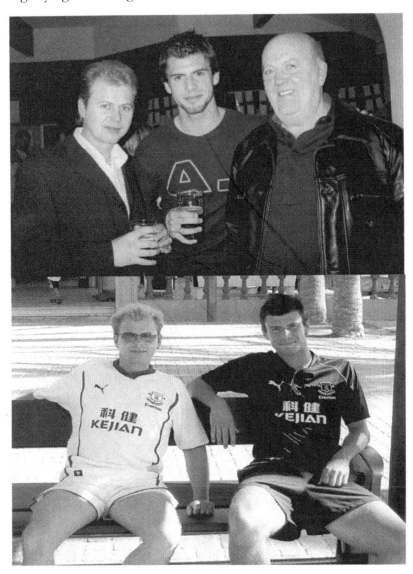

THREE RICHARDS ABOVE
DAD AND SON BOTH SUPPORT EVERTON F.C

Keith Alexander lifted his first silverware as Peterborough United boss. His side secured the Maunsell Cup with a comfortable win 3–0 at Northampton Spencer. Peterborough also gave Richard's home town 'Cobblers' a run for their money at home with a 1–0 win, with Simon Yeo being the goal scorer.

While in the professional game you never know who you may cross paths with: Richard told me that he had breakfast with the great Eric Pollard from the Emmerdale cast. He was with one of the other players, so I recall he said what a fantastic gentleman he was. He really enjoyed his time spent with him and was pleased to have met him.

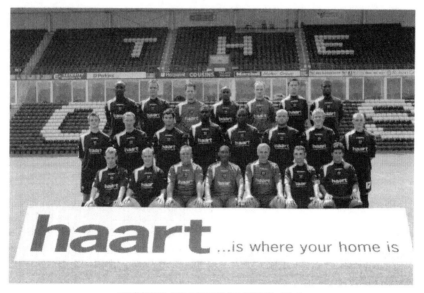

PETERBOROUGH UNITED F C
PERMISSION WAS KINDLY GIVEN TO USE PHOTO BY : JOE DENT

Moving on to just a few stories and highlights of the games Richard scored in. Please read between the lines.

5/08/2006 Attendance 4,890 Ref D McDermid. Peterborough United–4 Day 10, Butcher 32, Yeo 35, and Opara 77 minutes, Bristol Rovers–1 Igoe 52 minutes. Keith Alexander's first game as a manager of Peterborough kicked off in the strong summer sunshine. The supporters were saluting their first goal after ten minutes. Lloyd Opara beat two defenders and burst into the area finding Richard Butcher who laid the ball into the path of Jamie Day. Twenty-two minutes later Richard was on the score sheet himself after receiving the ball from Opara, side-footing two defenders and slotting home. With half time ten minutes away Peterborough went into a 3–0 lead

when Plummer headed a free kick down to the feet of Simon Yeo.
Seven minutes into the second half Rovers pulled a goal back as
substitute. Andy Sandell beat the Peterborough defence for pace and
laid the ball on for Igoe to score. It was fitting that man of the match
should go to Richard Butcher. Opara scored Peterborough's fourth
goal with a left-footed volley.

One of the greatest nights in Peterborough United Carling Cup
past came against a side from Merseyside. It was a 1–0 victory against
Liverpool.

The arrival of Everton for the Carling Cup was a dream come
true for our son as he faced his boyhood heroes in front of a packed
Posh full-house approaching 11,000 at London Road, the atmosphere
unique to those twin 4,000 terraces at Posh.

JOLEON LESCOTT & RICHARD BUTCHER

LEE CARSLEY & RICHARD BUTCHER

PERMISSION WAS KINDLY GIVEN TO USE PHOTOS BY : RICHARD WHITING
www.actionimages.com

19/09/2006 (CC) Attendance 11,000 Everton–2 Peterborough–1. I remember the game with pride. Richard and his dad both supported Everton. It was a proud moment in time. I can remember Tim Cahill asking our son for his shirt. Richard replied, "Why do you want my shirt?" and Tim Cahill said, "I collect all the shirts of the midfielders I play against." It was a really special moment for Richard to have swopped shirts with Tim Cahill's, he had it proudly framed with a photo placed inside it and the full names of both teams. His dad would have loved to have kept the shirt but we don't know what happened to it.

Richard's dad's proudest moment was when his son got to play against Everton, as he used to sit him on his knee as a child, and they used to watch the games together at Goodison Park. When our son found the time he took me and his dad to an Everton game. It was such a great day out for his dad, and he always bought an Everton shirt for his birthday.

Richard met some fantastic people through his football career. He admired Barry Fry and Darren Ferguson, but football wasn't just about money and glamour to him. He so enjoyed the game, although he knew there was never any guarantees in football that you would be playing when you moved on. He always saw it as a fresh start and a new adventure, but he would always look out for Gary Simpson and Keith, and he would always keep in touch with them, especially Gary (Simmo, as Richard called his friend).

However, it was nice when our son was at Posh because he was a bit closer to his family, and we were able to see him play that bit more as Oldham was quite a distance.

Another player our son was excited to play against was former England midfielder Paul Ince. He couldn't help Swindon Town from slipping to defeat against Peterborough United. Ince played a half as Posh ran out 1–0 winner. Paul Ince attempted to shut Richard down, but he was having none of it in the heart of midfield. Our son said "Paul is a great player. It was a proud moment to be able to play against him."

Richard also scored in the game against Hartlepool United 3–5 and Rotherham United 3–0 (FAC) and Torquay United 5–2 in 2006; he also scored in the MK Dons 4–0 home game 2007.

Ben Futcher and Simon Yeo share a story with us:

We remember when Butch drove us to Peterborough in the car. We always managed to get Butch to drive (no mean feat as he never liked paying for fuel). On the way home he had almost no petrol left (ten miles left in the tank, tops) so we stopped for petrol. Out Butch got and literally two minutes later he got back in the car.

"That was quick," we said. Then Yeo looked at the petrol cost and he had put £6 in. We couldn't believe it. His excuse was his girlfriend had the car in the evening and she would fill it up! He then drove home at 56 mph as he said it was the best fuel economy. Butch got loads of stick for that for quite a while.

Peter Gain feels Keith was hard done by at Peterborough:

Keith was a great manager and had done a brilliant job on a low budget, in contrast to Ferguson who had an unlimited budget to strengthen his squad. Even our midfield partnership did not really get a chance to sparkle at Peterborough, due to my hernia operation upon Butch's arrival, and then Fergie opting to leave him out. Add to that my best goal being that thirty-yarder into the top corner against the Imps, and it is safe to say that I did not have any good memories of Peterborough. It was satisfying in a way, as I had got some verbal abuse from the Lincoln faithful, but many did not know my true reasons for leaving, and actually not wanting to go. But it was the principle, you know, not greed—just getting what I had been owed and promised from the admin days. I got some real abuse after that goal as well, so looking back, safe to say, I didn't really enjoy my time at Posh.

Amongst the storm, humour always appears, with the lads deciding to play a trick on Butch to lighten the mood. With Richard asleep on the way down in the coach, Ben Futcher and Simon Yeo resolved to give the lad a bit of moral support and company. 'Futch' picked up Richard's mobile from the table and sent a message suggesting he was down and in need of a friend to text him, to all of his contacts. The first reply woke him, but he went back to sleep, the second saw him frown quizzically, before umpteen beeps were met with howls of laughter from around the coach. Sometimes banter is all you have to lift the gloom.

Gavin Strachan, son of Gordon Strachan, a great friend of Richard's, shares his thoughts with us:

Butch had a great friendship with big Ben Futcher, and I was lucky enough to gain an insight into this relationship at first hand during our time together at Peterborough. I used to meet the two of them at Newark where we would then share the journey into Peterborough. It was no coincidence that when Butch drove, the journey took a little bit longer. Butch's, shall we say, rather frugal nature, meant that he would not drive over 60 mph due to the benefits in fuel consumption. Whilst this was perfectly reasonable, it did make it rather embarrassing on the A1 as we were being overtaken by lorries, tractors, and, on occasion, I am pretty sure we got overtaken by someone on a push-bike! The abuse dished out to Butch by Ben was non-stop, but all taken in good humour.

This leads me on to another of Butch's great attributes. In a generation where a lot of footballers take themselves so seriously, Butch had the endearing ability to laugh at himself. In my role as Youth Team Manager at Peterborough United I often mention Butch in conversations with the lads. His fitness, desire to work hard, ability to recover from disappointments, and love for the game should act as an inspiration to all young players looking to make a career in football. I was one of the lucky few who had the privilege of spending a great deal of time with Butch, and I regard it as a huge honour to call him a teammate, but more importantly, a friend.

RICHARD BUTCHER PETERBOROUGH UNITED F.C
PERMISSION WAS KINDLY GIVEN TO USE PHOTO BY : JOE DENT

Richard's Mum Gail:

Moving on, our son knew his time was up at The Posh. He still had two years left on his current contract. Darren Ferguson put seven players up for transfer, but after a rumoured £50,000 bid from Shrewsbury had been knocked back, hometown club Northampton pulled out of making a move. Shrewsbury had made an enquiry in January. Richard was keen to make an emotional return to the Cobblers, and the local press was abuzz with the story, but they could not meet the wages and the fee. In the end, Richard weakened with agent Richard Cody's negotiating a hand by waiving any demand for a pay-off. Notts County got Richard for no upfront fee, but would agree to a substantial cut of any future transfer fee going to Peterborough. County also matched his wages and gave him a two-year deal.

Our son was impressed with the Notts County stadium; I was pleased with the professional way Richard left Peterborough United. Player and manager parted on good terms. Our son never liked hanging around. He always liked to know where he stood so he could weigh up his options and move on. Greed for money never got the better of him; he just loved to play football. But, by moving on, there are no guarantees you will get in the side. It just gives you a fresh start, and knowing a manager who wants you, just gives you that lift, and you start the slate clean and look forward to the new season with excitement and nerves.

I always said to our son, "I read the paper, Rich, nice write up." He would say, "Tomorrow's chip-paper, Mum." His words were, "You're only as good as your last game."

No offence to the media meant, but. I know he used to get annoyed with the marks given out by the papers. He used to say, "I am sure they're not even at the game. Some of the marks given out to players are totally wrong." Well, I guess it's one person's opinion. One thing you can say about football—once the manager leaves, his staff follows, so it's always a good idea to clear out and start all over again.

Manager Darren Ferguson

Darren Ferguson is a Scottish football manager and former player, currently in his second spell as the manager of Peterborough United.

Between his first and second stints with Peterborough, he also managed Preston North End.

As a player, Ferguson was managed at Manchester United by his father Alex Ferguson, but spent most of his playing career at Wolverhampton Wanderers and Wrexham in the lower divisions of English football.

Ferguson's first managerial appointment was as player–manager of League Two Peterborough United in January 2007. After two successive promotions, and guiding the club to the second-tier of English football for the first time in 17 seasons, Ferguson was relieved of his duties on 9 November 2009, with Peterborough United at the foot of the Championship.

Ferguson was appointed Preston North End manager on 6 January, 2010. He was dismissed on 29 December, 2010 after a string of poor results. On 12 January, 2011, he was again appointed as the manager of Peterborough United, where he took the club to the League One play-off finals at Old Trafford, and in this match won promotion to the Football League Championship, the club's third promotion in four years, with a 3–0 victory over Huddersfield.

Peterborough United spent two seasons in the Championship after winning promotion. On 4 May 2013, Ferguson's side were relegated to League One after losing to Crystal Palace 3–2 on the final match of the season.

Information about the club and Manager was found on en.wikipedia.org/wiki.

Richard was so privileged to have met Darren and when we heard about his family having a car accident I know at that time Richard was very concerned because with all that goes on behind the scenes of a manager's life and a footballer's life you never know what's around the corner, and your family and children are the most important people in your life.

But when these things happen, footballers and managers have to find the time to juggle it all and try and carry on. Everything is televised or in the papers. You can't hide away. We were so pleased that Darren's family were okay as the accident was very serious. We send our best to his family and hope they are all well. And thank you to Darren's father whom I wrote to for sending a Manchester United shirt to help raise money for my son's charity. We were so very grateful.

Manager Darren Ferguson said of his time with Richard:

When I took over at Peterborough United from Keith Alexander in January 2007, Richard was part of the squad I inherited, and it was obvious from the moment that I walked into the door at London Road that he was a player who always gave 100% both at training and in matches. He was a very good modern day box-to-box midfielder. He was always willing to learn and improve. He was a quiet individual. He wasn't one who would cause you any problems and he got on well with everyone in the dressing room. I worked with Richard for a short period of time and found him to be one of the nicest people I have met, and a true professional.

It was purely for footballing reasons that Richard departed the football club. It was a difficult decision to move him on, but he understood the reasons behind that decision and when we parted, we both wished each other the best of luck in the future. He was always going to have a good career in the game and I had no doubts that Richard would be a good player for the club he signed for, Notts County. He went on to make 80 appearances for them, scoring nearly 20 goals—an excellent return for a midfield player.

When I heard the tragic news of his death, it really came as a massive shock. Richard was one of the fittest members of the squad, and you just couldn't quite believe it. Everyone at Peterborough United was devastated by his loss. A year before, the manager I replaced, Keith Alexander, had passed away. Richard and Keith were extremely close, and I am sure they still are. Richard was taken far too soon and will not be forgotten.

Richard's family would like to thank Peterborough United Football Club for their kind words and support, and we as a family, alongside Richard, enjoyed our time spent with the clubs and fans. Richard enjoyed his time spent with Darren and was very proud to have met him.

Peterborough United

Peterborough United Football Club is a professional English football club based in Peterborough. Peterborough United formed in 1934 and played in the old Midland League, which they won six times, eventually being admitted to the Football League in 1960, replacing Gateshead. Their home ground is London Road and the club nickname is The Posh. After being relegated from the Championship on the final day of the 2012–13 season, the club will compete in League One, the third tier in the English Football League System, in the 2013–14 season. Their highest finishing position in the Football League ladder was 10th in the Championship.

Information about the club was found on en.wikipedia.org/wiki.

RICHARD BUTCHER PETERBOROUGH UNITED F.C
PERMISSION WAS KINDLY GIVEN TO USE PHOTO BY : JOE DENT

RICHARD BUTCHER PETERBOROUGH UNITED F.C
PERMISSION WAS KINDLY GIVEN TO USE PHOTOS BY : JOE DENT

RICHARD BUTCHER PETERBOROUGH UNITED F.C
PERMISSION WAS KINDLY GIVEN TO USE PHOTOS BY : JOE DENT

RICHARD BUTCHER : PETERBOROUGH UNITED F.C
PERMISSION WAS KINDLY GIVEN TO USE PHOTOS BY : JOE DENT

Peterborough United Games 2006–2007

Year 2006

5th August	Home Bristol Rovers	(L2) 4–1 SCORED
9th August	Away Boston United	(L2) 1–0
12th August	Away Wrexham	(L2) 0–0
19th August	Home Macclesfield Town	(L2) 3–1
22nd August	Home Ipswich Town	(CC) 2–2 won in pens
26th August	Away Notts County	(L2) 0–0
3rd September	Home Bury	(L2) 0–1
9th September	Home Darlington	(L2) 1–3
12th September	Away Walsall	(L2) 0–5
16th September	Swindon Town	(L2) 1–0
19th September	Home Everton	(CC) 1–2
23rd September	Home Hartlepool United	(L2) 3–5 SCORED
26th September	Home Barnet	(L2) 1–1
30th September	Away Stockport County	(L2) 1–0
6th September	Away MK Dons	(L2) 2–0
14th September	Home Shrewsbury Town	(L2) 2–1
21st September	Away Wycombe Wanderers	(L2) 0–2
28th September	Home Grimsby Town	(L2) 2–2
31st September	Home Swansea City	(JPT) 1–0
4th November	Home Accrington Stanley	(L2) 4–2
11th November	Home Rotherham United	(FAC) 3–0 SCORED
18th November	Away Mansfield Town	(L2) 2–0
25th November	Home Torquay United	(L2) 5–2 SCORED
29th November	Away Bristol Rovers	(JPT) 0–1
1st December	Away Tranmere Rovers	(FAC) 2–1
5th December	Away Hereford United	(L2) 0–0
9th December	Away Rochdale	(L2) 0–1
16th December	Home Chester City	(L2) 0–2
23rd December	Home Lincoln City	(L2) 1–2
26th December	Away Barnet	(L2) 0–1
30th December	Away Hartlepool United	(L2) 0–1

Year 2007

1st January	Home Walsall	(L2) 0–2
5th January	Home Plymouth Argyle	(FAC) 1–1
13th January	Away Darlington	(L2) 1–1
16th January	Away Plymouth Argyle	(FCA) 1–2
20th January	Home Stockport	(L2) 0–3 Substitute
27th January	Away Lincoln City	(L2) 0–1
30th January	Home Swindon Town	(L2) 1–1
3rd February	Away Bristol Rovers	(L2) 2–3
10th February	Home Wrexham	(L2) 3–0
17th February	Away Macclesfield Town	(L2) 1–2
3rd March	Home Notts County	(L2) 2–0 Substitute
10th March	Home MK Dons	(L2) 4–0 Substitute SCORED
24th March	Away Grimsby	(L2) 2–0 Substitute
31st March	Home Wycombe Wanderers	(L2) 3–3
7th April	Away Accrington Stanley	(L2) 2–3 Substitute
9th April	Home Mansfield Town	(L2) 2–0
14th April	Away Torquay United	(L2) 1–1 Substitute
21st April	Home Hereford United	(L2) 3–0 Substitute
28th April	Away Chester City	(L2) 1–1 Substitute
5th May	Home Rochdale	(L2) 3–3

10: Notts County 2007–2008

Former assistant manager Steve Thompson was given the manager's job in June 2006 and had guided the Magpies to 13th the season before. Richard liked Thommo's chit-chat and his management skills. He thought he was a great manager. He happily signed a two-year deal after Barry Fry had let him go on a free, plus a percentage of any sell-on, but Thommo would actually only last until the October when Ian McParland took over. Our son had a good working relationship with both managers, who did well given the financial turmoil going on behind the scenes at the League's oldest club.

RICHARD BUTCHER NOTT'S COUNTY F .C
RICHARD BUTCHER , STEVE THOMPSON , IAN MACPARLAND
WE KINDLY THANK NOTTS COUNTY MEDIA FOR USE OF PHOTOS

Local legend Ian McParland lifted the gloom. "Ian had played for the club for 9 years scoring 69 League goals in 221 appearances," Richard said. Peterborough did have offers on the table for him, so he could understand why they were reluctant to let him go to County on a free, but he dug his heels in and said he wasn't going anywhere but to Notts. He was determined to do well and make a difference and to get it right this season. Richard put pen to paper and signed on £1200 plus £100 goal bonus

Our son became the eighth summer signing at Meadow Lane in the summer of 2007, ending Steve Thompson's long chase for a midfielder. Richard was renowned for his passing abilities and sneaky goals. He made his name at Lincoln City where he was successful under Keith Alexander. Our son had two years left on his contract at Peterborough United, but knew manager Darren Ferguson had his own plans for his future team.

Thompson admitted he had been hot on the heels of Butcher all summer, and he was delighted to hear he had knocked back several offers from elsewhere in leagues one and two. Our son was keen to link up with Thompson at Meadow Lane. He was handed the number 23 shirt for the forthcoming campaign, as Richard and the team travelled to Devon for pre-season. Our son signed from Peterborough United—he made over 30 appearances at London Road. During his career so far Richard had made over 200 appearances—turning out for Kettering town, Lincoln City on two occasions, Oldham Athletic, and Peterborough United.

Richard made league two team of the week regularly. He was in contention to be crowned the league two player of the month for August 2007. The league had recognised his form and had nominated him alongside two other players: Morecambe's Jim Bentley, and Dave Hibbert of Peterborough United. He was also named in the Coca Cola football league as one of the league's two hotshots. He narrowly missed out on claiming Powerade league two 'player of the month' awards for August, finishing third.

A few things to tell you about our son Richard Butcher: his stamina was not just over the course of 90 minutes. While as a midfielder he would still be chasing lost causes deep into injury time, it is over a season that his condition came into effect. He was an extremely consistent player. Our son would give the same application on the first day of the campaign and the last. His game was his timing. He had the ability to be in the right place at the right time—a skill that cannot be taught. Whether it was a last-minute tackle or a match-winning goal, Richard ensured he would be in the thick of things.

Our son was a tall central midfielder. He used his height with great effect when heading the ball. He often helped out in defence and helped out with defensive set pieces. He also attacked the ball dangerously in the opposing penalty box. His energy showed him as a real box-to-box player who could cover a great amount of distance over 90 minutes. His great energy ensured that he could be in the midst of helping defend and attack, and, within seconds, he could be on the end of a swift breakaway. His finishing made him one of the most consistent goal-scoring midfielders in league two. He regularly found the net with all types of goals. He could let fly some spectacular long-range efforts or pop a tap in from inside the box.

He often effortlessly slammed home a loose ball to put Notts ahead against Grimsby Town. I found myself wondering where Notts would be without him or Kevin Pilkington for that matter. I felt at times Richard was misunderstood as a player; we take a look at the increasing importance of the midfield goal-getter and we ask, "Was our son too often overlooked as a summer signing from Peterborough United?" By a certain section of the fans it was Richards's tenth goal of the season; he had the potential to grab 15 or even 20, because of his ability to pop almost unnoticed at times into the opposition's area, added with his fantastic shooting from outside the box, which created one dangerous footballer.

Notts were much better with him in the side, and yet I found it bizarre that some fans were critical of him. What more could he do? Still, some fans look at other aspects of the game, almost desperate to find a weakness, and some would leave you out of their best eleven. I found that incredible. If you had taken away Richard's goals, Notts would have had six more losses to their name and have six points left—meaning they would have dropped to level points with second bottom Wrexham.

But if those ten goals of Richard's had been taken off Notts' goal difference, it would have been worse, and so the Magpies would have been inside the relegation zone only just ahead of the fierce Mansfield Town. Sure, Notts hadn't actually won in any of the games our son had netted in, and a tiny minority of fans even blamed him, but it was hardly his fault; and while his goals were precious, many suggested that it was all he had in his locker. For one—he would have been the first name on many a manager's first team sheet—no one else seemed to be able to get on the score sheet or score consistently for Notts at that time.

Richard was one of the most hard-working and fittest players on the pitch. He never moaned when he had been shifted about on the pitch to accommodate others, even though it is they who should be accommodating him. He has played his preferred central midfield, right wing, left wing and an emergency attacker. Our son was always one to put personal glory behind team success.

Richard's brother, Glenn, has a few words to say:

He would always set himself a target for goals: around 8 or 10. He would be happy with that, but although my brother did really well for Notts County, it just seemed to be that every time he scored it ended up in a draw. He was always delighted with his goals, but he so wanted to win a game with him scoring. He was a man on a mission, that's for sure, but to Richard it didn't matter who scored; he just wanted to win a game.

Footballer and friend Ali Gibb remembers:

In 2008 I signed for Notts County Football Club and walked into the changing rooms to be greeted by Butch parading around the dressing room with his shorts tucked into his underwear to elongate his legs. He had his top off with his muscles rippled after a succession of press-ups, and a tan which would suggest he had been in the Algarve for two weeks. I remember playing Macclesfield in a league match and watching Richard's pre-match ritual. He looked great—healthy and strong.

One particular day after discussing the options with his family, Butch arrived to training in a new BMW. So pleased at his new car, he showed various players around it in the car park. However, whilst the players were out training, one of the players retrieved his keys from his pocket and decided to hide the car in one of the garages where the tractors would normally park. I think he found it a day later.

Lawrie Dudfield remembers Richard's readjustment process:

Richard travelled from Lincoln to Nottingham and, at least three times a week, he would be late. Only five minutes or so, but enough to warrant a fine of £5. Richard was 'careful with his money' and battled his case for being late, blaming the car, the traffic, almost anything but himself, and offered to pay a pound which, to put it politely, got rejected.

One day Richard arrived for training and was wearing a pink pair of underpants. As a joke, a couple of the lads cut them to ribbons. Upset, Richard approached the Gaffer (Ian McParland) and told him they had cost him over twenty quid. "What colour were they?" inquired the gaffer. "Pink," Butch replied. End of conversation.

Richard was a lovely lad, everyone's friend, and did not have a bad word to say about anyone.

Friend Jason Lee:

I had been top scorer at County during the 2006–7 season with 16 goals. Richard joined the following season and there was an awful lot of banter between us. He told me he would score more goals than me, causing some healthy competition. Not only did he net more goals, he ended the season as the club's top scorer; no mean feat, considering he got 12 goals from midfield. Richard was a great character, we always had a laugh and a joke together, and he was one of the fittest players I have ever played alongside.

Richard's Mum Gail:

We knew how proud our son was to be playing at Notts County. Richard scored some fantastic goals and left us, his family, with some great memories. He really was proud to say he played at the oldest club in the football league. How proud can two parents be? He got on with all the players at Notts County, and formed a great relationship with manager Ian McParland. Both of them were so looking forward to the next season.

Our son's agent, Richard Cody, died during the course of the season. He had worked for Richard from his first year at Lincoln City. Richard Cody never told our son that he was ill; he just carried on working for Richard right up until the day he died. He was a prince amongst agents; he always looked out for our son, but he also kept in touch with us to have a chat about Richard or football in general. He never let on to us that he was so ill; he was such a lovely man.

Former footballing friend Gavin Strachan says:

I was very fortunate to have worked with Richard at Peterborough United and Notts County. Butch was an instantly likeable person. He had an innocence and naïveté about him which you could not help but find amusing. It was these traits which accompany some of my fondest memories of Butch.

One instance occurred during a game when we were both playing at Notts County. I cannot remember the opposition, but it was at home in the midst of a league 2 relegation battle. We had just conceded a goal, and myself and Butch were getting ready to take the kickoff to resume the game. At this point Butch looked at me and said, "I cannot believe this, what are we going to do?" I told him not to worry and that we will get a goal back and things will be fine. To my astonishment and great amusement, he replied, "No, it's not that. I have just bought a new car, and if we go down, I don't think I can afford the payments!"

We ended up winning the game, and I am pretty sure Butch got on the score sheet, which was an extremely good habit of his. Those who knew Butch would vouch that this story was not a lack of professionalism, but just the fact that he was a persistent worrier. In fact, Butch was about the fittest footballer that I ever worked with, and the number of goals he scored was due in a great part to this attribute.

Richard's Mum Gail:

I find this so typical of our son. He had just bought his new mini, which some of the players always took the Mick out of, with Richard being so tall. But he loved that car; I think it reminded him of his great Granddad's, as he always had a mini, and it was good on petrol, although Richard's was the new model. He was so sentimental; happy-go-lucky and funny at times. Richard then replaced his car with a BMW.

Manager Ian McParland called on his players to find a hero, and our son stepped up to fill that role. Richard bagged his 12th goal of the season securing County's league status in the ten games he had netted previously. The Magpies had never won a single game. It was a record Richard wasn't proud of, and certainly one he was frustrated with.

It was fitting that our son should get the goal and secure league two safety, and afterwards he couldn't hide his delight. It couldn't have gotten much better for our son. Obviously, with the record of never winning whenever he scored finally being broken, after he scored he thought to himself, "Should I have done that really, given my record this season?" He was, in a way, waiting for the ref to blow his whistle to stop play, because he couldn't believe he was on goal with that much time and space, but he was delighted to see the ball sneak in the top corner. Richard said, "I have broken my record. Now, I am so happy for all the lads and also the fans who were right behind us throughout the game."

There was such a long way to go after he scored, and time seemed to tick away really slowly, but when that final whistle went, it was such a great relief for everyone. Our son said he felt they all underachieved big-time that season, and to finally be safe was a big weight off all their shoulders. There must have been over 3,000 roaring fans willing the side to victory. Richard's goal was certainly crucial for the campaign, as his efforts preserved Notts' football league status for the next year, while a commanding performance from Russell Hoult saw the experienced goalkeeper record his seventh clean sheet in County colours. Congratulations to the both of them.

The stories and goals, and the excitement amongst the games will help you feel what Richard felt at the time in his career.

18/08/2007 Home Notts County–1 Butcher 82, Brentford–1 O'Connor 63 minutes. Smith played a long ball into the box and Brentford failed to clear; it fell to Richard Butcher who composed himself before drilling left-footed into the bottom corner from 12 yards. It was a clinical finish, and Notts could have won it in the end.

25/08/2007 Away Darlington–2 Wright 40 Miller 85, Notts County–2 Butcher 72, 90+4. Richard Butcher twice dragged Notts from behind. He had the last laugh, although he had to take a few choice words from his relative, Uncle Graham, who supported

Darlington. The breakthrough came with 18 minutes remaining. Richard started to move when he picked out Smith on the right. He fed Parkinson who whipped a low ball into the six-yard box, and the midfielder stormed in to turn it into the back of the net. The second goal Richard had other ideas. Matt Somner and Dudfield combined down the right before Dudfield crossed for Richard, who volleyed in from close range for a dramatic equaliser with seconds left in injury time. I remember so well our son had asked his auntie and uncle to the game. Graham, his uncle, supported Darlington, but sat quite happily with the Notts County fans; but Richard made them pay with two fantastic goals that ended the game at two all. But all jokes aside, his uncle was so proud of his nephew that day.

01/09/2007 Home Notts County–1 Morecambe–1. Richard Butcher popped up with three minutes left to grab Notts a draw. He stole the show again at the end with a late equaliser for the third game running. Somner gave the ball away and Morecambe broke as they looked to wrap the game up in the last few minutes, but Twiss blazed a shot over when he should have hit the target, and in the 87th minute Richard met a cross from Mayo from the left and headed into the far corner for the equaliser.

Our son always politely turned down a request for an interview. As a new player he was conscious of being seen to talk too much when he felt his football feet should be speaking for him.

6/10/2007 Away Wycombe Wanderers–3 Notts County–1. Butcher on 68 minutes to equalise for Notts. Sam beat the offside trap to get down the left and he looked up and pulled a great ball back for Richard who, despite a good hand from Fielding, found the back of the net.

6/11/2007 Away Barnet–1 J Puncheon Notts County–1 Butcher on 4 minutes. His goals alone have totalled four points for Notts all in the second half of the matches. Richard Butcher's goal on Tuesday was fortunate to say the least as his mishit cross was totally misjudged by Barnet goalkeeper Lee Harries, as the ball somehow found its way into the back of the net. Despite the effort it could have gone down as an own goal. Richard said, "It was certainly my goal. Despite a few of the lads saying it was an own goal, I am claiming it." He said, "It was on target, so it was my goal. I didn't mean it, though; it was lucky

Butch: The Wings of Football   201

because I mishit the cross, and it was a real fluke that the goalkeeper misjudged." Barnet's Jason Puncheon scored their goal.

22/12/2007 Away Dagenham & Redbridge–1 South 50, Notts County–1 Butcher. Ian McParland was a relieved man after a 10-man County held on for a point. Richard Butcher's 25-yarder gave Magpies a fifth-minute lead. Daggers levelled three minutes after the break through a Glen Southam penalty after keeper Pilkington fouled Jon Nurse. The Magpies played the best 45 minutes, but they could have had more goals with other chances not being converted.

There is just one report on a game Richard scored in that I have been unable to find. It was 26/12/2007 Home to M K Dons 1–2 but I am sure, if I remember rightly, it would have been a great goal.

26/01/2008 Away Morecambe–1 Baker 72, Notts County–1 Butcher 28 minutes. The long-awaited return of County defender Mike Edwards for his first appearance of the season after a terrible injury was certainly a ray of brilliant light for the Magpies' boss Ian McParland and the travelling band of supporters. So, too, was the first-half goal from the leading scorer Richard Butcher, incredibly his ninth of the season, that put the Magpies ahead and inspired hope of only a second away-win of the season. It was a wonderful strike from the midfielder that flew in the top corner of the net.

2/02/2008 Home Grimsby Town–1 Notts County–1. Richard Butcher proved a jack-of-all-trades as he hit a County goal. The much-travelled midfielder who figured on both flanks against Grimsby said, "I am not a wide player, but I'll do my best for the team wherever I'm asked to play." Richard's 59th-minute strike was soon cancelled out by former favourite Nick Fenton. Our son said, "If I didn't score all season and we could win a game, I will take it! Another way of looking at it is that we have only lost twice when I have scored."

It was the third different position that Richard Butcher, the club's leading goal scorer, had played in the last three games, having played right midfield against Morecambe, and in an advanced central role in the goal-less draw at Brentford. Richard showed incredible versatility in both those games. McParland said, "It's a bit unfair to the lad at times, but with the players we have got, that's the way it is. We played him on the left, and we wanted him to come in and support the strikers. We gave him a bit of a free role and he got his goal in the end."

The legendary manager Jimmy Sirrel was out on the pitch to celebrate his 86th birthday with the supporters that adored him. It was a strange coincidence that Richard's funeral took place at Lincoln City football club, with fans and friends paying their last respects, on 2nd February 2011, the date that would have been the legendary Jimmy Sirrel's birthday.

01/03/2008 Away Macclesfield–1 Izak Reid 22, Notts County–1 Butcher 72 minutes. Goal Hero Richard Butcher. The ball fell invariably just outside the penalty area and he lifted it over the Macclesfield keeper with a brilliant strike. Keith Alexander didn't enjoy seeing one of his old players come back to haunt him but admitted he watched Richard's second half strike in awe from the dugout. "He scored a magnificent strike; you can't do anything about goals like that," said the Silkmen's new boss.

The Magpies showed great resolve and mental courage to stage a second-half comeback at Moss Rose—the kind they will need for the rest of the season if they are to avoid the trap. Our son was delighted to net his 11th goal of the campaign but disappointed one of his goals has still not led to a victory so far this season. He said, "If I stay on 11 goals, or whatever I get to, the most important thing is that we stay in the League." It was the worst scoring record in the football league, with only 37 goals in 46 league games.

We could go on about the matches our son scored goals in; so many to mention, but they are all in the stats. Richard showed a good combative edge to his natural attacking game in the heart of the Magpies midfield, and he took his goals of the season with characteristic composure. He also made vital goal-line clearances to keep Notts in the lead.

26/04/2008 Home Wycombe Wanderers–0 Notts County–1 Butcher 66 minutes. Richard Butcher scored another priceless goal to secure County's League status and relieve the tension at Meadow Lane. It was the second time in three years County have gone into their last home game needing points to save relegation, and they could not hide their nerves. Richard, as he has done so often this season, stepped up after 66 minutes and County clung on to their slender advantage. Jason Lee prodded the loose ball into the path of Richard Butcher who fired in his 12th goal of the season. In the ten games he had netted previously, the Magpies had never won a single game. But it had finally been broken just at the right time. 7,327 fans once again in the Kop stand.

Ian McParland, speaking after securing safety, spoke of his delight for the supporters who were once again superb with over 3,000 roaring the side to victory from the Kop after a difficult season. McParland was pleased to be able to give the fans something to cheer about. "It had been a hard season for me and for the players as well, but the main thing is Notts County will be playing in the football League next season." Goal scorer Richard Butcher and goalkeeper Russell Hoult have both been handed spots in the team of the week select XI. Following the weekend's games in league two, Richard's twelfth goal of the season was certainly his most crucial of the campaign as his efforts preserved Notts' football league status for the year, while a commanding performance from Hoult saw the experienced goalkeeper record his seventh clean sheet in County colours. Our son showed a good combative edge to his natural attacking game in the heart of the Magpies midfield and he took his goals of the season with characteristic composure. He also made vital goal line clearances to keep Notts in the lead.

RICHARD BUTCHER : NOTTS COUNTY F.C
PERMISSION WAS KINDLY GIVEN TO USE PHOTO BY : NOTTS MEDIA TEAM

RICHARD BUTCHER : NOTTS COUNTY F.C
PERMISSION WAS KINDLY GIVEN TO USE PHOTOS BY : RICHARD WHITING
www.actionimages.com

Notts County Games 2007–2008

Year 2007

11th August	Away Grimsby Town	(L2) 1–1
14th August	Away Coventry City	(CC) 0–3
18th August	Home Brentford	(LC) 1–1 SCORED
25th August	Away Darlington	(L2) 2–2 SCORED TWO
1st September	Home Morecambe	(L2) 1–1 SCORED
7th September	Away MK Dons	(L2) 0–3
15th September	Home Dagenham & Redbridge	(L2) 1–0
22nd September	Away Rotherham United	L2) 1–1
29th September	Home Chesterfield	(L2) 1–0
2nd October	Home Hereford United	(L2) 2–3
6th October	Away Wycombe Wanderers	(L2) 1–3 SCORED
13th October	Home Bury	(L2) 1–3
20th October	Away Mansfield	(L2) 0–0
27th October	Home Wrexham	(L2) 2–1
3rd November	Away Accrington Stanley	(L2) 2–0
10th November	Home Histon	(FAC) 3–0
6th November	Away Barnet	(L2) 1–1 SCORED
17th November	Home Macclesfield Town	(L2) 0–1
25th November	Away Lincoln City	(L2) 1–2
1st December	Home Havant & Waterlooville	(FAC) 0–1 Substitute
4th December	Home Peterborough United	(L2) 0–1
8th December	Home Shrewsbury Town	(L2) 2–1
22nd December	Away Dagenham & Redbridge	(L2) 1–1 SCORED
26th December	Home MK Dons	(L2) 1–2 SCORED
29th December	Home Rotherham United	(L2) 0–1

Year 2008

1st January	Away Hereford United	(L2) 0–0
5th January	Home Stockport	(L2) 1–2
12th January	Away Bradford City	(L2) 0–3

19th January	Home Chester City	(L2) 1–0
26th January	Away Morecambe	(L2) 1–1SCORED
29th January	Away Brentford	(L2) 0–0
2nd February	Home Grimsby Town	(L2) 1–1 SCORED
9th February	Away Stockport County	(L2) 1–1
12th February	Home Darlington	(L2) 0–1
16th February	Away Chester City	L2) 1–1
23rd February	Home Bradford City	(L2) 1–3
1st March	Away Macclesfield Town	(L2) 1–1 SCORED
8th March	Home Barnet	(L2) 1–1
11th March	Home Lincoln City	(L2) 0–1
15th March	Away Peterborough United	(L2) 0–0
22nd March	Home Rochdale	(L2) 1–0
24th March	Away Shrewsbury Town	(L2) 0–0
29th March	Home Mansfield Town	(L2) 0–0
5th April	Away Bury	(L2) 1–2
8th April	Away Rochdale	(L2) 2–4
12th April	Home Accrington	(L2) 1–0
19th April	Away Wrexham	(L2) 0–1
26th April	Home Wycombe Wanderers	(L2) 1–0 SCORED
3rd April	Away Chesterfield	(L2) 1–1

11: Notts County 2008–2009

Notts County would sacrifice Ian McParland in the coming months. He would give every waking hour to the club, only to be cast aside. There was clearly a problem with strikers. Richard was looking forward to the season starting after saving the Magpies from relegation. On paper it looked to be a good squad from the previous season. With Richard hoping to reach the play-offs he set out with a great start; he was a goal mean machine for Notts County and was looking to get on the score sheet once more. He always started the season fitter and stronger than the season before with the excitement of getting on the score sheet once again. Again the stories and excitements are within the games.

9/08/2008 Away Bradford City–2 Thorne 22-61, Notts County–1 Butcher 72 minutes. Richard Butcher said scoring his first goal of the season counted for nothing; it was a well-worked goal with Myles Weston beating Arnison on the left wing and pulling back across into the path of Richard to coolly side-foot past keeper Rhys Evans.

30/08/2008 Home Shrewsbury–2 Hibbert 47, Symes 88 Notts County–2 Edwards 39, Butcher 75 minutes. Richard took his goal with characteristic composure on 75 minutes to put Notts back in front, arriving with typical timing to direct Delroy Facey's cross into the net from close range. Richard was also in the right place at the right time to clear off the goal-line just minutes after putting Notts ahead, and he very nearly snatched victory in injury time at the end of a swift counter attack, but miscued wide.

02/09/2008 Scunthorpe–2 Notts County–1 Johnston's Paint Trophy. Richard Butcher put Notts ahead with a superb left-foot 18-yard volley on nine minutes. Until the final minute it looked as if the Magpies would dispose of their League One opponents. Hayes equalised with a downward header at the far post in the first minute of injury time, and in the third minute he nodded home from a yard out after Russell Hoult had made a superb reaction save following a goalmouth scramble.

27/12/2008 Home Aldershot–1 Charles 51 mins, Notts County–2 Johnson, 55, Butcher 94. Fans paid their final respects to former manager Jimmy Sirrel before the game. The game went deep into injury time; the fans knew there was one more act to be played out. Somehow it was fate for them to win on the day they paid tribute to Jimmy Sirrel, the most famous and successful manager in the club's history who died at the age of 86. It was the first league win of the season against the club where Sirrel ended his playing days and began his coaching career, which only made it more fitting. It all seemed to be happening in slow motion when Richard Butcher met Jamie Clapham's measured cross and directed a header back across goal over Nikki Bull. The keeper back-pedalled frantically as the ball looped in the air; it went in and the game burst into real play. It sparked memorable scenes of celebrations. Boss Ian McParland ran down the touch line punching the air, the players mobbed Richard who stood with his arms raised triumphantly to the heavens and Notts supporters erupted out of their seats. There was joy and relief and pure unadulterated excitement that Notts had clinched a victory in the most dramatic of circumstances. They had done it for Jimmy. 6,033 fans chanted 'there's only one Jimmy Sirrel'. I can tell you as a mother and father, our son was so proud to be a part of that day. Richard's words were, "That was one of the most important goals to me."

Jimmy Sirrel's birthday was February 2nd. (2nd February 1922 – 25 September 2008). He was a Scottish football player and manager, best known for his management career. Sirrel started his career with Celtic before moving to England, spending most of his playing career with Brighton & Hove Albion.

He started his management career in the Fourth Division with Brentford. Sirrel then moved to Notts County where he achieved promotion to the Second Division, and then, after a spell at Sheffield United, he returned to Notts County to achieve promotion to the First Division for the first time since 1926. He is regarded as a legend at the club, with the County Road Stand at Notts County's Meadow Lane named after him.

Information about the club and Jimmy Sirrel was found on en.wikipedia.org/wiki.

21/10/2008 Home Gillingham–2 Mullingan 39 Southall 63 Notts County–2 Butcher 65 Facey 79 minutes. Richard Butcher's strike was the first time Gillingham had conceded a goal at home in five games, in a record of four wins and draws. In our son's own words, "it's a hard place to come back from 2–0 down and to get a point is great. Not many teams will come here and do that," added Richard. "It just shows the character and the belief we have got in the squad this season. I didn't think we would come back from that last season. It was a great finish from Del to get the equaliser, and I was pleased to get a goal."

08/11/2008 Away Sutton United–0 Notts County–1 Richard Butcher. Notts County claimed their place in the second round of this season's FA cup with a first round victory at Sutton United. Boggy conditions had dominated the play, and we took the lead at the plucky non-league outfit fifteen minutes from time with Richard Butcher's headed home with a Matt Hamshaw's excellent cross from the right.

15/11/2008 Away Barnet–0 Notts County–4. Jonathan Forte made a dream debut as he netted a hat-trick to steer County to their first league win in seven games. Forte, who this week arrived on a one-month's loan from Scunthorpe, fired home from 12 yards in the 14th minute to double County's lead after Richard Butcher had opened the scoring with an 18-yard volley seven minutes earlier. Forte claimed his second in the 32nd minute, slotting home from close range, before securing the match ball on the stroke of half time with a six-yard finish.

30/11/2008 Home at Meadow Lane Stadium F.A Cup round two Notts County–1 Kettering Town–1. Our son's words: "I owe my career in part to the people of Kettering Town football club because when I joined them at 18 I was still in two minds about whether I would make it as a professional footballer. I was given a chance at Rockingham Road and I took it with both hands, thinking it might be my last. This was one game I was looking forward to."

Richard did get on the pitch only to suffer an injury—a stress fracture of the fifth metatarsal led him to leave the pitch, which led to surgery to have a screw fixation and bone grafting that was also recommended. This would leave him on the sidelines for up to 6–8 weeks after the operation. He suffered a serious infection with his foot oozing with poison. The foot opened up and, for a time, he thought he would lose his foot. The frustration showed as the healing time lingered on. Swabs were taken and medication was given, but I have to say, when I saw his foot I was very concerned; it was a frightening time.

RICHARD BUTCHER : NOTTS COUNTY F.C
PERMISSION WAS KINDLY GIVEN TO USE PHOTO BY : NOTTS MEDIA TEAM

One joke our son shared with us is that he felt the FA Cup was jinxed and that by lifting the cup it had caused his injury. He felt upset that he was on a good goal-scoring run for Notts County, but it would be some time before he would be back on track. Richard had also chipped in 14 goals with his time at Kettering. He made his debut away at Folkestone. It was his first taste of success. Kettering town gained promotion from the Southern Conference in the last game of the season. How good it felt to achieve promotion! It was extra special for our son because he was relatively new to the game and it was his first taste of success at any level.

Speaking for Richard about the conversations we had after he got injured with his metatarsal in which surgery was required; within the space of less than a week he was asked to go back in training working on his upper body strengths, which was far too soon. He also felt there was a lack of equipment to help support his injury, which he feels didn't help his recovery, and may have contributed to his serious infection. It was Christmas when he phoned me to tell me that his foot was oozing with poison; the wound had opened up. I really have to say I did think he was going to lose his foot, it looked so bad. This really did set him back; he wanted to score more goals this season. 7/3/2009 Notts County Away to Shrewsbury Town which ended 2–3 featured another show-stopping goal from Richard Butcher.

Our son really did enjoy his time at the oldest league club. He was a proud lad, and we were proud of him, but it did get to him a bit knowing that all the hard work he had put in didn't warrant a new contract. He did really feel hurt by that. I think he felt maybe behind the scenes a certain person didn't like him too much. Sometimes people take a dislike to you without even getting to know you, which can lead to you not getting a new contract, as in any walk of life. Whether this is true or not, it's what our son felt and said at the time. Behind the scenes sometimes you can be polite and well-mannered, I know. He said a certain board member would not answer him whenever he spoke to him. He used to say, "I don't know what I have done wrong."

Our son moved on with a happy smile to pastures new. He was surprised he didn't get 'players' player of the season' voted by teammates, but that's life, as Richard would say. He thought it was a fantastic club to play for, and he was so honoured to have been given the opportunity to play for such a great club.

Richard was now at the end of his contract; he had given up waiting for Ian McParland's offer long before this game and, although the manager had told him he wanted to keep him, others had already signed deals. He did not blame the manager because things were being taken more and more out of his hands, nor did he want to because Lincoln had come calling and Jacko wanted him to go home. He knew that the Magpies needed a huge cash injection to keep them going; it was coming, everyone knew that, but Lincoln felt safe and secure with so many fans that he had come to know as friends.

We knew Richard had so many positive Magpies memories but the parting of the ways was imminent. Richard had some great times at Notts County, but hanging on wasn't his style. You could tell his time was up and, as a family, we really found this hard to believe as our son, on a personal level, had done really well for the club, and it just shows—even if you do well for a club, this still doesn't guarantee you a new contract. We really didn't feel he got the credit he deserved, but that's football. It was time to move again—a footballer's life is never settled—'a new start and new beginnings'. I wonder how many times a footballer has said that in his lifetime. Richard even took his little dog, Charlie, in for a bit of training and to meet all the staff, and they all fell in love with him. But at a later date we soon realised that, with England manager, Sven-Goran Eriksson, waiting in the wings to take over, Ian McParland's hands would be tied, as it looked like he didn't realise what his own future would hold.

Richard claimed the 'Junior Magpies' player of the season' award at Meadow Lane. All the Magpies' squad and management were in attendance in the Masson suite to join the younger supporters for their end-of-season awards night. At this event a number of the junior Magpies were presented awards from the first team squad for their efforts this season. The squad also posed for photos and signed autographs, and took part in a quiz with the youngsters. Twelve-goal Richard, who scored the winner against Wycombe Wanderers, claimed the top award after a productive season. After claiming the award, he said he was delighted to have received the award and would like to thank all those youngsters who voted for him. "They obviously know their stuff, that is for sure."

After Richard left Notts County, fans sent letters of support and wished him well as they couldn't believe he had been released. Thank you to those fans; my son really was grateful for your letters. I still have them today.

Richard would often get fan mail from people all around the world. He would always reply with a letter and signed photograph.

We would like to thank Notts County football club for giving us some great memories of Richard's career. They will stay with us forever in our hearts.

We will finish with a great friend, Jim Rodwell. During two years at the club Richard made 93 appearances, scoring 20 goals, and became a popular figure with the Meadow Lane faithful.

Jim Rodwell pays his respects:

This is like the worst type of déjà vu. Less than a year after saying goodbye to a great friend in Keith Alexander, we are all united in grief for Butch. I first met Butch when he came to Rushden & Diamonds as a raw 17-year-old. Even then he was full of life and character. He looked after my boots, and I can say, without fear of contradiction, he was the worst boot boy I had ever had. However, that didn't stop him from expecting a large cash tip at Christmas! Anybody that knows me will tell you how tight I am, so getting money out of me was a herculean task in itself, but he always managed it! You just couldn't help but like Butch. He was infectious and great fun to be around.

He always made the training ground a better place to be; of course it was at Kettering where Butch really made his mark, before Keith took him to Lincoln City where he became the polished professional we all remember. I watched him play for the Imps on many occasions, and he was invariably their best player. For me, he was probably their best midfielder in the lower leagues. I always took great pride and pleasure in watching him.

It was only in the last tragic week or so that I realised how much Butch was a part of the folklore at Notts County. He was a hero for many of our fans for almost single-handedly keeping Notts in the football league with 12 goals from midfield and scoring the goal against Wycombe that secured our league status. Our Facebook page has been overwhelmed with tributes. Ultimately it's not as a footballer that I'll remember Butch, it's as a friend, and as a decent human being—far more important attributes than just being able to kick a ball about. We will always miss you pal, but never forget the smiles and the laughs we had with you. Our hearts and prayers go to your family, and all those who had the privilege of knowing you.

Notts County

Notts County Football Club (often known as Notts or County or by their nickname The Magpies) is a professional football club based in Nottingham, England. Formed on 28 November, 1862, Notts County is the oldest football team in the world to currently play at a professional level. Between 1888–89 and 2012–13 they played a total of 4,710 Football League matches—more than any other English team. They currently play in League One of the Football League, the third tier in the English Football League System. County play their home games at Meadow Lane in black and white striped shirts.

Information about the club was found on en.wikipedia.org/wiki.

RICHARD BUTCHER WITH NEPHEWS ROBBIE TOP LEFT AND KYLE TOP RIGHT
AND COUSIN RACHEL BOTTOM LEFT AND BOTTOM RIGHT RICHARD WITH CHARLIE

RICHARD BUTCHER : NOTTS COUNTY F.C
PERMISSION WAS KINDLY GIVEN TO USE PHOTOS BY : RICHARD WHITING
www.actionimages.com

Notts County Games 2008–2009

Year 2008

9th August	Away Bradford City	(L2) 1–2 SCORED
12th August	Home Doncaster City	(CC) 1–0
16th August	Home Darlington	(L2) 0–0
23rd August	Away Luton Town	(L2) 1–1
26th August	Away Wigan Athletic	(CC) 0–4
30th August	Home Shrewsbury	(L2) 2–2 SCORED
2nd September	Away Scunthorpe United	(JPT) 1–2 SCORED
6th September	Home Bournemouth	(L2) 1–1
13th September	Away Accrington Stanley	(L2) 1–1
20th September	Away Exeter City	(L2) 2–2
27th September	Home Aldershot Town	(L2) 2–1 SCORED
4th October	Away Port Vale	(L2) 2–1
13th October	Home Brentford	(L2) 1–1
18th October	Home Mansfield Town	(L2) 1–1
21st October	Away Gillingham	(L2) 2–2 SCORED
25th October	Away Chesterfield	(L2) 1–3
28th October	Home Rochdale	(L2) 1–2
1st November	Home Bury	(L2) 0–1
8th November	Away Sutton United	(FAC) 1–0 SCORED
15th November	Away Barnet	(L2) 4–0 SCORED
22nd November	Away Dagenham & Redbridge	(L2) 1–6
25th November	Home Wycombe Wanderers	(L2) 0–2
30th November	Home Kettering Town	(FAC) 1–1
14th February	Home Barnet	(L2) 2–0 Substituted

Year 2009

17th February	Away Macclesfield Town	(L2)1–1 substituted
21st February	Away Bury	(L2) 0–2 substituted
28th February	Home Bradford City	(L2) 3–1 substituted
3rd March	Away Darlington	(L2) 0–1 substituted
7th March	Away Shrewsbury	(L2) 2–3 SCORED
10th March	Home Luton Town	(L2) 0–2
14th March	Home Accrington Stanley	(L2) 1–1 substituted
17th March	Home Gillingham	(L2) 0–1

21st March	Away Bournemouth	(L2) 1–0
28th March	Away Lincoln City	(L2) 1–1
4th March	Home Chester City	(L2) 1–2
11th March	Away Rotherham United	(L2) 1–2
13th March	Home Grimsby Town	(L2) 1–2
18th April	Away Morecambe	(L2) 0–1
25th April	Home Dagenham & Redbridge	(L2) 0–3

12: Lincoln City FC 2009–2010

Richard made an emotional return to Lincoln City. Our son's words were: "Sincil Bank would be the perfect place to reignite my career." He discussed a move with Peter Jackson and he described Jackson as "the sort of manager I would like to play for." He had waited out at Notts County, but a new deal was not forthcoming. County fans were surprised to see him leave after being their top goal scorer and saving the club from relegation. The fans sent cards to wish him well. Our son admitted he was shocked, after being given indications he would be offered a new deal after scoring 20 goals in his two seasons.

Peter Jackson said that, on the face of it, it was an easy decision for Richard to make. Our son said, "I feel at home at the club. When I look back at my career, my days at Lincoln stand out. There were a lot of highlights, like making the play-off finals," he added. "But the thing I remember most is the great relationship I had with the fans. I'd be so proud to put on the shirt again." Richard was full of joy at returning to the Imps. He was looking to settle at Lincoln City, going back to a club that treated him with great respect. He really did love the club and was looking forward to getting that fantastic atmosphere back that the fans so graciously handed out. He really did feel at home.

Peter Jackson was faced with some financial limitations at Lincoln City with his pre-season signing, but our son and the players were looking forward to a great season. Peter Jackson made Richard his first summer signing. It was a return of a goal-scoring hero. Peter said of the signings, "In the three seasons I was at Sincil Bank the budget was cut, so the likes of Sinclair, Beevers, N'Guessan had to go, to balance the books. The replacements had to be free transfers, loans, or young and hungry lads, certainly with talent, but you know, maybe 1 in 3 of your teenage gambles will pay off given the pressure, but I had no doubts in the meetings with Richard. He was tall, fit, an all-round athlete with great technique who could get you a goal from deep with either peg. That's just what the team and the strikers need, a lad with the engine to help out at both ends of the pitch, who can chip in with 8-10 goals a season. That is massive for a midfielder, and that is what made him one of the top catches at our level. Butch was not a Premiership player, but he deserved a crack at the Championship.

But back to those doubts. Although I didn't, Richard did have, and even though he loved the club, failure would ruin a deep relationship he had with the fans, so, naturally, he did not want to jeopardise that with a move. I told him about my doubts at a return to Huddersfield, then on the verge of going under, but I had done it and wouldn't swap that memory for the world. It was then that the optimist came out in him; he was such a genuinely nice kid with a great attitude. He was keen to put in the hard work from day one.

Our son got on well with Iffy Onuora and Simon Clark who were doing the day-to-day coaching. Iffy, who is now an equalities officer at the PFA, was also a big Everton fan like Richard. Our son knew, with the financial restriction, that no one could possibly know how well the team would blend.

Friendlies were celebrated in style at Arsenal XI and Sheffield United, with both owned by the Blades chairman. United were also favourites to sign Danny N'Guessan, according to the dressing room grapevine, although Leicester City won the deal. Although Richard looked forward to playing in these games, he knew the club would be ill-prepared for league two opposition when it hit them full-on in August. But, unlike other senior players, he kept quiet and respected the manager's decisions.

Our son enjoyed the game against Arsenal. He was very proud to be Captain on the day. It was a real proud moment for him to be a part of such a great day. The family really enjoyed the day out.

Richard signed for Lincoln on a grand a week plus goal bonuses. He was happy with that. It meant he could save a bit more, looking to his future life after football. But things didn't quite work out the way he would have liked.

Moving on into the season Richard knew he had not really pleased the fans. They were getting frustrated at the way the club was being run on and off the field with the manager not having the financial backing; the team would not have time to gel. And there was no financial scope for new signings. Our son knew that, being one of the highest earners, the knives would be out. He was always a worrier. When he was up he was up, but when he was down, he was down. He would always put an unselfish ninety minutes into the game with little rewards. If he was to keep his two-year deal, the side and style would have to change.

At times he slowly started to regret his move back to Lincoln as the fans got increasingly frustrated. He knew it would be a long season. He felt Peter Jackson was a great manager. Not all of the board wanted Peter Jackson to go, but a majority voted Peter out. Richard's loyalty always sat high with the manager, but a new manager and team style was on the agenda. There was one thing you could say about Peter Jackson; he wore his heart on his sleeve—he would fight till the last—and he had passion and a great love for Lincoln City football club. His health suffered with his illness. I know our son was worried for him, and so were we when we heard his news, but even though he was so ill, he was still there doing his job and working hard for the club he loved.

RICHARD BUTCHER AND MANAGER PETER JACKSON
LINCOLN CITY F.C
PERMISSION WAS KINDLY GIVEN BY THE MEDIA TEAM & JOHN VICKERS FOR USE OF PHOTOS

Peter Jackson talks of his time at Lincoln:

From the time I arrived at Lincoln I knew the pressure and potential of the club and those fantastic supporters. We needed to get out into the media more, especially Sky Sports and the local connections of the BBC. I told the chairman this, and that we needed to start by trying to at least make Lincoln into everyone's second team. PR is free, and we certainly needed to shake off this sleepy little club tag with so much development going on elsewhere in the City. Then again, you need all the help you can get with 91 teams above you in the league.

There was no doubt we would survive, and we did. Then I formed a genuine life-long affection with the fans that really did help me through my illness. The send-off, the huge card, and signing that massive 'Lord of The Imps' shirt; these, along with the positive sentiments of the fans, those red-and-white-striped Imps, they are what you take with you through the dark days.

Managers are ultimately judged on results, and, although we would have had enough to stay up, we did not win enough at home, with too many draws. Coming into the Darlo Cup game, a director had given me the heads-up that we had to win. We did not. And when Steff Wright came up to me and said, "Leave things for now, we will speak in the morning," I knew my time was up. It was such a shame to leave in front of just 500 fans, after I had forged such a bond with those fantastic Lincoln City supporters.

Richard's Mum Gail:

Richard shared his thoughts with us about manager Peter Jackson. "He was a great guy. I really got on well with him. He was a motivator and had a great personality and was approachable and easy to talk to. I was sorry to see him leave Lincoln City."

Simon Clark took over as first team coach and Tom Spall took over as acting assistant manager. The mood in the dressing room changed, and the style of a passing game gave Clark a winning start. The players worked hard with Iffy Onuora. Our son rated that Simon had the desire to achieve the attacking strengths. Richard returned to his former strengths in the game. Young LJL, a talented player, made a mistake, but our son encouraged the lad and told him he would grow, and to forget it. He said, "You have the ability to go far, keep going."

Richard showed the Lincoln fans what he had become since he had been away. Simon Clark told the players he would be making a full pitch to the board for new signings. He praised the lads for their contributions. Simon Clark got money for a couple of loans, with Barry Fry helping out with Sergio Torres on a month's loan. Our son would have to start rethinking his career sooner rather than later. Lincoln had no money and needed to bring in new players.

Chris Sutton and Ian Pearce were given the new manager's job. Richard knew that, once this happened, managers like to bring in their own playing staff. Chris Sutton soon started to criticise him, although to start with he praised him, telling him he was the best player at the club. Our son worked well alongside Sutton in training. He was enjoying the challenge. Who wouldn't? To get the chance to train with a great player in his time. Chris Sutton soon used the old trick that is used so widely in football terms: lack of fitness. Managers used this to buy them time. A number of players failed the fitness test, but Richard didn't. Sutton felt he had the best technique at the club and was very complimentary towards him telling him he would play a role.

Manager Chris Sutton

Chris Sutton is an English professional football player. In his career, he played from 1991 to 2007 for Norwich City, Blackburn Rovers, Chelsea, Celtic, Birmingham City, and Aston Villa. He scored over 150 career goals in over 400 league appearances spanning 16 years in the English and Scottish Premier Leagues. He was capped once by England. He also played in midfield or attack, although usually in the latter role as a striker. He was a very physical player; he was also a fairly prolific goal scorer throughout his career, and was joint top goal scorer (with Dion Dublin and Michael Owen) in the FA Premier League 1997–98 season. He scored many goals which made him particularly effective from set-pieces.

Information about the club and Manager was found on en.wikipedia.org/wiki.

Our son soon phoned Simmo, his best pal, in the hope they could be reunited. He was looking forward to meeting up with Keith and Gary when a deal was agreed upon. Although Sutton's regime was something Richard enjoyed and was playing to his strengths, our son said Sutton was never approachable or friendly, but he inspired and demanded that the players try to improve. Our son felt this was just what he needed—the approach seemed to be working on the pitch.

Richard was an unused substitute in the game against Morecambe, but was surprised to get a call from two rival managers on the Sunday—both asking if he wanted to join them on loan. His name had been circulated, along with four others, as being on the transfer list. On the Monday, Chris Sutton asked if everyone had enjoyed the rest of their weekend, to which Richard replied, "Not really, as I found out I had been transfer listed, thanks to a manager making an enquiry." Chris Sutton then took our son into his office describing him as a bad egg, and saying that he did not want or need bad eggs on his team. This was not unexpected. We were also aware that a new manager would look at the wage bill and would quickly realise that his wages would fund two more players.

Richard would now spend training sessions running around a field with Sam Clucas (his mum actually complained to the club at the way her young son was treated) until he managed to find himself another club. Now frozen out completely, Richard was not surprised. It got worse as our son collapsed that Saturday evening while he was out with friends. Ian Pearce, to his credit, quickly came to check on him and, although tests again revealed his slightly enlarged heart, which is perfectly normal for an athlete to have, because the muscles are naturally bigger, there was no reason for him to cease his profession as a professional athlete. After three days of tests, Richard returned to the training ground. In a two-minute meeting Chris Sutton asked him if he was fit to which he replied "yes" and the manager said "well, off you go then." He did not look at him once during the discussion, and our son was left in no doubt that his days were very much numbered.

We remember the incident well. We rushed up to Lincoln Hospital to find out what was wrong with our son. It was a long drive from Northampton and upon arrival Richard seemed fine. We were aware that he had been under a lot of stress through being made to run so hard and being pushed out of the side completely. He would phone us from time to time and say, "Mum, I don't know if I can take any more." The mental side of things was getting to him. I just tried to encourage Richard to carry on and to try to take no notice as I know full well he was one of the better players at the club and the issue was really the wages he earned.

It was a Saturday night, the only bit of free time the players get. Richard didn't go out much, but I will say this: when a player is not used to drink, and they are as fit and healthy as our son was, when they do drink it hits them hard. Our son was always the sort to drink water, fruit juice, and milk most of the time apart from an odd Saturday night out. After all, he is only human, and it was in his own time. Our son left the hospital with nothing found wrong with him.

In any other job in life you would never have to put up with the sort of treatment that our son did, as other companies would not allow this to happen. Each and every day he dreaded going into work not knowing what the day would bring. Even though Richard was so fit, he was pushed to the limit, and your body can only take so much, not to mention the mental side of things. He was also supportive of the younger lads who were suffering, too. Our son would put his arms round other young players to try and lift their spirits up, and he would pass on the advice given to him by past players who had given him support over his career—professionals like Duane Darby and Carl Heggs. But he was upset for the young lads as this sort of treatment can destroy a young player's career and confidence. The management have their job to do but the effects can be difficult to live with.

Richard was given the all clear at Lincoln Hospital with nothing untoward found wrong with him. I can only say the stress of the treatment he received at the time did not help our son at all and I believe that's why he ended up in hospital. He would always keep his head down as he was taught to do over the years by other players when things were not going right. Answering back can give the club the right to break your contract and he wasn't that sort.

Richard and Sam kept running around that field, doing their own training, long after the squad they were so isolated from; the other players had packed their kitbags up for the day. They both knew they were never going to get into the reckoning, let alone the side. Our son had plenty of pearls of wisdom for the young lad, as the two were cut off from the main squad and forced to just endlessly run around the training ground. He kept the young lad's spirits up at a time when the harsher side of football life threatened to ruin his career. Signed by Peter Jackson, who described him as 'a real find', the ex-Lincoln College lad was destined to become little more than a publicity stunt, facing the 'moving on' process despite not being given a chance to show his ability. His choice to turn down a scholarship in the States for Lincoln City appeared to be a wrong one.

When managers change there is always a risk that you will not fit in with the style of play or formation. As this had clearly happened, he had to hope that his agent and contacts could get him a loan move. Richard often talked of his time running around that field, and he knew that, with the manager keen to free up the budget, the endless runs and isolation from the squad is a time-honoured psychological way to force a player out. This would ensure a player either elects to move to another club, or, in frustration, commits a breach of contract that would benefit the club. Fines of up to two weeks' wages or the ability to negotiate a reduced severance deal allow the club to save money, needed to fund loans or even a new signing. The tricks of the trade that managers use were falling into place. Richard and Sam tried to work through the season with Sam being determined never to breach his contract; they were forming a close bond. They both worked hard and kept their heads down and helped each other through this rough period they were both having. Meanwhile the manager was looking for new signings.

Sam Clucas had this to say:

The first time I met Butch was on my first day training with Lincoln City whilst on trial. I was obviously nervous and scared, only being 18 and at my hometown club. But straight away the first person to talk to me and welcome me was Richard Butcher and this made me feel a little more at ease and welcome. Every morning as I'd arrive at the training ground the first person to say good morning and ask if I was okay was always Butch. He was a lot older than me and sometimes older pros at clubs don't talk to you or help you, but Butch was the opposite and always spoke to young lads and gave them advice and helped them through.

We became good friends at football and outside and we would regularly, well almost every night, play FIFA online against each other and have forfeits for losing, such as making the cups of tea in the morning. He would often lose and always blame his dog saying he got in the way when playing.

During my time at Lincoln I wasn't playing, and the manager singled a few of us out and didn't want us training or playing games despite doing nothing wrong. Being young I didn't know what I had done wrong, but Butch was always there helping me and telling me that I would get my chance and not to be disheartened even though me and him would often be running around the pitch on our own—whilst the kit man and chef would train instead of us. So many days I felt like giving up, but being such a nice and down-to-earth lad, Butch was always there to put a smile on my face and cheer me up. You won't find anyone who will have a bad word to say about him. He was a good friend and a top man. He's sorely missed, and, without him, I don't know if I could have dealt with the situation at Lincoln. So I owe him a lot.

Richard was forced to chew over the 'what ifs', having left Notts after being their top scorer the previous two seasons. Chris Sutton offered Richard a severance package. This occurred a couple of days after the Chesterfield game but he declined to take it as it was insultingly low.

Sutton could have felt sorry for Sam and Richard but he didn't. When our son was going through a rough time the manager could have taken him under his wing. Our son really felt his football career was coming to an end. He applied to be a fireman at the fire station near Sincil Bank; he was accepted and even got through the first round. When I asked him why he would want to do this, he felt at that time he didn't know if he could go through any more. Richard bided his time, staying professional and polite as he always was; he would give everything he had on and off pitch.

Macclesfield threw him a life line. He had some hard times and a lot of ups and downs, but he lived his dream. He was charming, likable, and would give his time to anyone. He liked to keep things simple using his payoff from Lincoln. His mortgage came first. He paid a large sum of money of that for a bit more security. That way he could live within his means with his wages reduced to the £700 a week he would get from Macclesfield. Our son always had his priorities the right way round. He never liked credit cards and saved for a rainy day. He knew his career would come to an end at some point, but just when you don't know. With the rent he would now receive from his two houses in Lincoln, this would help with his cut in wages, and would enable him to move back to his house in Swinton, Manchester.

As parents you go through all the good and the bad. It affects you just as much as it does your son. The incredible twists and turns in football life follow you week in, and week out, even though it's your son's chosen career. But we followed Richard's dream along with him, and sometimes it would even affect our night out with friends as we also would be on a downer. When things weren't going right, people were always quick to pick up on when Richard wasn't playing, but when he was doing well, no one seemed to ask. You would walk down the street and someone would say, "See, he's not playing today," with great delight, not knowing he was injured. Or people would ask how much money is he on, as if his wages should be an open book for everyone to know, or, "I see he's on the bench today."

Our other son, Glenn, would also go through torment with comments like, "I bet you wish you were a footballer like your brother." That really used to upset me, or people would stop and talk to Richard and totally ignore the fact that his brother was standing right next to him. Richard found that upsetting, too. Glenn was so proud of his brother. He would race home from work as he was a tiler at the time, asking how his brother and team are getting on when he couldn't make the games due to work commitments. He would also come running in shouting and race up the stairs announcing "Richard scored, Mum" so very proudly. Richard's dad, when joining Carlsberg, had to miss certain games due to his shift work, so I would listen to the game on the internet and text him the half-time scores. He would love it when his son scored, and even the lads at Carlsberg would look out for him.

If we could not make a game, our Saturday would be to put the commentary on the internet as soon as the game started. We never missed one game that way and if we could not make it Richard always called after a game to have a chat with his dad, win or lose. We always had a tea break at half-time and one thing's for sure, we never got used to our son's name popping up on the television when he scored. His dad used to tape all his goals, sometimes sitting up late to catch a glimpse of the one he had missed due to work. We loved Jeff Stelling; what a fantastic job he does. Jeff very kindly showed the programme we had done for the memorial match that we did for

Richard at Northampton Town FC to raise money for the Richard Butcher Memorial Trust. He even sent a letter of support. Our son would have been so proud to have received a letter from Jeff whom he admired so much, as we did.

Lincoln City

Lincoln City Football Club is an English professional association football club based in Lincoln, Lincolnshire. The club is a member of the Conference National following relegation from the Football League. The club plays at the 10,120-capacity Sincil Bank, and is nicknamed the Imps after the legend of the Lincoln Imp. They have also been known as the Red Imps. Traditionally they play in red and white striped shirts with black shorts and red and white socks.

Information about the club was found on en.wikipedia.org/wiki.

Manager Gary Simpson

The New Manager Gary Simpson is an England former footballer and manager of Conference National side Lincoln City. As a player he was a midfielder. He played for Boston United and Altrincham amongst other clubs. He acted as a coach and assistant to Keith Alexander at a number of Football League clubs, and upon Alexander's death in March 2010 he replaced him as manager at Macclesfield until March 2012.

Simpson started his career with Stoke City, making more than 100 reserve team appearances, before joining Boston United in the summer of 1980. He remained with the club for five seasons, skippering the club in the 1985 FA Trophy final, before leaving to join Stafford Rangers, Weymouth and Altrincham.

Simpson moved on to his first managerial role becoming Player/Manager at Gainsborough Trinity, winning the club's first ever Manager of the Month award in March 1993. Having been in charge at the Northolme for three years, following a 3–1 home defeat to Whitby Town on 9 October 1993 Simpson resigned from his role with Leighton James succeeding him in Trinity's hot seat. He quickly signed as a player for Arnold Town operating under the stewardship of his one-time Boston United manager Ray O'Brien. He became something of a cult-figure with the club, helping them secure the Northern Counties East League Northern Division One Title for

1993–1994 before joining Hyde United in September 1994. He debuted in the 2–1 Northern Premier League away defeat to Boston United on 14 September and spent a month with the club before leaving. He won nine England semi-professional international caps and also captained the Middlesex Wanderers touring side, playing games in Indonesia, Holland and Hungary.

Information taken from en.wikipedia.org/wiki and from Gary Simpson.

RICHARD BUTCHER LINCOLN CITY F.C
WE KINDLY THANK THE MEDIA TEAM AND JOHN VICKERS FOR THE USE OF PHOTOS

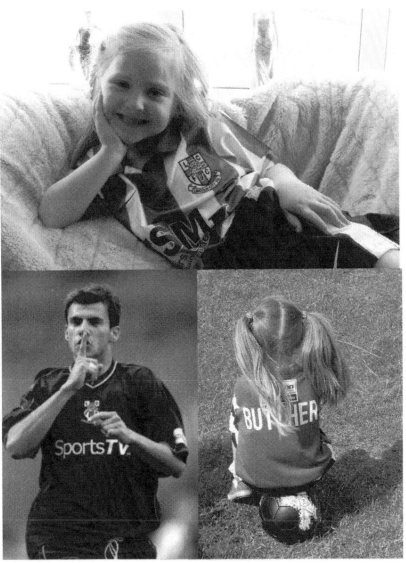

RICHARD BUTCHER'S NIECE ELISE IS ENJOYING WEARING HER
LINCOLN CITY FOOTBALL KIT, WHICH WAS KINDLY DONATED
BY PHIL KIME

Lincoln City Games 2009–2010

Year 2009

8th August	Home Barnet	(L2) 1–0
11th August	Home Barnsley	(CC) 0–1
15th August	Away Accrington Stanley	(L2) 0–1
22nd August	Home Burton Albion	(L2) 0–2
29th August	Away Dagenham & Redbridge	(L2) 0–3
5th September	Home Darlington	(L2) 3–0
12th September	Away Bournemouth	(L2) 1–3
19th September	Home Shrewsbury Town	(L2) 0–2
3rd October	Home Aldershot Town	(L2) 1–0
10th October	Away Macclesfield Town	(L2) 1–0
17th October	Away Northampton Town	(L2) 0–1
24th October	Home Torquay United	(L2) 0–0 Substitute
24th November	Away Rotherham United	(L2) 0–2 Substitute

13: Macclesfield Town 2009–2010–2011

Richard had turned to friend Gary for help during a distressing three months at Lincoln while he had not breached his contract despite being removed from the squad and was denied the chance to get back into the side at Lincoln. As hard as it was, our son had heard many a story over the years about this being part and parcel of the game. Players can leave at no cost to the club, but our son hung out for a 'pay up' and the player and the club agreed to a settlement. This was the first time Richard had ever been paid up from any club he had played for in his career; because of his age and the bills he had to pay, he was advised to stay put until an agreement was reached. But, in truth, you really don't have a choice. You have to wait it out in the hope something will come up. In the meantime his experience and skill would carry him through.

Manager Keith Alexander managed to stretch the Macclesfield budget by £500 a week; this was helped by Andy Scott who paid this out of his own pocket. Richard was forever grateful to Keith and Gary and, of course, Macclesfield. The one-month loan deal started on Tuesday 9th February 2010. Our son loved being back with Keith and Gary again. He felt reborn. At first, while on loan, he would drive back and forth from Lincoln to Macclesfield sharing the travelling with Keith Alexander. This was the daily chore they would have to follow. Once his move became permanent, he would move back into his house at Swinton near Manchester, which he left while playing for Oldham.

I have to say Keith Alexander was a fantastic manager. Our son was so very proud to be a part of his squad at Macclesfield Town. Keith had achieved so much in his career, which will be talked about more later. He was such a great guy with a big heart and a brilliant sense of humour. Our son so loved being around him. We will move on and talk about a few of the manager's highlights and our son's games but first, when Richard made his move to Macclesfield more permanent, what would he find on his arrival?

When he got back to Macclesfield he found that his house, which he had bought when he moved to Oldham, had been damaged to a stage where he could not move back in. Our son phoned us while we were on holiday for his dad's 50th birthday, November 2010, to tell us what had happened. Richard moved in with friend Ben Futcher for a while until things got sorted out. When we returned from holiday, his dad then went up and helped to restore the house. His dad had spent a lot of time helping him to fit out his first home in Lincoln. Richard also got married on Sunday 6th June 2010, at Hemswell Court, Gainsborough, Lincolnshire. So with Richard's move up to Macclesfield, the house needed to be sorted out ready for him to start a new chapter in his life.

We always followed our son's career keenly. It didn't matter what country we were in, we always talked to him on the phone, and still found an internet place to listen to the games. Richard and his dad still had the chats they always had about the match, no matter how many miles they were apart.

A few stories and highlights within the match reports:

01/2/2010 Away Gigg Lane League: 2 Attendance 2,169 Ref J. Moss. Bury–2 Low 29 pen Bishop 79, Macclesfield–1 Butcher 26 minutes. It started well for the Silkmen when Sean Hessey's shot on goal was deflected to Richard Butcher who made no mistake with his shot, but three minutes later it all turned sour when Ryan Lowe and Colin Daniels both went up for a 50-50 ball and the referee awarded a spot kick when Lowe tumbled to the ground; the striker converted the penalty himself. The match looked to be ending all square, when Bury substitute, Sam Hewson, broke clear and despite the claims that he was at least two yards offside, he was allowed to continue and set up Andy Bishop to score the Shakers' winning goal.

23/02/2010 Away Attendance 4,813 Ref Oliver Langford. Macclesfield–1 Grimsby–1. Richard Butcher who was the Silkmen's most potent attacking threat all night had two chances to open the score when the hosts took the lead with only their second real chance of the first half. A cross from the left wasn't cleared and fell kindly to Jamie Devitt, who cut back onto his right foot and struck a sweet left-foot shot past Jon Brian in the Silkmen's goal. A change of tactics saw Mathew Tipton replacing Ben Wright, with the Silkmen moving to 4-4-2 formation and back on track, and what a goal it was from Richard Butcher, with his second since arriving at Moss Rose from Lincoln City; he curled an exquisite free kick into the net from 35 yards. The result saw the Silkmen maintain their eight-point gap over the Mariners and stretch their unbeaten run to three games.

Lincoln had won to push the Silkmen to 20th, but Gary Simpson also realised the value of our son's contribution. "Richard's goal against Grimsby was vital as both sides were heading down. The Mariners had gone one up, and Butch had given them the lifeline they needed. We had got him working on free-kicks but that brilliant 35-yarder into the top corner blew everyone away. That goal was vital as it kept us safe while Grimsby continued to run out of games and the points they needed to save themselves."

Keith had been right to warn the Silkmen that Rochdale would bounce back and they did with a one–nil. Chris O'Grady stabbed home from six yards on the hour to win a close encounter that suggested Macclesfield deserved at least a point. Richard walked in the wrong changing room upon his return to Notts County to be greeted by Steve Cotterill who had just taken over at the 7th placed Magpies. He would go on to win 14, draw 3 and lose 1 of his games in charge. The fact that Richard's old club would win the League put the 1–0 win over Macclesfield into context. Our son received a standing ovation from the Magpies; he had been the leading scorer for the Magpies in the previous two seasons, both part of a struggle to avoid the drop.

Keith, Gary, and our son drove home together after the Notts County game, and talked about Richard's performance, and Keith's kid's homework, and a game plan for the Hereford game on the Saturday. As our son said goodbye and shut the car door, he never realised that would be the last time he would speak to Big Keith. As the last non-family member to see Keith alive, he always wished he had said more, even thanked him once again for giving him the opportunity to keep his dream alive at Lincoln, Peterborough, and Macc. Richard spoke about Keith's bout of hiccups a few weeks before; he had discussed this with us and we had recently seen a TV programme on the subject. We told our son and talked about this, relaying how a hospital in the UK had missed the symptoms only for a ground-breaking scan in Japan to reveal a tumour at the top of the spine with a gentleman on TV who was suffering with hiccups. We didn't know if this was the same symptoms or not but it just sounded strange that Keith was suffering with hiccups too.

Keith Alexander passed away on the morning of Wednesday 3rd march 2010 aged 53, leaving his family and, of course, extended family—the fans of Lincoln City, Grimsby Town, Peterborough United, and Macclesfield Town, were left with a massive void that we can never ever fill. He died having just returned from a game at Notts County, leaving Gary Simpson, his friend. Keith died as a result of a brain bleed from a long standing condition, having only returned to work two weeks before. Richard's heart went out to Gary, who was juggling personal grief with the media and trying to lift the team up. They needed to stay up for Keith. Flowers and tributes were pouring into Moss Rose, Richard and teammates were fighting back the tears, and fans' reactions brought home what a big part Keith played in their lives. A book of condolence was opened with photos of Keith, and floral tributes from fans were displayed on the London Road terraces. On the evening of his passing, England played a friendly match against Egypt when all the England players wore black armbands as a tribute to Keith.

211 Macclesfield fans travelled to the Hereford match. The players came out for their warm-up in tops inscribed 'Rest In Peace, Gaffer' which they threw into the crowd. A minute's silence was held before the match. At the end of the match, both players and directors went to the Macclesfield fans and home fans remaining to applaud. On this day, at matches from the Premier League down to Coca-Cola league 2, all players wore black armbands, as did some of the match officials. There was a minute's silence held at some of the games while others applauded a fantastic manager and great friend in the footballing world.

I thought it would be nice to put this into in our son's own words. Richard struggled to contain his emotions in his heart-wrenching tribute to Keith Alexander admitting; "I loved him to bits. I am still struggling to take it all in because when I left him, he was absolutely fine. Looking back I thought maybe I should have been looking for signs that something was not right, but honestly, there was nothing wrong. I was totally stunned and shocked to hear the news ... That's what makes this so hard, because it was out of the blue, and it's so sad he simply knew how to get the best out of me, as he did with all the players ... His man-management was exceptional, but he was a friend, too, and having travelled with him daily to Macclesfield, there would never be any awkward silence ... The best times I had as a player were under him, and it's funny, because we both agreed that our playoff years at Lincoln were the best of our careers. He took them to the playoffs four times in a row. He was regarded as one of Lincoln's most successful bosses, and was the sport's first full-time black manager. Keith Alexander transformed the club and the finances after they had been plunged into administration."

Our son's last loan game for Macclesfield came in at 1–1 draw at Accrington. He was denied any further part for this season at least. As Macclesfield was moving a point clear of Sutton's Imps, now fourth from bottom, he had to go back from his loan spell. Richard left Macclesfield, but Gary told him he would be back soon. They were both still trying to get their heads around Keith's death, and would have to prepare themselves for Keith's funeral. He was such a massive loss to them both and to Lincoln City and Macclesfield football club.

Manager Chris Sutton was trying to force Richard out as cheaply as possible. By having him running endlessly around the field he almost made him crack under the strain. The desperation and huge downer had seen him apply to the fire service because Chris Sutton had all but extinguished the spirit that had seen him make it, against all the odds, in the game in the first place. The advice from his trusted group of friends and family suggested he wait patiently until the club made the right offer. Lincoln agreed a hefty pay-off that was sufficient to allow him to go to Macclesfield on almost a third of his Lincoln contract.

Plans were being made for Keith's funeral at Lincoln City Cathedral; the football world was united in mourning as it bid farewell to Keith Alexander. A catalogue of stars joined friends and family of the Macclesfield Town Manager at a packed funeral service in Lincoln Cathedral. Thousands of well-wishers were lining the surrounding streets. The hugely popular Alexander made history as one of Britain's first black managers. Keith was a role model for many black players in the modern game. It is a legacy to be proud of. Keith Alexander, alongside assistant manager Gary Simpson, had the ability to form a fantastic side, and their ability to help the players gel was no accident; they worked extremely hard on the chemistry to bring the team together not just as players but as friends too, on and off the field. He will be sorely missed, but through his memories in those young men he chose as his canvas and many people whose lives he touched—his spirit will live on. Manager now Gary Simpson continues to wear his yellow socks in Keith's memory.

With the sad loss of Keith, Richard went back to Lincoln City. Gary and Macclesfield wanted him, but their budget could not stretch to a grand a week, Sutton's previous annual income. Gary Simpson would rebuild our son's confidence again when he rejoined Macclesfield on just £700 a week; this was less than half the money Richard was used to, but he weighed up his options for the future. Although he had been offered more money elsewhere, he was looking to the future for life after football. In doing his physio course and being able to play football at the same time, our son started studying at Salford University. We would visit Richard often and the things he would come out with were so funny. He would dance round the house telling you about every bone and muscle in his body. He really was learning fast and was so enjoying his time at Salford University.

Reunited again with manager Gary Simpson, Richard's words were, "I'm only 29, so I think I've got a fair bit of playing time left. But it's true that you start looking to life after football, and I've been taking a physiotherapy course at Salford University. I am in the first year of a four-year course. Whilst I have got one eye on that as a career in the game after finishing playing, I'm still focused on getting out on the pitch.

"If I take care of myself, there is no reason why I can't still be playing at the end of the course, or even a couple of years beyond that. When you're in your late twenties and you get an injury, people will usually try and blame it on you getting older, but it's no different than something you could pick up at 20-21. Really, either way you need to work hard and get on with getting fit again ... watching a game is certainly easier than playing. You see so much more of the game; it makes it very easy to see where you might think that other people might have done something wrong or made the wrong decision. But you know that when you're down there, it's not as simple as that. The only highlight of being injured is that I got to watch Jeff Stelling on Sky Sports.

"If we lost, I would keenly look out for the other score lines in the hope they had gone our way. It's so important that you stay fit and mentally strong when injured and also try and support your team as best you can from the side lines, even though it's frustrating."

It's so nice for us, Richard's mother and father, to put things in the book in our son's own words and thoughts on the game and his life. I think it helps people see the way our son thought and what he was thinking at certain times in his career, and also the heartaches he felt.

He always found Christmas a great time of the year, a family time which he so missed out on due to his career, because around this time games are coming through thick and fast. There is one song that sticks in my mind. Richard always sang to me when he was driving home for Christmas. The song was, "I am driving home for Christmas," and he used to phone on his way home, using hands-free, mind, to say "Mum is the turkey on?" He used to be playing the song full blast singing along to it to me. I know Keith and Simmo used to find our son's taste in music a refreshing change compared to other young footballers as it was 50s and 60s; the sort of music they liked to hear. Richard once said Keith could not believe how he knew all the words to these great old songs. They were a throwback to his Teddy Boy days, when we used to take him and Glenn to the Jets concerts.

28/12/2010 The last game we saw our son play in was at Oxford United v. Macclesfield Town when he gave me a late Christmas gift. He said "Sorry, Mum, didn't have time to wrap it," with that Richard Butcher smile that could fill so many hearts. Christmas was always a special but unique time for us as a family—given his professional commitments. We really did love Macclesfield Town; we so loved the family atmosphere the club could bring. We had been up to see Richard just before Christmas, but the snow was really bad, so we were a bit later than usual to do the normal routine. We still treated him like a child at Christmas, putting his presents in a row. He so loved Christmas and took us shopping around Manchester to buy some gifts for the family.

At Macclesfield Town our son began the season as a regular starter before two knee injuries saw him out of action from the end of August until December, either side of a short return in October.

Richard's professionalism shone through once more and he was rated by most as the fittest player at the club and was desperate to return to action to win his way back into the side before Christmas. Although his final match in a home game was against Rotherham, his final goal came the match before. As always there was a touch of the spectacular as he fired a crisp volley during an away game on the 01/01/2011 trip to Bury at Gigg Lane which ended 2–2. Richard was popular around the clubs as a player and teammate; he was a powerful Athletic midfielder who had a knack of scoring spectacular goals.

On the topic of our son's knee injuries: yes, on that day Richard had phoned us early in the morning as his little dog Charlie had also hurt his leg going for a wee. I remarked that it was as if he had come out in sympathy. He took him to the vet's, only to phone again later to say he had done his other knee in training. We could not believe it and nor could Richard.

On the evening of Sunday 9th January, 2011 Richard rang us, his parents. In truth, he always found it easier to talk to us when walking the dog or when he was by himself having a bit of quiet time. He spoke to his dad at length, putting the football world to rights as they always did, and discussing the Macclesfield team that just seemed to need a bit of luck to fulfil its potential. My son then spoke to me, his Mum, about everyday life, and said he had just finished his course work set for January. He was pleased about finishing—that he was keeping on top of things and seemed happy.

Never taking football for granted, our son wanted something to go into, as he felt he had maybe 2 or 3 years left to make some money from the playing side of the game. He had only been able to afford to take the contract offered by Macclesfield due to his payoff at Lincoln; the only time he had done so in his entire career. Peterborough had seen him go against agent Richard Cody's financial advice since he chose to play as opposed to waiting it out for a payoff.

Richard was also keen to find out how his brother was settling. He was in the process of moving into a house and, of course, we were helping Glenn to set things up so Richard was looking forward to getting down to see the place finished, Richard had looked at the house on the internet to give his approval. He finished off by saying, "I love you, Mum, goodnight. I'll talk to you tomorrow." But I never knew what was going to confront me and my family the very next day. Our son sounded happy; he never said he felt unwell. His brother Glenn had called in to see us and was going to phone his brother later that evening but it was late; he said "I will phone him tomorrow," not realising he would never get that chance to speak to him again.

I remember, though, it was really strange that evening, as our dog Rex seemed really unsettled and was constantly whining, almost as if he knew something was wrong. He kept looking at me and whining, which is not like him. He had me in and out of bed. If only I sensed something was wrong; but how could I?

On the 10th January 2011 Richard did not appear at training, and with no answer on his mobile phone, life-friend Gary Simpson called Ben Futcher, who lived just around the corner from our son. Ben went round to find his car in the drive and Charlie, the dog, yelping and barking. Ben alerted the police, who had to break in, and then he had the harrowing job of identifying our son once the paramedics had gone through the formalities that confirmed the tragic loss. The official time of death is logged by the paramedics at 14.15 on the 10th January.

Lifelong friend and mentor, Gary Simpson, takes us through the events as they unfolded:

As the day unfolded you just knew something was up. If it had been traffic, he would have rung; if it had been any problems, he would have rung me. I started ringing every 20 minutes during the training session, then tried Futch (Ben Futcher), and finally got hold of him as we were preparing for home. Ben lives just round the corner from Butch, and when I asked him if he had seen him he replied, 'Yes, just the day before, and he seemed his normal self, but I'll pop round to put everyone's minds at rest.'

Ben rang me and told me he was there; the curtains were closed; the car was there and his dog was barking like mad. I told him to smash a window, but he couldn't find anything so he said he would ring the police.

It took an age, and I had already dropped Hammy and Wedge back and was back in Sheffield when I got the call from Futch. In the pit of my stomach I was expecting the worst the longer it had gone on, for he would have been in contact earlier, otherwise. Butch and I had formed a great bond. Some even reckoned he was like me—teacher's pet. But Futch's tone and emotions gave it away straight away. The police had broken in, gone upstairs to find him lying in bed and had called the emergency services. Poor Futch had to identify his mate's body. That's got to be hard to deal with. It was so hard to get your head round. It was like numbness, as Butch had been the fittest lad I had ever come across, and his physique looked like it had been chiselled from marble. It hit home that if this could happen to Butch, it could happen to anyone. Coz Richard lived life and ate right, determined to put his career first, because fitness was the biggest part to his natural box-to-box game.

That is what hit the players, and that it could happen to any of them. Butch was not only a nice kid, but he worked hard to stay at a peak, and that meant he was first or at the forefront in terms of fitness within the Mac squad at the time. So it shocked all the lads, and made it harder to lift them, than when the Gaffer died just 10 months earlier. Then, there was a unity and a determination to do it for him. But having lost one of their own, and in the way it happened, it was harder for them and for me to get our heads round it, and it would take longer for everyone to take it on board and respond.

Richard's Mum Gail:

It was the most shocking experience of my life. When I heard of our son's death I was standing in Richard's brother's house, cleaning up as you do. The call came early afternoon, I answered the phone, it was his wife; her only words were, 'are you alone?' I said, 'yes,' she just said, 'Richard is dead.' There was a pause, then it hit me, I screamed and called her a liar, then ran frantically around the house not knowing what to do. I ran to the car… kept telling myself it's not true… I got to Carlsberg and asked them to get Richard's dad and brother… but all the time not believing what had happened. We all jumped in the car still not wanting to believe a word. We then raced around to tell the family… my mum threw herself on the floor… calling for Richard, and yet I stood there not knowing what to do. The media soon put it out on the TV before all the family knew… as we went back home and raced off to Manchester. There was an accident on the way which held us up, too. We understand the media were doing their job, but this caused extra distress and pain to our family.

The situation was made worse by the media, with half the family having to go into overdrive to tell the rest of our nearest and dearest quickly, so they wouldn't find out second hand via the TV and radio who deliver the headlines with speculation even in the absence of the full facts and showing no regard for our family's feelings. Half of our family found out via the media circus.

The drive up to Manchester to see our son's body was hell. I kept thinking, It's all a lie, he's going to phone me in a minute. Please God, don't let it be. My phone kept ringing. I don't want to talk to anyone why are they ringing me? I remember the silence between all three of us—the cold and disbelief and denial—this is not happening. How his dad drove to Manchester I will never know to this day. I was told that people had already been on the internet chat sites trying to guess what my son died of, and were giving their thoughts, on which some remarks were not very nice, yet some were passing on their sorrow. It was all too fast and all too quick. I couldn't even put the radio on, or the TV. I didn't want to believe any of it.

I was trembling and shaking, the emotion still as fresh as the tears that were streaming down my cheeks. The rain was pouring down as we all sat in silence on that agonising, long, long drive from Northampton, none of us wanting to believe what had happened.

On arrival, no one could believe it as the nightmare continued when we went in to see Richard. He lay there, so still, looking so beautiful. My heart was bursting, wishing him to wake up, so perfect he looked. I kissed his head and told him I loved him, still believing he would wake up any minute. His dad and his brother found it so hard to hold back the tears, his beautiful son, and brother to Glenn. They both embraced Richard still not believing what had happened.

I noticed he had put the new pyjamas on I had bought him for Christmas—a fresh white top with gray trimmings and gray trousers. We fell apart when we saw his lifeless body, our son's normal joking jolly self completely drained away. As a child Richard used to pretend he was dead as a joke, but it really hit us that there was to be no 'just messing about Mum, sorry' as our son, just 29 years, old slept in peace. Upon arrival at our son's Swinton home, where he had died overnight in his sleep, his clothes and shoes were everywhere strewn over the house; his car sat in the drive, but there was no evidence of a break-in or suspicious death. It was at this point that reality started to set in. Not wishing to open up the agony for all parties, but here is where our grieving process began to be interrupted. Not being classed as the next of kin, due to Richard marrying just seven months earlier, there is a horrendous 'one step removed' nature to the grieving process for so many parents and siblings under UK law. Our son was so young, he wasn't 50 or 60. He hadn't been married 20 or 30 years like us, his parents. With tears streaming down my cheeks to this day when discussing my lovely boy, I try to convey what can best be described as a harrowing journey.

All of a sudden you realise you have no say in what happens to your son, a part of you for almost three decades, cradle to—well not even grave. No one could give us answers to questions; even at the hospital, talks were held with the coroners with no involvement from us, his parents. All of a sudden we were in a stranger's house, where no one seemed to have the time or authorisation to answer our questions. It comes across as if they don't care, although they cannot. We hated having to leave our son for one minute, but after two days of torment we returned to Northampton still unable to properly grieve.

When our son was moved to Lincoln all three of us, Richard's brother Glenn, Mum and Dad, stayed in a hotel together for the three weeks before the funeral. We were offered the chance to stay in a house that was up for sale but it wasn't very inviting; we just wanted to be with Richard every minute so we could try and make some sense out of what had happened. I couldn't leave him for a minute although we weren't allowed to stay with Richard all day; so many people wanted to see him and say goodbye, our time was limited. We would wander around Lincoln in between our visits not knowing what to do, unable to eat anything for feeling sick and so ill with the news our family seemed so far away.

The family followed the day after Richard was moved to Lincoln, to stay for a night to say their goodbyes to our son, but even the funeral arrangements almost passed us by, too, even down to not being able as a mother to have flowers on my son's coffin; and I was taken to the florist to pick some flowers but the shock of them not being put on his coffin was too much to bear. As a mother and father it's very difficult having to step back from the one you love so much, not being able to choose the clothes he wore, or to be able to talk about him at his private ceremony as a family. His childhood and dreams were all dismissed—where he came from—where he grew up. As a Mother, you reach out for your son; your heart is wrenched in every direction. That maternal instinct moves in more than ever. He was our baby, our boy. We brought him up for 29 years. We needed to be close to him, touch him, kiss him, to try and make some sense out of what had happened, and every small detail and word that was spoken meant so much to us.

With Richard's 30th birthday coming up Macclesfield arranged a tribute which coincided with their next home game. The club kindly let off 30 doves, yet it still seemed to be for someone else, as we could not get our heads round what had happened, let alone believe it was our son that had gone. All I could think of was, *I was meant to be at my son's now with him celebrating this day*. Macclesfield were so kind to all the family; they looked after us so well.

Manchester police had phoned us on a couple of occasions to ask about our family history; there are no sudden deaths in the family.

The Forensic Toxicology and Medical Reports by the Coroner also failed to deliver any closure to our son's death, which was concluded to be one of natural causes. The alcohol levels were miniscule (13mg), there were traces of acetone too, but that would have had more to do with Richard's low fat diet which was so central to his fitness regime. Our son had suffered a collapse in 2009 one Saturday evening while out with friends, during his third stint at Lincoln, but he was discharged and told he could go back to playing football the following Friday. Although a slightly enlarged heart was found, this was natural for a sports person to have. The report does make mention (by Richard's wife) that our son had experienced fourteen months of chest pains, and that he had coughed up phlegm every morning, which would sometimes contain blood. However, the medical experts did not find any scarring suggesting that this could have led to Richard's sudden and premature death. There was no scar tissue found on our son's heart to suggest this at all. There were no blockages to the main arteries to the heart. Our son's heart was sent to London and Sheffield for seven months of tests; nothing was found wrong. If you had a slight heart attack without knowing there would have been scar tissue damage shown on the heart; there was none.

It was mentioned in one of the reports that Richard's lungs were very heavy and this is not found in sudden cardiac deaths; however, this has been seen in similar previous cases to this, where the patient has suddenly died of swine flu.

All I know is, call it mother's instinct if you like, if Richard had suffered with chest pains there is no way mentally he would have been able to keep it to himself; he would have told someone if he was worried about anything like that. He was that sort of person, a worrier; he would not have been able to continue playing football with that worry on his mind. He was very close to us, his parents, and Lincoln City manager Gary Simpson. Richard would have been checked at every club he played for; you have to pass a medical and for the number of years Richard played professional football something would have been picked up. They are checked more times than an average person would be in their lifetime. It's really difficult when the media say he had a rare heart condition; it was so rare they couldn't find anything wrong with him.

Richard had certainly been ill in the run up to the tragic events, as he revealed in the regular phone calls he made to us his parents. It is well known that professional footballers have long received a flu jab to prepare them for the winter months. Some say they are told they have to have this done, or if they are ill they will lose a week's wage, but at the time of our son's death this had been replaced by an annual combined swine flu and flu inoculation; so I was told by my son. I expressed my concerns to him and was very upset that he had this done because of what I had heard about the vaccine. This was also mentioned by www.telegraph.co.uk on the 20th September 2010.

Richard had called us the morning after his latest jab and he certainly sounded very rough. He told me that he had the swine flu and flu jab combined. Not one for man flu, he said that he had a real rough night and had been shaking so badly in bed that he had thought about calling an ambulance. Against my advice he still intended to go into training to 'run it off', even though two of his teammates were too ill to face training, one of them being Paul Morgan. I said, "Please don't go into training like that. You sound so poorly." He said, "I will be okay, Mum. I will run it off." Richard, being Richard, would never have missed training—not for anything. Six weeks later, after having the vaccination around November 24th 2010, our son had died on January 10th 2011.

I don't know if this had something to do with our son's death, I just want to find out why our beautiful son, so healthy, so fit, just died. We have no answer as to why this happened, and this is something we have to live with for the rest of our lives. There are no reports of sudden death in our family. All grandparents have lived well into their 80s, even 90s. It has taken me two and half years to pluck the courage up to read the report myself. It really is not a nice thing to have to do to read about your son in that manner. I have since written to the coroners asking if they can re-open my son's case, as they keep slides up to ten years.

I also wrote a letter to the Attorney General and received a letter back from them advising me that if I want my son's case reopened I have to apply to the High Courts. I also have to have the Attorney General's consent; they advised me that the coroners may oppose my application and if they do I could be liable for my costs as well as theirs if I was refused by the coroners for the case to be reopened into my son's death. It all depends on whether you have any new evidence to support your application. I just wish at the time of Richards death I had found the courage and strength to have attended the coroner's hearing in Bolton so I could have said more about how I felt regarding the outcome of their report as it is something I don't agree with and will always be unhappy with. But with the media attention surrounding Richard's death, it wasn't really very private and my emotions were running so high.

Richard did seem to work through his bout of illness after having the vaccine, but there have been recorded instances, though rare, that suggest fatalities have occurred when too much of the vaccine gets into the bloodstream, as might happen with an athlete when training. The process can then lead to the shutdown of the muscles, of which the heart is one, with cases of people dying in their sleep; another unanswered question that keeps us from some kind of closure. Millions turned down the vaccination because they were concerned that it had not been fully tested; at the time there were possible links to narcolepsy, a rare condition which causes people to fall asleep suddenly (www.telegraph.co.uk).

We were told Ben Futcher, a very good friend of our son's, identified Richard, and this must have been so hard for him to do. We are so grateful his best friend could be there for him, and we know this was something he will never forget, and it will live with him for the rest of his life. They were great friends. And manager Gary Simpson, it was a massive shock to him, as he was like a second dad to our son. Simmo thought the world of him. We are very grateful that he has kept in contact with us throughout and has been a massive support to us both. It's really difficult to say, but, as a mother and father, we had to chase up where our son's death had been registered. We didn't even have a copy of his death certificate sent to us.

Once we got a copy months later, it said Richard had a potential abnormal conductive pathway but there were no signs or proof of this at all. They said it's like looking for a needle in a haystack. Everything came back inconclusive.

The years go past, but it always seems like weeks to us as parents; people move on, but we can't move on. We never will; we need to know why our son died. Any parent will tell you it doesn't matter how many years go by; the loss always seems like yesterday. We have family and friends who have also lost a child also, and I do find some comfort alongside them in some strange way, because they do know how we feel, and they can relate to all I have to say. They don't look at me as being strange, as they can relate to what I am saying.

We thank Chairman Mike Rance and Andy Scott along with everyone at Macclesfield football club who have shown us so much respect since our son's passing. Andy Scott kindly sent a tree to our home for us to plant in Richard's memory. It really is lovely; it flowers in January. Keith's son Matt Alexander also came to see us at the hotel while we spent three weeks in Lincoln.

We could not leave our son for one minute. I had to stay in Lincoln to be with him. The Macclesfield staff and players had a collection for us, to help with the three weeks' hotel bill. We had been advised to contact the PFA, but we were told they had never come across this before, so we didn't call again. We wanted to spend every precious minute we could with our son.

The last day we saw Richard before his funeral was so precious. He was laid out at the funeral director's just behind Lincoln City football club. We could hear people passing by when leaving the football ground. We kissed him and put our arms around him to tell him we love him. It broke our heart to have to leave him. Upon leaving the funeral director, we were told one of the cars had been cancelled, which was meant to take Richard's grandparents from Lincoln City football club to the crematorium. I got back to the hotel and phoned them all, as I was worried about them finding their way around when leaving the football ground.

About 1,000 people were at the memorial service at Lincoln City Football Club ground at Sincil Bank. They had come from all over to pay their last respects to Richard. We left the hotel that morning and a car picked us up. Our son, Glenn, stayed at the football ground and we, Richard's mum and dad, would leave from our son's house in Lincoln, and would follow the hearse. I could see the hearse waiting and my heart sank, still not believing what had happened.

Richard's brother Glenn would wait at the ground ready to help carry his brother alongside Richard's football friends, and Manager Gary Simpson, and physio Keith Oakes. We arrived at the ground and my heart sank as the coffin was taken from the hearse. I noticed my flowers were not on the top of the coffin. I was heartbroken; there was no room for my small wreath. We followed the coffin into the ground, and we were overwhelmed with the amount of people who had come to say their good-byes.

The service at the ground was lovely with everyone talking about Richard's career and what a lovely lad he was. We were so overwhelmed I just couldn't look at anyone. I still didn't want to believe what was happening. We then moved onto the crematorium with the hope everyone would follow as they were all close friends of our son at some point in his career, and some had travelled such a long way.

I am sorry if people were put off coming to the private service. It really is not what we wanted, and nor would Richard. On arrival at the crematorium I so hoped everyone would follow. The service began and I just stared at the coffin still thinking this is just a bad dream; I will wake up soon, and it will be all over. I really felt lost— no mention of Richard growing up and his life before football, or even us, his mum and dad. I was heartbroken. It was like I didn't even know or feel a part of my son's life. In one verse that stood out in my mind was that my son had been transferred from our family to another. My family were so upset; some had to be held back as the service went on, so I was told afterwards. When your child passes away and you have spent every waking hour looking after their every need, it's very difficult to take a step back. Somehow you feel like you don't belong and you're on the outside looking in and you're looking at a child you once knew; he's gone, he's not there anymore to answer your question or to have an opinion to tell you what he feels. If your child falls, as a parent you're always there to pick them, up no matter how old they are. It's so hard to let go; the truth is you never do.   Even to play the CDs we listened to when we used to travel up on our visits I find so hard. I hope one day we will be able to return as we have so many great memories of our time spent with Richard in the place we called our second home. Everyday life is difficult; at certain times we would have travelled to see Richard and would have spent time with him but when you live year to year without that routine and you don't get to spend that special time together as a family anymore you can't just replace it with something else. There will always be a great hole in our hearts and that routine will always be missing from our lives. Richard's brother Glenn will always feel like something is missing, not having big brother to have a chat with, or to take his daughter Elise to visit. Richard would have been so proud of her.

I really thought the service was lovely at the football ground. They could not have done Richard any prouder, but the private service should have been about Richard's whole life I thought at first, maybe it's just me thinking in this way; but many people talked to me afterward and felt the same. I look at photos of our children growing up and the fun times we had but it's like a snapshot of time itself; where did that life go? Was it real? Did it really happen?

It's like looking into a looking glass back at a life you once knew. Richard was our son before a footballer, just a young beautiful boy who grew up into a fantastic funny and kind young man.

Many a time we have been told we need to talk to someone like a counsellor. My husband tried and so did Richard's brother Glenn to try and come to terms with our son's death but it didn't help; the one thing they can't say is "I can make it better, here you go, here's your son and your life back", because that's what you want to do, to go back in time and to have your life all over again and to see that funny boy once again that made you smile and laugh and hugged you and loved you and made you feel so special and privileged to be his parent.

We thank Lincoln City FC for allowing the funeral to take place at their club. They did a fantastic job and Richard would have been so proud. And Fran (Fran Martin) was so very helpful and kind. We would like to thank the many people that attended the funeral. You were more than welcome to come to the crematorium as most people had travelled such a long way. So many of you were great friends of our son at some point in his life or through his football journey that saw him realise his dream.

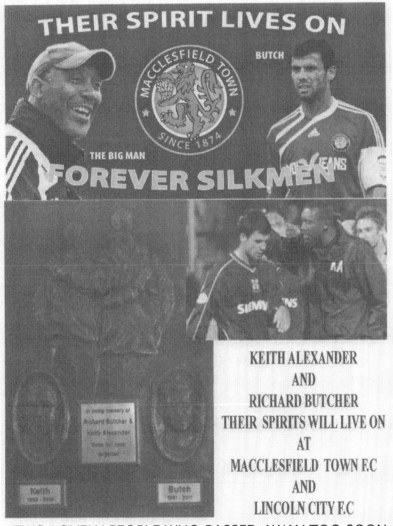

TWO LOVELY PEOPLE WHO PASSED AWAY TOO SOON
GOD BLESS THEM BOTH

We are so proud of the fans' flag that flies high in Richard and Keith's memory, not to mention the portraits, and the plaques that hang at Lincoln City and Macclesfield Town. The 30 white doves that were released on our son's 30th birthday were lovely, but things didn't really feel that real because it still felt at the time that they must be for someone else. The treatment we received from Macclesfield Town was outstanding; words cannot express how we feel. Thank you to all the football clubs that Richard played for, for sending flowers on the day in his memory, and a player from each club came to represent their club. Our son's uncle Steven proudly represented Northampton Town and placed the flowers on the pitch. And thank you for all the letters and cards that were sent and the book of condolences. We thank the fans for their kind messages; we are so very sorry we didn't get to read them as there were difficulties behind the scenes.

Our return back to Northampton was the hardest thing we have ever had to do, leaving behind our life with Richard. You step in the door still waiting for the phone to ring, the football matches carry on just the same; names pop up of football friends of our son's on the TV. You hear their names, but not Richard's any more. The phone stops ringing ... the silence is unbearable; you decide to go for a walk but people cross the road to avoid talking to you ... The world carries on in the fast lane, but you stand still just waiting for that text or the phone to ring to say, "Hi Mum and Hi, Dad." The waiting to hear if Richard's coming home to be laid to rest; life goes on for others, but 'we' stand still. The word that is used so often is that you need to move on, like you have just buried your .... The thing is, as any parent knows, you will never move on from losing a child. They are 'you', a 'part' of you, like a jigsaw puzzle that can never be fixed. Every birthday, every Christmas, we miss him so much. Someone kindly asked does it get easier with time? And my answer was, "No, it never will. It will always be like yesterday, no matter how hard we try."

But we can be proud, especially of the Kettering, Macclesfield and Lincoln City and many other clubs our son played for where Richard will live on. How lucky are we to at least have that, as many others don't. He made us so proud to be his parents, and he made his brother so proud, too. Northampton and Lincoln's funeral directors arranged for Richard's homecoming, along with his wife who brought him home with her family and friends; because Richard had only been married for just seven months and was only just twenty nine years old, being Richard's parents we wanted our son home, as he had no children and it would have been a long way for us to travel as we got older to visit his grave if Richard had stayed in Lincoln.

The things you think about when losing a child are so alien; normally they would be burying you but when it's the other way round you choose your grave alongside them, which feels so strange having to think like that. It's not natural having to do that.

Richard's football kit was buried with our son, only signed by his great friend Gary Simpson. Before our son finally arrived home to his resting place seven months after his death, photos of family and Keith Alexander were also laid to rest with him, as well as personal letters and cards telling him how much we love him.

Even the burial was in two stages with us, Richard's family, having to pay our respects after the grave had been filled in Father George, with whom our son had spent a lot of time through growing up, blessed the ground. Prayers and music were played in the open air. Richard's brother chose 'Tears in Heaven' and his dad chose 'Bring Him Home'. Flowers were laid, and candles were lit and left burning all night. A pair of football boots I bought specially for the grave, with our son's name on, stood proudly in the centre. A photo of each football club he played for lay elegantly around his grave to show what a great career he had, and the lovely white ornamental doves sat proudly on top to represent Macclesfield Town as they released them for his 30th birthday.

The lack of closure and unanswered questions only continues for us, with official bodies (with far more powerfully-funded solicitors than we the family have the financial backing or wherewithal to take issue with) who are unable or unwilling to explain the actions and undertakings subsequent to the death of one so young.

A few months later a shoe box arrived. Inside was a ring I had bought Richard's dad at the age of fifteen. I had bought him a new one, and our son asked if he could have it. He wore the ring in every match he played in, and would kiss it before every game. There was a watch I bought Richard when he first joined Lincoln City, to congratulate him on getting his first league contract. The watch had stopped working. I had just had it mended just before Richard died. He was so pleased, as the watch meant so much to him. There were also two gold pens I had bought for him with his name initialled on them.

Glenn, Richard's brother, was asked to travel to Lincoln to collect a box with some of his brother's things in it. On his arrival the box was placed in his car. No cuppa was offered by the player who was to pass these over to him, so he just jumped back in the car and returned straight back home. His heart was broken. All these items were put neatly in what was Richard's room. We can't bring ourselves to look at them even to this day, but I will never part with them.

Richard's father also suffered a heart attack in 2013, leading to a triple bypass; this had no connection to our son's death. The problems that Richard's dad suffered would have been undoubtedly found in the first autopsy if our son had suffered with the same problem. The Doctors at Harefield reassured us there was no connection after filling them in with our family history and Richard's death.

The scars clearly show even over the years. As a parent it never leaves you, it never goes away. It's like a cancer that just keeps building up and eats away at you bit by bit. It's so easy to trick people for a few hours with a smile and to look happy because that's what others want to see. Then you shut your door and go to bed, and it's always in your head. You try to sleep. You toss and turn within the hope it's just all been a bad dream.

The fantastic little club Macclesfield Town retired Richard's squad number 21 as a mark of respect for their former midfielder. They wanted a way to ensure that our son's memory lives on, explained the club chairman Mike Rance. So, since our son's death, no player has ever been given the No 21 shirt, and Richard's name continues to appear on Macclesfield's official website and Match Day programmes. There is also a plaque and wall-to-wall portrait at Macclesfield Town in memory of Richard and Keith Alexander. And a plaque is proudly mounted on the wall at Lincoln City's football club.

A memory shared by Paul Morgan:

When Butch left Lincoln for Oldham I missed my weekly rendezvous. But then, lucky for Macclesfield Town FC, Butch signed for them where I was now playing. I managed to talk Butch into going to University to study physio, which I had been doing for the past 3 years, convincing him that he would need something to fall back on after football, but mainly so I could meet up with him at the coffee bar in Uni to talk old times! Not a day passes without thinking about Butch. He was more than a team mate, he was a friend.

Richard's Mum Gail:

Former Lincoln City player Gary Taylor-Fletcher also paid tribute to our son. He was seen by millions after scoring Blackpool's opener in their encounter with Kenny Dalglish's Liverpool side. It was instrumental in the Tangerines 2–1 victory and the midfielder dedicated his goal to his friend. The two played alongside each other for the two seasons at Lincoln City. Gary and Richard always had a bit of banter between them as my son supported Everton and Gary supports Liverpool. It was so kind of Gary Taylor-Fletcher to dedicate his goal to him. He would have been so very proud. Gary's T-shirt said 'for Butch U Blues'. He would have definitely smiled at that.

Gary Simpson speaks of his loss:

I was closer to Richard than any other player I've worked with. I was the one who first spotted him playing in non-league and convinced the big man to give him his chance at Lincoln. So to lose both of them in the space of ten months is extremely hard to take. He was like a son to me, and I'd kept in touch with him throughout his career, and, of course, was delighted to get him to come to the Moss Rose in the summer. As a manager, I felt he was all you could ask for. He had everything a modern-day footballer should have: a good engine, an eye for goal, fully-committed, and an overriding desire to win games of football.

If anything, and we spoke together about this on many occasions, he was probably too nice. With that extra bit of aggression I have no doubt he could have played at the highest level. But that was also one of his strengths. He was just a great lad, and it has been a pleasure to have worked with him over the years. I'm just so glad he signed off at Bury with a goal, and it means a lot to me that he ran over to the bench to celebrate.

You couldn't ask for a better professional than Butch. He was a great person, and a great role model for the younger lads, and it's an understatement to say that he leaves a massive void in our lives. My heart goes out to his parents, brother, and family.

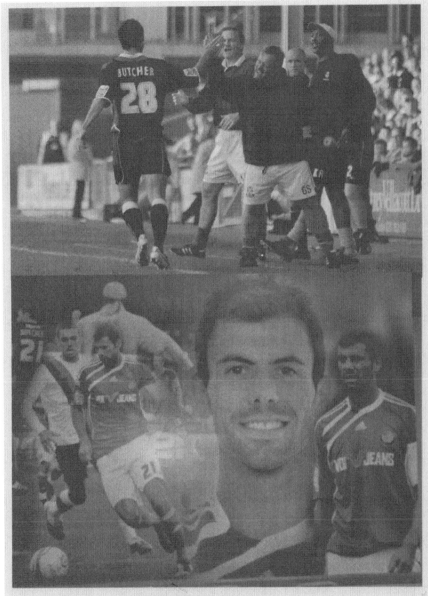

GREAT FRIEND GARY SIMPSON ABOVE AND PORTRAIT OF RICHARD BUTCHER
AT MACCLESFIELD TOWN FOOTBALL CLUB

Richard's Mum Gail:

There's one thing I would like to say in this book and that is how important the lower league clubs are to the league itself. What would life be like without them? Never mind your championship clubs or premiership clubs, whose wage bills are far too big in my opinion, when we have clubs like Northampton Town, Lincoln City, and Macclesfield who struggle week in and week out.

I have to take my hat off to people like Andy Scott and Mike Rance who have worked so hard for the love of Macclesfield Town and who place their hands in their own pockets with their hard-earned money to keep their club alive.

And then there are managers like Gary Simpson who, I know, burns the candle at both ends. He runs around night and day to try to unearth a football gem on shoe string wages. But he does it for the love of Lincoln City as he did at Macclesfield Town. Some of the wages these managers are on are no bigger than an electrician or a plumber or less. The same with the players, but when you get a manager like Gary Simpson come after you to give you that big break, snap it up, because you never know where it might lead.

You don't put the money first if you want a chance in a career in football. You have to start somewhere to get your lucky break, because there really isn't loads of money to be had early on in your career, but you still can earn a living from something you enjoy doing. You have to establish yourself in a regular first-team spot to help you get noticed, and to help keep your foot in the game, or you can easily slip by the wayside. There are a lot of players that get released every year and they are all looking for a new clubs. These clubs have to survive and, with the fans support and all the hard-working staff behind the scenes, we have to remember they really do go beyond their port of call.

Richard often followed my cousin Paul's career with pride as he also once played for Macclesfield Town. Football can take you to such wonderful places. Early on in our son's career he too looked into going further afield to carry on his career if things hadn't worked out for him. Paul was an inspiration to Richard because of what he had achieved; it's nice to show the younger generation how far a football life can take you and the great distance that can become between you and your family.

Paul Wright had the pleasure of playing for Macclesfield Town under coach Sammy McIlroy, but left after one season after being offered a scholarship to play in the United States and this is what he went on to achieve: In Central Connecticut State University men's soccer Paul was back for his fifth season as the team's assistant coach in 2010. His job and responsibilities include recruitment, player development, scouting, and various administrative duties. Prior to joining the Blue Devil staff, he starred for CCSU from 1995-98, and had been coaching high school and club soccer since 2000. He also had been playing professionally in both the US and Spain. As a player under Green, Paul was a two-time All-Mid-Continent-Conference performer as well as an All-New England honouree twice. He also tied the NCAA single game record for goals, scoring eight against Maryland-Eastern Shore in 1995. He added an assist in that Blue Devil victory, setting a CCSU single-game record with 17 points. He also ranks third in the program record book for single season points (50, 1996), second for single season goals (23, 1996) and tied for eighth in single season goals (14, 1995 and 1997). After graduating from Central in 1999 with a Bachelor of Science in Exercise Science and Health Promotion, Paul played for three seasons with the Western Massachusetts Pioneers. The Pioneers were National Champions in Paul's first season and went to the semi-finals the following year. He continued his professional career with the Philadelphia Kixx of the Major Indoor Soccer League in 2002, reaching the league finals in his only season.

A native of the Rock of Gibraltar, Paul divided his time playing professionally with coaching stints for the boys' soccer programs at Plainville High and Maloney High. He was also the Director of Coaching for Wethersfield youth soccer. Paul holds a USSF 'A' license, the highest coaching license offered in the U.S. He is coaching youth soccer and is currently the boys director of the olympic development program in the state of connecticut. Paul lives in West Hartford with his wife, Emily, and sons, Liam and Freddie.

RICHARD BUTCHER, MACCLESFIELD TOWN F.C
WE KINDLY THANK MACCLESFIELD TOWN, PETER HILTON
& MEDIA TEAM FOR USE OF PHOTOS

Mike Rance, Chairman, Macclesfield Town F.C:

The season had been a challenging one at Moss Rose as the Silkmen finally succeeded in returning to the conference football after a 15-year stay up in the football league. In the small hours, between long days attempting to plan a bigger stage, I simply can't help dwelling on the thoughts of 'might have been'. How would things have turned out if Richard had been around to set the perfect example for our talented but inexperienced squad? When Richard agreed to join the Silkmen I was delighted from the first day of training. Disciplined on and off the pitch, he set the tone and he was a role model for the younger players, exemplifying just how they should set out to make the very most of their talents.

Richard was proud to be a professional footballer. Never arrogant, he was always aware that it was a privilege to be allowed to pursue a career playing the game he loved. And he was truly a credit to the game. In an era dominated by publicity and image, he quietly and effectively exemplified the potential that football has to be a positive force in the world.

Few players generate such empathy, few connected so well with football fraternity. With Richard it was always a case of 'what you see is what you get' and people simply liked what they saw.

In Lincoln the year before, the city where just a few months before we'd gathered to bid farewell to Richard's erstwhile mentor, Keith Alexander, we mourned Richard's loss and celebrated his life. I was able to say then that he would be sorely missed, but his spirit, through the memories of all who knew him, would truly live on.

At Moss Rose, I can now say with absolute certainty that he was, and it does!

Macclesfield Town Football Club

Macclesfield Town Football Club is an English football club based in Macclesfield, Cheshire. The club played in the Football League from 1997 until relegation to the Conference Premier in 2012. The club was formed in 1874 and the team play their home games at the 6,355 capacity Moss Rose stadium.

The 2011–12 season was Macclesfield Town's 15th consecutive season in the Football League and their 13th consecutive season in the fourth tier of English football which, until their relegation, made them the then longest-serving members of League Two.

Information about the club was found on en.wikipedia.org/wiki.

RICHARD BUTCHER & MANAGER GARY SIMPSON
MACCLESFIELD TOWN F.C PHOTOS BY : PETER HILTON

MACCLESFIELD F.C CAME TO NORTHAMPTON TO PAY
THEIR RESPECTS TO RICHARD

BROTHER GLENN SHOWS HIS TATTOO WITH PRIDE

Macclesfield Town Games 2009–2010

Year 2010

9th February	Away Bury	(L2) 1–2 SCORED
13th February	Home Accrington Stanley	(L2) 0–1
20th February	Away Bournemouth	(L2) 1–1
23rd February	Away Grimsby Town	(L2) 1–1 SCORED
27th February	Home Rochdale	(L2) 0–1
2nd March	Away Nott's County	(L2) 0–1
6th March	Away Hereford United	(L2) 2–0
9th March	Away Accrington Stanley	(L2) 1–1

Lincoln City Games 2010

Year 2010

27th March	Home Northampton Town	(L2) 1–1 Substitute
17th April	Away Shrewsbury Town	(L2) 0–1 Substitute
8th May	Home Macclesfield Town	(L2) 0–0 Substitute

Macclesfield Town Games 2010–2011

Year 2010

7th August	Away Stevenage Town	(L2) 2–2
10th August	Away Leicester City	(CC) 3–4
14th August	Home Shrewsbury Town	(L2) 0–1
2nd October	Home Northampton Town	(L2) 2–0 Substitute
5th October	Home Crewe Alexander	(JPT) 2–4 Substitute
11th December	Home Gillingham	(L2) 2–4 Substitute
28th December	Away Oxford United	(L2) 1–2

Year 2011

1st January	Away Bury	(L2) 2–2 SCORED
3rd January	Home Rotherham United	(L2) 0–2

14: Richard Butcher Memorial Pitch

I didn't know whether to talk about this or not but my son was honest and true to his word, and he would have said, "Mum, you go ahead."

Since Richard's death we have been determined to channel the pain into something more positive to raise money for our local community for a football pitch and club house that is very much needed in our local area of Far Cotton Northampton for the wide-eyed future footballers in honour of our son, Richard, a hard-working lad who lived the dream and who was born and bred in Far Cotton, Northampton.

The first event we held in Richard's memory was to try and help raise money towards the plaques at Lincoln City and Macclesfield Town, but one of the players decided he wanted to raise this alongside his teammates and he didn't really need our help so we respected his wishes. An open day was held for the plaque to be hung. A neighbour kindly told us about it as he had read about it in our local paper; I was delighted to receive a photo of the plaque.

We would like to say that we are very proud of the plaques that proudly hang at Macclesfield and Lincoln City football club.

So after our first event at The Saint Rugby Club we raised £10,000. I really didn't know what to do with the money at the time, so I involved the football teams and managers in our local area and asked for some advice from one of our local councillors. The local teams talked about not having good football facilities and they needed a football pitch with club house and wondered if there would be some land within the area where we could raise enough money for this to happen as there has been nothing like this before in our local area, especially in Richard's lifetime and ours. So we took it on board knowing the local kids were desperate to have a footballing place they could call their own, with no glass and needles and dog foul which has to be removed by the parents before a match can take place.

So I said I would set a petition up to see what sort of support we would get to help us with their plight. Within a couple of months 2,000 people signed the petition in our local area. Well, after that, what could I say? So I set about approaching the council with football team managers in tow and Councillor Geraldine Davis and Councillor Tony Clark to see what could be done.

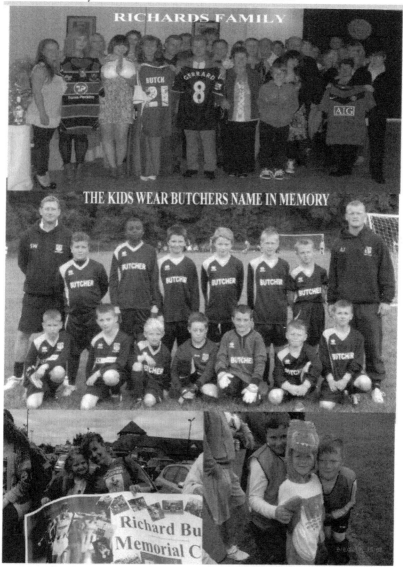

RAISING MONEY FOR THE RICHARD BUTCHER MEMORIAL TRUST

The first task would be to look for land within the local area. We must have looked at ten pieces of land to talk to the council about. Only one ended up being suitable. So we all sat round a table with the council and talked about a piece of land at Eagle Drive,

Northampton, which a local councillor, being my next door neighbour, pointed out to us at our local residents' meeting. To see if it would be possible for this to happen there, he organised for us to meet up with Councillor Mr M. Ford who showed me and my husband the land. The council kindly said they would investigate this for us; however, there was an equestrian centre to consider across the way from this piece of land. We thought, well, this would not be a bad idea as children love horse riding. If this could happen it would bring more of an income to them as well as give the kids and local teams a football pitch and club house to play on and to hold their trophy events all in one place.

There also was the Golf complex next door and the Marriott Hotel, but things didn't go as smoothly as we would have liked. We have to remember that this was only in the talking stages at this time in 2011. Nothing was set in stone. The local elections were due to run in our local area and everything turned into a frenzy regarding the land and the football pitch. It really was a living nightmare, as it was the very councillor who had pointed the land out to us in the first place. Rumours were being spread that we would try and put people out of business if the pitch was to go ahead. Well, this was not the intention at all.

To cut a long story short, the local elections turned our fantastic idea into an ugly one, to say the least. Our nerves were shattered. Everywhere we looked, leaflets were being put out with wrong information on them, so I felt. Nasty remarks were being blasted by text sent in to the local radio and Facebook pages. I felt I was being used as a human football for political trappings.

Then we started to hear about a battle that I had never heard of—not even when I was at school—that took place in the area where we would like the pitch to go, but no one had heard of this in our local area, or maybe just a handful of people. We have always shown great respect for any battle and loss of life that has ever taken place The Battle of Northampton (War of the Roses) is now on the map, although a Golf Complex was already built on the area and so was the Marriott Hotel. I wrote to the Queen to find out some more information about it, and her secretary kindly replied, but it didn't seem to show that it actually took place on the piece of land we were looking at. A Battlefield report was done by the council, but it still could not prove exactly where the battle had taken place, but an archaeological dig will be one for the future in the hope it will clear matters up.

**SALFORD UNIVERSITY RAISING MONEY
FOR THE RICHARD BUTCHER MEMORIAL TRUST
WHERE RICHARD WAS STUDYING**

I really could not believe how something that we were trying to do for the good of the community could turn so nasty and personal. I really felt I had let Richard down and, at times, I felt I couldn't carry on. I didn't even want to go to his grave as I felt I had let him down. My health and my husband's health have suffered due to the wrong attention that has been given which needn't have been. I am just a mother who has tried to do something good from a tragedy that should never have happened. If a parent should lose their child, grief and depression can cause the daily routines to be so difficult. I don't understand why a big fuss has been made just for asking about a piece of land, when it could have just been talked about like normal human beings.

I had followed everything the council had asked me to do. I had to prove I could raise funds to even get charitable status, which I have done.

Our nerves were shattered to the stage we nearly suffered a breakdown, not to mention the embarrassment of the whole storm that awaited us. Some people, including a local football team, pulled out of their support, not knowing which way to go. Community was turned against community. This really did sadden me as everyone is quite close and knew us so well after living in the area for over 40 years—a place where I had grown up and my son too. My sister-in-law suffered a brain tumour; my husband suffered a heart attack, and was taken very ill; my sister's husband found out he has cancer. I also lost my brother-in-law Steven at the age of 52 not to mention my Dad who is also very poorly.

But I still am trying to fight on through the storm, just as my son did at times in his career. He was my inspiration to carry on. How I have kept going God only knows, but my charity means so much to me, and I have great respect for the community and the support given.

Complaints were made to the Northampton Borough Council to their legal department for the way things had been dealt with, but to no avail. I also contacted the Legal Government Ombudsman, but they said they were unable to help. I really felt hurt and upset with the way things had been handled. I had nowhere to turn to express my feelings on the matter. The phone stopped ringing. I found it so hard to face the days ahead.

I didn't think I should mention this in the book at one point, because it's in Richard's memory, but the one thing Richard was is honest and true to his word and would always speak the truth no matter what, so maybe that's where I get my energy from to keep going and keep trying. I do feel a lot of what has happened could have been worked out with us all sitting around a table, and it should never have become a political matter in any way, shape, or form, as we are reasonable people and easy to talk to. A local councillor had pointed out the land; my son had spent time in his home while growing up, but politics seems to rear its ugly head in everything we do in life, and has no thought for feelings or how destructive it can be to someone's life.

At times, I couldn't face even leaving the house. I struggled so much and was still suffering with Richard's death and still do, but I set this charity up for the good of other people to try to help in the best way I can, and to try and keep myself going. I am very proud of what has been achieved by myself and others who have supported the charity. I thank you all so much for the support you have given us. But what I can say is that I can hold my head up, as it is the first time anyone has even gotten close to trying to make something like this happen. It is just a shame our son had to die to try and achieve something the kids have always needed and wanted.

Richard's spirit will live on, especially through the professional clubs like Macclesfield Town and Lincoln City FC and all the other clubs our son played for in his career that are mentioned in this book, and not forgetting the fans that will always remember him.

We also shouldn't forget all the hard work we have put into the charity and the local shops that have supported us. 'It's A Gift', 'Cost Cutter', 'Collins Coffee Shop', 'Co-Operative food store', 'Sandra's Florist' our local Butchers, Delos Community, 'Amy Group Service Limited', and 'ASDA', and, of course, and our Far Cotton 'Loco Club' and many more and we must thank all our professional football clubs from the premiership down to the conference in giving us signed football memorabilia to help raise money for the charity, which gave us a massive kick start on our first event. And thank you to all the ex-professional football players and managers who have helped in raising funds with a memorial match held at the Cobblers in Richard's memory. They made the day so special; it's hard to believe how many people Richard met through his career who thought the world of him, and not forgetting the public who believed in what I have been trying to do.

RAISING MONEY FOR THE RICHARD BUTCHER MEMORIAL CHARITY

I didn't wake up one morning and say I would like a football pitch and club house named after my son; I started my charity because of the support given. It will be fantastic for all the community and our local business to get involved and to help build a fantastic community project where many can be remembered by their children and grandchildren in future generation to come. No staff gets paid from the charity; all the hard work that has been put in is from the heart. Wrist bands, T-shirts and balloons and sweets given out to the community are all donations from our family. At least five football kits were donated to our local teams by us, Richard's family. Macclesfield Town football club invited and paid for a local team to come to their ground at Moss Road and kindly donated an away kit and home kit in Richard's memory, which was presented on their football pitch amongst the fans. The team renamed themselves the Butcher Locos. Footballs and winter coats were also donated; we thank Macclesfield Town for their support. A local kids' team, Delapre Dragons run by Ashley Jarvis, wear their kit with pride. They wear Richard's name on their shirts in memory; the football kit donated by us Richard's family. I want to thank Neil Jarrett, a close friend of Richard's, for his support on the accounts side of things; he has donated his time to help me with the charity at no cost, as everything has been a learning curve for me. Every penny you donate goes to our charity. I thank you all from the bottom of my heart. A song in Richard's memory has also been written and will be sung by Daniel Knight, called Angels with Tears, to help raise money for our charity.

Since our Local Northampton Borough Council is in full support of the Memorial Pitch, I am sure land will be found very soon as promised. All proceeds after printing costs will go to the Richard Butcher Memorial Trust, although I have paid for the book to be published out of my own pocket, so there is no loss to the charity. The public will always be kept informed via our website: www.richardbutcherfamilymemorial.com.

Richard never gave up on his dream. He always had a supportive family behind him and good family values bred into him. That's what my charity is about. Although this book is sad in places, it's also a celebration of his life.

The Richard Butcher Memorial Trust (Registered Charity Number 1151743) wishes to help other young footballers, and give them a chance to follow in his footsteps. We started out as a one-off fundraiser event at the Saints Rugby club Northampton on the evening of 29th May 2011 and were overwhelmed with the response and went on to do a second event which was held at the Cobblers football ground, where all the ex-professionals took part to pay their respects to Richard. We also involved local teams to see what support we would get from the public; again we were overwhelmed by the support given. We then obtained charitable status on the 31st January 2013 after proving we could raise funds. By the end of August 2014 we have already raised more than £30,000.

RAISING MONEY FOR THE RICHARD BUTCHER MEMORIAL CHARITY

As Mr. David Mackintosh, the leader of Northampton Borough Council succinctly puts things:

I first met Richard and Gail Butcher in December 2012 only months after they had lost their son. Despite obviously grieving for their beloved son, I was struck by how passionate they were to create a lasting sporting legacy for him, and to give other young people from Far Cotton and Northampton a chance in life to make a difference through football and sport.

The Richard Butcher Memorial Charity has already made a big difference and raised lots of money to honour the memory of a popular young footballer to create a long-term legacy. Northampton Borough Council is committed to working with Richard and Gail Butcher and is currently looking at options to create an impressive long-term legacy to provide sporting opportunities to young people for years to come.

Many of the local children have never had the benefit of proper coaching, or even special changing rooms, let alone safe facilities for parents to watch them play. Richard succeeded because he had two parents who backed him and made sacrifices. Few others are fortunate enough to have that head start. The Far Cotton Memorial Pitch and Club House will provide a friendly environment that will encourage single parents, caregivers, and relatives to support optimistic budding players who want to follow a local lad's path into the people's game. Outside of football use, the Charity will encourage other local bodies to use the facilities that will be accessible to disabled and able-bodied patrons alike.

Your purchase of this book or e-book will help those dreams become a reality, so I thank you so much for reading this book. Richard would have been amazed at the fact that a book had even been written about him, but I wanted to share his story and mine with you. God bless you, Richard—you gave—you died—your memories will live on forever.

PHOTOS TAKEN BY : RON FITZHUGH

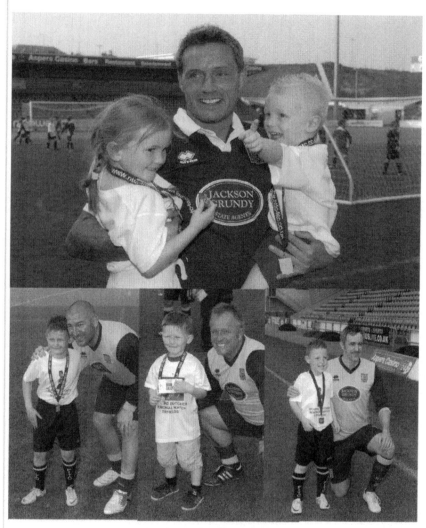

RICHARD BUTCHERS MEMORIAL MATCH
NORTHAMPTON TOWN F.C

RICHARD BUTCHER'S MEMORIAL MATCH, NORTHAMPTON TOWN F.C
PHOTOS TAKEN BY RON FITZHUGH

WE KINDLY THANK RON FITZHUGH FOR THE RICHARD BUTCHER
MEMORIAL CHARITY PHOTOS

CHARITY MEMORIAL PHOTOS
ERIC BRISTOW SUPPORTS THE NUMBER 21 SHIRT ON HOLIDAY
THANK YOU TO EVERYONE WHO TOOK PART

15: New charity XPRO for former professional footballers

The **Organisation of Ex-Professional Footballers**, or XPRO, has been set up to support the health and welfare of retired players by providing financial assistance and legal help. They have been granted charitable status.

The charity, which is headed by the former Stoke City defender Geoff Scott, is keen to dispel the idea that former footballers don't need help because they are all pampered millionaires. "Most footballers are not wealthy at all," says the charity's website *http://www.xpro.org/*

It is only a very small number of today's top players who are very wealthy. The vast majority of ex-professionals will have enjoyed only very modest earnings during their playing careers which are typically over by their early 30s. XPRO has been registered as a charity with the purposes of education, relief of poverty, relief of disability and community development. The charity wants to support research into the possible link between heading the ball and dementia, brain damage, and Alzheimer's disease in ex-footballers.

If in any emergency please contact: telephone 08444 120401 email *info@xpro.org*.

I have to say I have been in touch with the ex-pros for help and guidance with issues I can't talk about, but they have been a fantastic support to me and my family. So if you need any help or support please don't hesitate to contact them; they are fantastic people, and they are there to help with any issues you may have.

I think it's great what these people are trying to do, especially trying to help the lower league players and their families. They need all the support they can get at a time when their career comes to an end through injury, or retirement, or even death. The players and their families need someone they can rely on at a time when they most need someone.

I have to say Geoff Scott is an amazing man. He is suffering himself with his own serious illness, but he has still found time for me and my family in a time of need, and we are very grateful to him and the ex-pros for their support.

16: On The Spiritual Side of Things: Do You Believe?

Yvonne, a natural clairvoyant medium, tells us:

Hi, my name is Yvonne. I am a natural clairvoyant medium. I have been asked by Richard's mum, Gail, to write a little of the experience and evidence we have shared together from the spirit world. I first met Gail three years ago when she booked an appointment with me, for a reading.

When I opened the door I saw a very heartfelt, but very sad lady; not unusual with the work I do. Rachel, Gail's niece, was also with her. I put the kettle on, and we started to talk. I became aware of a dark handsome young man standing behind Gail, then I saw a pair of new football boots and so we began. Spirit allowed me to bring evidence for Gail and Rachel of a personal detail and memories, too, of Richard's life and passing. For the last three years I have continued to see the family as a friend, and as a medium. Richard always shows his love and lets Gail know how he feels about what's happening in their lives. From a personal point of view, I feel humbled and honoured that spirit brought me into Richard's family's life, and all I can hope for is that I and my spirit family have brought a little comfort to Gail and her family, and especially to Richard himself.

Richard's mum, Gail:

On our first meeting when I first met Yvonne I really could not believe it as she talked of Richard and his new pair of football boots I had just bought for him to place on his grave, on which I had also had his name embroidered, on the side. She also talked of Keith Alexander, who was Richard's manager, who had passed just ten months before. That's when I knew, and felt she was talking about my son.

She talked of the plaques that would be placed at Lincoln City football club, and Macclesfield town. She said they would be honoured by both clubs, which soon came true.

I can remember when my son Richard was around ten years old and he cooked me a breakfast along with his brother Glenn for Mother's Day. They both brought the tray up with a cup of tea and the plate was swimming with everything you could think of: sausage, bacon, eggs, beans, tomatoes. I really had a job to eat it. No one would know about that day—only Richard.

There was a suit my son had bought and he phoned his dad to tell him about it. We had been out shopping ourselves, and his dad had bought exactly the same suit. It was really strange how that happened. No one knew about that, only us, his family.

One day I was really struggling to even get out of bed after my son's death, as any parent will tell you when losing their child. The phone rang out of the blue. Yvonne said, "Are you okay, Gail?" I replied, "No, I am so low today." She replied, "Richard said, 'Why have you taken that black ribbon out of your hair?' Richard said it looks nice." Well, I nearly fell through the floor. I had been on my own all day and I had pulled the ribbon from my hair, because I thought I was too old to wear it and threw it on the floor. How would she know that?

Yvonne also talked of the football kit that was buried with my son, which, I might add, no one knew of, and there was only one person who had signed the kit and that was Gary Simpson, my son's manager.

These are just a few personal things Yvonne talked about. There are so many to tell you. Richard wasn't a great believer when alive, but he knew I was. If anyone would try to reach us, it would be my son. Yvonne also came through with my grandparents, too, and I have to say she was spot on once again.

Yvonne Goodsell www.angelic-peace.co.uk E- mail: contact@angelic-peace.co.uk

17: No Will

First of all, I can't stress enough how important it is to make a will at any age, whether you are lucky enough to be wealthy or not. Some of us only own one home. Some of us are not even lucky enough to have that, but even personal things are really important, and maybe you want them to go to the right person in the event of your death.

But sometimes you can be lucky enough to have more than most, and these things need to be dealt with, if you are able to, before your death. But we have to remember that each and every one of us will die at some point. Not all of us will be lucky enough to know when this is going to happen, as my son didn't at just the tender age of 29 years old.

You may have been married more than once and have children from either marriage, or perhaps you were not so lucky as to have children at all. Or you may have a live-in partner. Everybody's circumstances are different in our ever-changing upcoming future generation.

In my own experience regarding my son's death, I found the whole thing really hard to deal with as a mother, because I thought, and was advised professionally, that I have no rights to see or read anything that I was named on if the deceased is married even for a short time. Even a qualified solicitor was unable to get me the documents I wanted to see. This cost me very dearly as regards finances and heartache.

I was advised by a friend at the time, two-and-a-half years after my son's death, that I could write a letter under the 1998 Data Protection Act to request this information for myself. According to the law, I was allowed to see any documents with my name on them. The documents were sent to me and they arrived with most things blacked out, so I could not read parts of the document. Forgive me, if it seems that I should know these things at the ripe old age of fifty, but unless you come across this sort of thing in your lifetime, you really don't know what to do.

My son held a document in his mother's name, as he told me himself. I was named as the full beneficiary. On contacting these people regarding the document, I was steered away, with them advising me I was not named on the document which was UN-true. I was only following up what my son had told me. But I was made to feel like I was doing something wrong, and that I shouldn't be asking the question.

Although my son died intestate—this means he had no will for those that don't know—this document did not come under the estate, so it was a separate issue. My husband alongside many others may fill these forms out at work. It's called an 'expression of wishes' form. You can name whomever you wish on this form. It could be your mother, your sister, your wife, your husband, or a friend, or any other person you wish. It is entirely up to you whom you want to name on this form. You can name at least three people if you wish, and leave them all a percentage each. They don't even have to be related to you.

I do feel, whether there is a will or not, if you, the public, or myself, name any person or family member on a document, your wishes should be granted. It is his or her wish for this to be carried out. This should be legally binding, as these are your last wishes, and you have signed the form, so no one should be able to change that in the event of your death, as it is not for others to decide after your death, as you are not here to defend yourself or your rights.

You should always take notice of the small print, as this is not entirely true; the company you have taken the insurance out with can or may change this at will or the company the document is sent to may change and decide who they think it should be paid to, either a percentage or all. A board of trustees who have never met you or your family members can sit around a table and decide where they think the money should go after your death if your circumstances have changed since you last filled the form out. But you may have left the form for a few years, or just months because you didn't want to change the form; although your circumstances had changed, this was your last wish. You also have to remember that you don't receive a copy of your 'expression of wishes' form to keep for your safekeeping, so unless you have been told by your loved ones that you have been named on the form, you might never find out because you may not be contacted by the company. I must admit, I can't speak for all companies, but this is based on my own experience which I am sharing with you.

So it is very important for people to read what they are signing and always ask questions. Please take the time to investigate any paperwork or insurance policies that you are given to sign, or your wishes may not be granted, and also check that you have a copy of the signed document.

We don't always write a will. It's natural to forget with such a busy life, but your UNtimely or UNexpected death, young or old, can leave heartache behind you no one can fill. I feel everyone who is named on any document, regardless of a will or not, should be contacted by the insurance company. A copy should be given to you for safekeeping. Your family should not have to contact them.

If you have named your children, your mother, father, daughter, son, brother, uncle, auntie, or a friend, you should let them know they are on your paperwork. Losing a loved one is bad enough without having to fight afterwards and having to prove to insurance companies that you are named as the beneficiary, because without a copy there is no proof.

Legal documents can sometimes prove very awkward. My father has a very old insurance document left to him by his mother. She had taken it out for him as a small child. There is only his name on the document alongside his mother's. But when he tried to process the document all these years later, at the age of 70, he was told he would have to get his brother's and sister's permission, which they don't have a problem with. But what I don't understand is that this document was taken out by my father's mother for him in his name by her, and yet they won't pay it out without the permission of his brother and sister, who are not named on the document. I really do feel the law should be changed, because, if his brother or sisters were not alive anymore, who would they be asking him to get permission from next, his daughter's?

My life has been very difficult since my son's death. I don't feel any respect has been shown to us as Richard's parents on this side of things; we have been made to feel we should not ask questions and it should be a closed book. In the future what I would like to see happen in my son's memory is that all footballers should have to make a will. They should be asked to update things every time they move to a new club; they should be given the option to change things if they wish if their circumstances have changed e.g. they got married or had children or have a live in partner; or they have the option to keep things as they are because they are happy with it. This should become part of their contracts to help support them and their families. Full names and address of your loved one should be on the forms and a copy should be kept for safe keeping. You should also pass a copy onto your family member so they have a copy too. We all say when something happens that will never happen to me but no one knows what's round the corner; my son didn't and nor did we.

I took a look at a nomination death in service form that a friend received through work and on the form it states the trustees have discretion over who should receive this payment but will normally respect your wishes.

And then the form goes onto to say: it is very important that you complete this form to tell us the trustees to whom you would like this benefit paid.

On the other side of the form it says the nomination constitutes only an expression of my wishes and is not binding on the trustees and the trustees have complete discretion over the payment of any death benefits.

After reading this form, which I feel contradicts itself because we are being asked to name family members on a form to whom we would like to leave our money to, we seem to be really signing a form for certain companies and their trustees to do as they wish in the event of our death.

18: The future

I really wish I could end the book on a more positive note. Many meetings have been held with Northampton Borough Council. We were told that once we achieved charitable status we would be given the lease for the land at Eagle Drive, Northampton.

At one point the council had brought on board Northampton Saints as regards the land at Eagle Drive, which we read about in our local paper Northampton Chronicle Echo; but after talks with them and explaining there was not enough land for all, they kindly withdrew from the land.

This only leaves the Richard Butcher memorial pitch and small club house and the equestrian centre across the road who uses some of the land for grazing. We have always supported the equestrian centre as lots of children love horse riding and we were reassured by the NBC that there is enough room for both.

We have constantly looked for other land, but have been unable to find anything that suitable and available.

We were advised by NBC that we could continue with the land at Eagle Drive, Northampton but this would take time as an archaeological dig needs to be done, with the arguments over where the Northampton Battle actually took place still ongoing, so the charity has offered to do this with the help of councillor Tony Clarke.

So we are continuing with the land at Eagle Drive unless other land becomes available. Land is so very hard to come by in Far Cotton, Northampton. I really hope this is all sorted out very soon as we have followed all that NBC have asked us to do.

I really wouldn't like to have to move the memorial pitch out of Far Cotton through land not being available as we were led to believe there was and we would be given a lease, and because of Richard's local connections.

So we continue to raise funds for the memorial pitch and club house unless we are told by Northampton Borough Council that this can't happen as we have been led to believe it will. I really do hope there will be a second book with pictures of the memorial pitch being built by all the community, and look forward to the day when young footballers can use the facilities. So if there are members of the public out there who know of any other land or you would like to come forward and help us please do.

I am told we need to have a regular income as regards the charity but with no land as yet this is very difficult; it's hard to get companies on board to help support us with having no lease for the land yet, so all we can do is work hard with our charity events to bring the money in to help carry on with our project.

But at worst a lot of other good charities can only gain from what we have tried to achieve with your help. At best there will be a new facility for the youth of the area to enjoy and make good use of.

We can reassure the community and the public we will always involve them and will let them know what happens.

Many thanks to Northampton Town for their donation of a full football kit to be used to raise money for our charity in memory of Richard.

Made in the USA
Charleston, SC
03 December 2014